Toward a New Science
of Educational Testing
and Assessment

SUNY Series, Teacher Preparation and Development

Alan R. Tom, Editor

Toward a New Science of Educational Testing and Assessment

Harold Berlak, Fred M. Newmann,
Elizabeth Adams, Doug A. Archbald,
Tyrrell Burgess, John Raven,
and Thomas A. Romberg

State University of New York Press

This book was prepared under the aegis of the National Center on Effective Secondary Schools, and was supported in part by the U.S. Department of Education, Office of Educational Research and Improvement (Grant No. G-008690007), and by the Wisconsin Center for Education Research, School of Education, University of Wisconsin-Madison. The opinions expressed are those of the writers alone and do not reflect the views of the supporting agencies.

Published by
State University of New York Press, Albany

For information, address State University of New York
Press, State University Plaza, Albany, N.Y., 12246

Production by M. R. Mulholland
Marketing by Bernadette LaManna

Library of Congress Cataloging-in-Publication Data
Toward a new science of educational testing & assessment / Harold
    Berlak . . . [et al.].
        p.   cm.—(SUNY series, teacher preparation and development)
    Includes bibliographical references.
    ISBN 0-7914-0877-9 (alk. paper).—ISBN 0-7914-0878-7 (pbk.:
alk. paper)
    1. Educational tests and measurements—United States.
    2. Educational tests and measurements—United States—Validity.
    I. Berlak, Harold.   II. Series: SUNY series in teacher preparation
    and development.
    LB3051.T635   1992
    371.2'6'0973—dc20   90-28708
                                                               CIP

10 9 8 7 6 5 4 3 2

Contents

Tables and Figures

1

The Need for a New Science of Assessment

Harold Berlak

Introduction

The idea that schooling for all is essential for social progress and economic growth grew up alongside the development of industrial capitalism during the tail end of the nineteenth and early decades of the twentieth century. By the 1990s, the aspiration for universal schooling has come a long way toward realization, though many American youth still do not complete secondary school.[1] While universal provision of schooling is still widely seen as a noble, if unrealized goal, there is a growing consensus that the system of public education that has evolved over the course of this century in the United States is in serious trouble. Public officials, corporate leaders, and ordinary citizens are increasingly dissatisfied with the quality of the education provided by the nation's schools to the great majority of children. While the margins of the American political scene, left and right have long been critical of schools (albeit with quite different ideas of the problems and solutions), with the exception of racial desegregation, discussions of elementary and secondary schooling policy over the last 25 years were virtually absent in the national media, in the platforms of the national political parties, or in campaigns for national state or even local public office. For brief interludes, following the launching of Sputnik in the late 1950s and in the mid-1960s during Lyndon Johnson's "war on poverty," public attention focused on schools, but this interest was not sustained.

This changed in 1983 with publication of *A Nation at Risk,* a report of the National Commission on Excellence in Education (1983). It made national news with its assertion that American education was threatened by "a rising tide of mediocrity," and with its frequently cited lines: "If an

unfriendly foreign power attempted to impose on America the mediocre educational performance that exists today, we might well have viewed it as an
act of war. As it stands, we have allowed this to happen to ourselves. . . . We
have, in effect been committing an act of unthinking unilateral disarmament.''

Why this report received so much attention is a matter of some conjecture. Very serious problems, particularly in, but not restricted to, inner city
and poor rural schools, had existed and been widely known for many years. In
spite of the report's claims to the contrary, what had changed were not the
problems[2]—though undoubtedly they had gotten worse—but the public's and
elected officials' response. The reason for wide notice of *A Nation at Risk* had
more to do with the particular historical moment it appeared than with the
originality or profundity of its analysis. In the early eighties, the failures of
the US economy had just begun to penetrate the nation's consciousness—
dominating the news were the galloping US trade deficit; the failures of US
industry; plant closings; and dramatic increases in unemployment, particularly in the older industrial cities. What this report offered was an explanation
for these apparently inexplicable events, an explanation which was eagerly
embraced by the mainstream press and corporate America, and widely repeated in the national media. The report told the American public that a major
cause, if not the major cause, of America's fall from grace as the world's pre-
eminent economic and industrial power was the failure of the nation's schools
to educate a competent, dedicated work force. This was a palatable diagnosis
of the nation's economic malaise that suited the times. It placed blame, not on
the basic structural problems of the US economy, nor on the failures of corporate leaders and politicians to address the changing world economy, and to
do something to relieve the accumulating social problems and the gross dis-
parities between rich and poor; but on the politically impotent: the nation's
elementary and secondary school teachers, nameless educational bureaucrats,
and unskilled and/or unmotivated workers.

A Nation at Risk was not the work of right-wing ideologues. Terrell
Bell, who initiated the report, and who was appointed by Ronald Reagan as
his first secretary of education, was at the time widely regarded as a middle-
of-the-road professional, and the eighteen-member National Commission on
Excellence Bell appointed included, among others, the retired chairman of the
board of Bell Laboratories, two professors from Harvard and University of
California at Berkeley respectively, four university presidents (including
Yale), a former governor of Minnesota, the immediate past-president of the
National School Boards Association, two principals, two school board members, the superintendent of schools from Albuquerque, and the 1981–82
teacher-of-the year, a high school foreign language teacher from an affluent
suburb of New York City.

Whatever its deficiencies, the *Nation at Risk* drew public attention to the schools, and this, attention contrary to the expectations of many, has continued to the present. The report and the wide attention if received stimulated responses from virtually every organization and group with an interest in educational policy. Since 1983 countless reports, articles, and books have been written or commissioned by every major foundation, dozens of minor ones, policy think-tanks across the political spectrum, associations of corporate executives and educational professionals, teachers' unions, children's and parents' advocacy groups, formal and *ad hoc* organizations of state and local educational officials, as well as by individual journalists and scholars. While there are major differences in the policy recommendations, very few reports contest the *Nation at Risk's* view of the economy, and none with dissenting views have received wide public notice.[3]

All this talk about education did, however, galvanize latent public discontent with the schools and create a political climate for change. Since 1983 virtually every governmental agency and administrative unit at the state, county, and school district levels that held some responsibility for elementary and secondary schools has initiated and implemented some reforms. State legislatures, governors, state and local education officers, the major foundations and think tanks, the two leading national teachers unions, and even the 1988 presidential candidates, Bush and Dukakis, felt the need to respond to the clamor for educational excellence.

Many of the responses can be passed off as media hype and political rhetoric. But there were also many concrete measures undertaken. I make no effort here to recount and analyze these efforts in any detail, a monumental undertaking far beyond the purview of this chapter. However, some effort to make sense of these intended reforms is essential if we are to understand the current movement for developing new forms of educational assessment and testing.

An Analysis of the Reform Movement: The Role of Testing

Two competing tendencies about how political decisions should be made and who should make them are represented by recent efforts to reform the nation's schools. One tendency is toward decentralization of authority and decision-making by those who are most immediately affected by those decisions. This view is often coupled with a distrust of centralized authority and a disdain for experts and intellectuals. From this perspective, "bottom-up" change is valorized along with direct, grassroots or participatory democracy.

The second tendency in this society is toward centralization of authority and decision-making, with responsibility for the difficult decisions left to the man or woman at the top—the CEO, the chief of staff. In the case of schools, the superintendent or principal must be a tough-minded leader, able to shape up the troops, delegate responsibility and hold subordinates accountable for their performance. Efficiency and immediate, demonstrable results are valorized, and while democracy is not necessarily rejected, it is representative democracy and delegation of authority to those who know best which is endorsed—with little tolerance for participatory democracy, which is seen as chaotic and in the end as encouraging the lowest common denominator in terms of process and product.

The relative strength of these two tendencies and the ambivalence many Americans feel about how to reform schools are evident in the multiplicity of proposals advanced and policies instituted since 1983. The language that has dominated the discourse about school reform has been that of crisis, of disaster, of imminent threat to the very survival of the nation. I have already quoted *A Nation at Risk* with its military metaphors. Here are the words of *A Nation Prepared,* the second-most influential report, published by the Carnegie Forum on Education and the Economy (1986), created and supported by the Carnegie Corporation of New York:

> American's ability to compete in the world markets is eroding. The productivity growth of our competitors outdistances our own. As jobs requiring little skills are automated or go offshore and demand increases for the highly skilled, the pool of educated and skilled people grows smaller and the backwater of the unemployable rises. Large numbers of American children are in limbo—ignorant of the past and unprepared for the future. Many are dropping out—not just out of school but out of productive society.
>
> As in past economic and social crises, Americans turn to education. They rightly demand an improved supply of young people with the knowledge, the spirit, the stamina and the skills to make the nation once again fully competitive. (p.2)

In times of national crisis, it is no surprise that the strongest impulse by politicians most directly responsible for schools is to use their authority by employing the tools they understand and know best. In the United States, basic responsibility for schools resides with the states. Eight years after publication of *A Nation at Risk* virtually every state had instituted a combination of top-down measures intended to raise educational standards. These measures include requirements for academic courses, new or strengthened controls over textbook adoptions, mandated use of state curriculum guidelines which in some instances are closely aligned to required tests, and more prescriptive regulations for certifying teachers. But, by far the most common measure is statewide testing programs throughout the grades that, in effect, increased the proportion of education dollars spent at the state level, and strengthened the control of the state's chief educational officer and/or state department of education.

While it is difficult to generalize about several thousand school districts, many, particularly the larger urban systems, responded much like state departments of education by tightening and centralizing bureaucratic control over curriculum, pedagogy, grading, student discipline, and personnel selection. In addition to the newly devised or revised state "basic skills" tests, and the standardized achievement tests which have been used for many years almost universally throughout the grades, some districts instituted their own district-wide tests, in some cases going so far as to specify textbooks for each grade level, and to link mandated tests to these texts.

The role of the federal government under Reagan-Bush is contradictory. On the one hand their administrations greatly reduced or eliminated programs supporting educational research and development, curriculum and staff development, as well as programs that aided particularly needy populations, using the justification that schools are primarily the responsibility of local and state governments. On the other hand, the Department of Education, whose elevation to cabinet-level status was bitterly opposed by Reagan and right-wing groups prior to 1980, in the ensuing years became an increasingly active instrument in efforts of right-wing forces within the federal government to shape local and state schooling policy through, for example, selective enforcement of and in some cases opposition to agreements reached by local and state school officials and the courts on civil rights issues, active advocacy of a national core curriculum, national assessment, and so-called "freedom of choice" plans which would, in effect, divert public funds to private schools. Among the more visible efforts by the federal government to shape schooling practice is the annual media event staged by the secretary of education upon publication of the "wall chart," which ranks the states' educational performance based on standardized test scores. In some instances a form of this annual ritual is repeated by states publicizing rankings of school districts, and by the central administrations of school districts releasing to the press rankings of individual schools within districts.

What explains the enormous emphasis on tests? I have suggested that a primary reason for this emphasis is that tests are a means of maintaining centralized control, providing those higher up in the educational bureaucracy (central office administrators, school board members, state education officials, legislators, etc.) with relative rankings of organizational units (classrooms, schools, districts, etc.) and/or students and teachers. This, however, is not an adequate explanation since it does not account for widespread popular support for the use of tests. While there is increasingly vocal criticism of tests among professionals and by the national media, there is still remarkably little evidence of widespread discontent with current forms of testing. Indeed, many support increased testing, including African-American, and Latino-American parents who are convinced that their children, who consistently score lower on standardized and criterion-referenced tests, have been and continue to be victimized by low expectations on the part of teachers and school officials. For many within these communities, the only credible indicator of improved educational performance is improved performance on standardized tests. The irony in this is that, while the demand for more professional accountability is certainly justified, any gains on such tests are often temporary and local. The technology of these tests assumes there will be winners and losers, and in our society the winners are invariably the more affluent and the losers the poor and powerless.

Efforts to reform schools from the center continue, but a counter tendency toward more democratic school-level control has become more visible recently for several reasons, including organized opposition to centralized control by teachers unions, parent groups, and local school boards, and a growing conviction that mandating changes from above has not worked. What a few years ago was a fringe view that genuine changes in the end must occur in individual classrooms, which is not possible without active participation of teachers and without a large measure of autonomy within each school, has become increasingly accepted as the common wisdom by the public policy establishment and the mainstream press.[4]

Several states while tightening centralized control, have encouraged school–level decision–making by altering state regulations to permit principals and teachers more say about school expenditures, curriculum and staffing. Also several districts scattered across the country—New York City, Buffalo, and Dade County, Florida, are the most frequently mentioned in the press—not only tolerate but appear to foster school-level decision-making. However, although talk about, and arguments for, teacher empowerment and school-level governance are commonplace, it is the rare exception rather than the rule for central office bureaucracies to yield power.

This ambivalence over who should call the shots, the authorities at the center or the local school community, is probably nowhere more clearly exemplified than in the previously cited Carnegie report, *A Nation Prepared*. On the one hand, the report celebrates the role of the teacher and provides what it calls "a scenario," a hypothetical example of a high school run by the school staff in close collaboration with the local community. On the other hand, however, the report makes no recommendations as to how centralized administrative control by school districts or the state is to be relinquished. Its key and sole concrete proposal is creating a new National Board for Professional Teaching Standards which would, in effect, centralize the certification of an elite cadre of master or lead teachers whom they assume would transform the schools.

If there is any consensus after almost eight years of intensive public discussion and activity, it is that tinkering with regulations and issuing more administrative mandates will not suffice, and that what is needed is *perestroika,* a basic restructuring of the entire system. *Restructuring* is one of those words like *democracy* and *accountability* that have an inexhaustible number of possible meanings, each aflame with ideological passion. At very least it implies an unfreezing of the central office bureaucracy and a shift in authority and the power of decision-making from existing to new formations.

In spite of the calls for *perestroika,* decentralizing authority, and empowering teachers and principals to institute changes from below, there has not been any wide-scale restructuring of the system. Except for some well-publicized exceptions, the evidence is that, overall, the system has become more and not less centralized over the past eight or so years. (Sarason, 1989) While there are several interconnected factors at work, one—if not *the*—single most significant in holding the current system in place, indeed in strengthening the current structures, is testing. Not any tests, but the *particular forms* of standardized and criterion-referenced testing which have become the main instruments of reform. Here we have the major paradox of the reform movement of the eighties: significant improvements in the quality of schooling are impossible without structural changes, but increased dependence on mass-administered tests at all levels has had the effect of strengthening existing structures and forms of control. The culprit is not educational assessment and testing *per se.* Rather, the argument I make here and in Chapter 8 is that the particular forms of testing in widest use for increasing accountability are rooted in a social science paradigm which takes as a given the necessity for centralized control.

Use of such tests are not the sole cause for the failures to restructure schools. *Re*-forming schools or any social institution is a complex business. It requires a commitment by national, state, and local, public officials, and professional educators to critically examine their own long standing practices and patterns of organizational control. It takes persistence and inordinate courage by leaders and governing bodies to dislodge entrenched, centralized bureaucratic power. If we know anything at all about politics and human behavior, it is that many endorse the need for change, but few risk challenging the many vested individual and institutional interests in maintaining business-as-usual. There are thousands of organizational entities, and tens of thousands of individuals within national and state governments, colleges and universities,

foundations, publishing companies, and central offices of local school districts whose power would be greatly diluted or lost if the current system of
assessment were significantly altered.

The historically unparalleled growth in the use of mass testing as the
chief instrument of school reform over the last several years has produced a
counter-reaction as evidenced by increasing public criticism in mainstream
journals and the popular national press questioning the credibility of these
tests, and by a resurgence of interest in alternative forms of assessment. Two
recent studies, the first conducted by the National Center for Fair and Open
Testing (Medina & Neil, 1988) and the second by the National Commission
on Testing and Public Policy (1990) document both the growth of and interest
in the development of alternative forms of testing, and the resistance to use of
current forms of testing by many mainline educators and citizen and professional groups. Skepticism of multiple choice tests, which for many years was
largely confined to progressive critics and to academic traditionalists, is now
voiced regularly in such places as the *Washington Post, New York Times, Wall
Street Journal, Newsweek,* and even on prime time television documentaries.

The two reports cited above and a publication of the National Center on
Effective Secondary Schools at the University of Wisconsin (1989) document
in detail the deficiencies and problems with these tests. They show that the
short-answer, closed-ended format precludes the assessment of higher-order
thinking and mastery of complex material, that test items are frequently bi-
ased in subtle and not so subtle ways, and that dependence on these tests as
the primary indicators of school quality and for making judgments about students abilities and achievements distorts schooling policies and practice in numerous ways.[5]

Though I (and all the writers included in this volume) would concur
with most of these criticisms of the commonly used forms of educational
tests, and that there is a need to develop alternatives, I do not focus here on
critique nor on reviewing and examining proposed alternative forms of testing. Rather my purpose in this chapter is to raise questions about the theoretical foundations of the widely used forms of achievement testing, and to
foreshadow the argument for a theory of testing and assessment, that is com-
patible with current interest in restructuring schools by dispersing power and
shifting responsibility away from the center, towards local school districts and
to the teachers and principals within individual schools.

Though there is critique in this volume, and discussions and exemplars
of alternative forms of assessment, the book is primarily an effort to examine
the theory and practice of educational assessment, and a modest step toward
the development of a new paradigm. This book supports the view that fundamental changes in the way we think about education and the process of
schooling must accompany the effort to rethink assessment theory and prac-

tices if we are to realize the aspiration of providing all the nation's children with schools which serve their best interests, the interests of the communities they live in, and the interests of the nation as a whole.

I must forewarn the reader that this book does not pretend to provide a fully articulated and coherent perspective on the theory and practice of educational assessment. The lack of unity and consistency of argument across chapters is, in part, a function of its history. Supported by a grant from the US Department of Education's Office of Educational Research and Improvement to the National Center on Secondary Education at the University of Wisconsin, I collected and edited a set of papers which were intended to provide some fresh perspectives on the testing and assessment question drawing upon work commissioned by the Center and from the existing assessment literature. This task was completed in 1988. In the course of this work, it became increasingly clear to me that some of the researchers whose writings I had collected and edited were pressing the limits of the familiar testing technology and moving in the direction of abandoning and replacing the measurement paradigm which has predominated for at least the last sixty years. Five chapters in this book are revised and edited versions of papers selected from that earlier collection, and three chapters (Chapters 1, 6, & 8) were written expressly for this volume. The first and last chapters are an effort to illuminate the arguments for a new assessment paradigm, arguments which I saw as largely submerged in the work of the writers of the other papers. In none of the chapters, except Chapter 5 by John Raven, and my two chapters, is there a self-conscious effort to articulate a case for a new science of testing and assessment. Although I make my case drawing freely from the work of others, from the writers of the other chapters, and from sources I cite in the endnotes of my two chapters, I alone must be held responsible for the way I have interpreted and used their work.

Foundational Assumptions of the Current Paradigm

I will state what I see as the four foundational assumptions of the paradigm which underlies virtually all standardized and most criterion-referenced tests. In so doing, I will also state four "counter assumptions" which are intended to foreshadow the argument for the development of a new testing and assessment paradigm.

Before proceeding I will clarify several commonly used terms:

Test Technology. Test technology refers to the structure of a test, the ground rules and conventions used for its construction, the procedures and protocols for scoring and summarizing results, and the matrix of practices required for everyday use.

The tests I refer to here are those generally composed of a relatively large array of short questions of "items." Each item includes a problem presentation—a sentence, paragraph, set of statements, a chart, graph, picture, or mathematical equation followed by a set of four or five possible responses, one of which is designated by the test-makers as the correct or best possible answer. The individual taking the test makes a selection and blackens a space provided, generally on an separate answer sheet which is subsequently machine scored. There is almost always a time limit for completing the test. Scores are usually computed by counting correct responses and subtracting this number from the number of incorrect responses. A variety of statistical operations is employed for summarizing test results so that they may be used for comparing scores of individual or groups. Some variations of this technology should be noted, which generally do not represent a significant change in a test's technology. A desktop computer or terminal may be used to present items to the test-taker and to tally responses in lieu of the printed test and answer sheet. Also, some tests may include open-ended test items, those which require a writing sample or solving a math problem. In scoring such items, responses are assigned a number by a person trained in the use of a set of scoring conventions. The scores are then treated in the same way as those derived from multiple choice items.

Standardized and Criterion-Referenced Tests. A distinction is commonly drawn between "standardized" (or norm-referenced) and "criterion-referenced" tests. Among the best known of the former are the California Achievement Tests, the Iowa Tests of Basic Skills, and the Standard Achievement Tests (or SAT). Criterion-referenced tests include virtually all National Assessment of Educational Progress (NAEP) tests and state-mandated "basic" or "essential" skills tests.

Standardized tests do not depend upon setting educational standards as is often assumed. The concept of standardization in this context refers to tests which are constructed in such a way that allows a standard score, grade equivalency, or percentile to be computed, thereby permitting comparison of an individual's score, percentile, or a group mean to those of another individual or group. Such comparisons are possible only if the test is "normed." What this requires is that during a test's development, it was administered to a sample of test-takers, and the distribution of their scores was compared statistically to a so-called "normal" distribution. The slope of such a distribution is bell-shaped, hence the commonly used term *bell curve*. A normal or bell curve does not appear naturally. To the contrary, test-makers attempt to compose test items so that there will be a suitable ratio of correct to incorrect responses. If too large a number of test-takers chooses the correct responses to sets of items, these items would be revised or abandoned even if there were unanimous consensus that the items tapped an educationally significant body of knowledge or set of skills. The reason is that the items must "discriminate," that is, produce the proportion of correct to incorrect answers required by a "normal" distribution.[6] The technology of standardized tests, contrary to popular belief, do not warrant making *qualitative* statements about a person's (or group's) performance. The only claims which are warranted is how an individual's score or percentile (or group's mean or mean percentile) compares with others who have taken a version of the same test.

Though there are a number of recent efforts by the NAEP and several states to depart from the usual closed-ended format, the items in the vast majority of criterion-referenced tests are indistinguishable from those included in a standardized test. The major difference is that criterion-referenced tests are not normed. A panel of educators decides what percentage of correct responses constitutes passing or minimal competence. This score serves as the criterion for making judgments about an individual's or groups' competence or level of achievement. In practice, someone selects a score which sets the minimum number of items students at a particular grade level must answer correctly in order to be considered minimally competent in a given area— mathematics, reading, or whatever. Criterion-referenced tests (with some significant exceptions) also warrant only quantitative statements about how an individual's score or a group's mean (the group may be a single class, a school, a set of schools from a district or entire state or region) compares to the mean of another individual or group, or to an established criterion score.

It is important to note that in recent years, there have been efforts to develop so-called "performance-based" tests. The intent is to create assessments which avoid the multiple choice format and more closely approximate real tasks, such as conducting an experiment or writing a job application letter. While some of these efforts succeed in breaking the boundaries of the conventional testing paradigm, most do not depart significantly from the conventional standardized and criterion-referenced test technology. Rather than presenting four or five alternatives to choose from, a score is assigned to the test-takers' "free" responses (recorded on paper or computer) on the basis of previously-determined criteria. Aggregate scores are then treated in more or less the same way as those derived from multiple choice items. For all practical purposes most such assessments are rooted in the conventional psychometric paradigm.

Scientific Paradigms. Scientific endeavor in any area rests upon a set of *a priori* assumptions shared by persons who engage in that endeavor. With reference to testing, this means that those within the educational testing and evaluation community who design and construct educational tests, or who administer and interpret their meaning to others take for granted a set of beliefs, values, and practices. (or "puzzle solutions"). It is the foundational assumptions and practices taken as normal within a particular community of scientists which Thomas Kuhn, a well-known historian of science, calls a *paradigm* in a widely quoted book, *The Structure of Scientific Revolutions,* first published almost thirty years ago. A paradigm may be seen as what Michael Foucault calls a "regime of truth." A regime of truth in science is a set of practices and discourses taken as given in everyday scientific activity and which implicitly defines what are and are not considered legitimate scientific questions and methods.

What is significant to my argument here, and to the thesis of this entire volume is Kuhn's claim that paradigms or regimes of truth in science are transient and that the history of science is itself a history of paradigm breakdown and replacement. Paradigms are replaced because anomalies and problems appear that cannot be explained or be fruitfully addressed using the commonly accepted language, ground rules, or "puzzle solutions." Over time scientists develop new paradigms—that is different concepts, sets of "puzzle-solutions," and a constellation of beliefs and values[7] which appear to address the difficulties. It is these changes that constitute revolutions in scientific thinking and practice, and while they are infrequent, major transformations are to be expected sooner or later. In the meantime, normal science continues more or less undisturbed, as the old regime erodes and in time is replaced by a new one. Periods of transition and change, it should be added, are unsettling if not tumultuous because the new paradigm threatens existing interests and the institutional arrangements that hold the current regime of truth in place.

The scientific paradigm that undergirds standardized and virtually all criterion-referenced tests which has been in the process of breakdown for the last two decades has reached a critical stage. Standardized and criterion referenced tests, rooted in an anachronistic paradigm, are a major barrier to the renewal and restructuring of the nation's schools. As we enter the last decade of the twentieth century, it is becoming apparent, at least to those outside the testing and measurement establishment, that the assumptions which are intrinsic to the technology of standardized and most criterion-referenced tests are untenable. Out of the ashes of this paradigm, from the many varied and imperfect efforts underway to solve the practical problems of assessing educational achievement, is slowly emerging a new paradigm, one based on a set of foundational assumptions that are in sharp contrast to those that underlay the current paradigm.

The paradigm that is foundational to current forms of standardized and criterion-referenced tests I label the *psychometric* paradigm; the emerging one, a *contextual* paradigm. There is some risk in the use of these terms, as there is in any effort to classify and simplify complex ongoing human activities into categories. The distinction is helpful insofar as it helps to clarify the issues and distinguish significant differences in efforts to develop alternatives to the most commonly used forms of testing and assessment. The implication

that all tests and assessments may be classified in terms of two mutually exclusive categories, however, is potentially misleading and confusing because
the distinction also may obscure significant differences within and similarities
across categories. As Doug Archbald's and Fred Newmann's summaries of
alternative forms of assessment show (see Chapter 7), some efforts appear to
embody aspects of both paradigms.

It should also be underscored that the psychometric paradigm must not
be considered as synonymous with *quantitative* methods, and the contextual
paradigm with *qualitative* approaches. It is certainly true that psychometric
assessments rely heavily on quantification and statistics, and contextual assessments more often than not employ qualitative methods. However, quantitative measurement and the use of statistics are not necessarily inconsistent
with contextual approaches, and qualitative techniques are sometimes used in
ways that ignore or bypass social context.

Assumption 1: Universality of Meaning. By universality I mean a view that
there is or can be established a single consensual meaning about what standardized or criterion-referenced tests claim to measure which, in effect, tran-
scends social context and history. For example, a standardized reading test
purportedly indicates a person's ability to read in the real world, not just in
the testing situation, and "ability to read," it is assumed, has a more or less
universally understood and accepted meaning. Further, it is assumed that
scores on a given reading test indicate individuals' level of reading ability—
regardless of their or their families' history, culture, or race; regardless of
gender, whether they live in Nome, Alaska or Newark, New Jersey; regardless
of whether they have gone to a school with a first-class library or no library
at all, and whether they reside in an affluent suburb or an area with high
and chronic unemployment. The assumption of universality, in effect says,
that a reading test score has essentially the same meaning for all individuals
everywhere.

Within the discourse of psychometrics, postulated attributes or capacities of persons (their reading ability, or academic achievement in a particular
area, for example) are called *constructs.* A standardized test of academic
achievement presumably measures the *construct* of "academic achievement";
a criterion-referenced test of basic or essential skills measures the *construct* of
"basic" or "essential skills." The term *construct* may sound strange and may
perhaps be considered superfluous to non-specialists in the field of educational measurement. This term became commonplace in the field of mental
measurement after its use in a seminal article by Lee Cronbach and P. E.
Meehl titled "Construct Validity in Psychological Tests" (1955). According
to Cronbach and Meehl a construct "is an intellectual device by means of
which one construes events. . . . It is a means of organizing experience into

categories. . . . Construct validity, then, is involved whenever a test is to be interpreted as a measure of some attribute or quality which is not 'operationally defined''' (pp. 281–82). The use of this term acknowledges an obvious but sometimes ignored fact that human attributes or capacities are not tangible, directly observable, or measurable. Thus, a reading test does not, indeed cannot measure reading directly. Rather, if the reading test does what it claims, it measures a construct the test-makers have labeled ''reading'' or ''reading ability.''

How do we know whether a test measures what it claims to measure, whether a test in fact measures authentic reading ability or genuine academic achievement? The response a traditional testing expert gives to the question of whether a standardized or criterion-referenced test measures what it purports to measure is that this determination depends upon the adequacy of the case a test-maker makes for the test's *construct validity.*

Establishing construct validity of a test requires getting things straight between (1) the world of human events and experience, (2) the construct label, and (3) the test. This entails establishing what Cronbach and Meehl refer to as a ''nomological net,'' which is ''a rigorous (though perhaps probabilistic) chain of inference'' from an empirical body of knowledge and a logical analysis of the meaning of the construct. Almost thirty years later, Cronbach (1987) stressed that ''the argument [for test validation] must link concepts, evidence, *social and political consequences and values''* [italics added]. Thus, in order to establish the validity of a test of academic achievement within the framework of the psychometric paradigm, for example, one would need to assume that the construct of ''academic achievement'' has a stable, universal meaning, or that unanimity on its meaning is both possible and desirable, *and* that it is possible to reach consensus on the desirability of the social and political consequences of the test's use.

The counter assumption: plural, and contradictory meanings. In Chapter 8, I examine in some detail the basic controversies and contradictions in contemporary America over education and the functions, purposes and practices of schooling. I demonstrate that the assumption that there can be a meaningful nationwide statewide, district-wide, or even schoolwide consensus on the goals of schooling and on what students should learn and how they should learn is untenable. I also argue that in a muticultural society which values difference, consensus is undesirable. While it is perhaps understandable that in the 1950s some would hold the view that consensus on basic educational beliefs and values is possible, from the vantage point of the 1990s this view is naive. The premise of what I call a contextual paradigm is that a plurality of meanings, and differences and contradiction in perspectives are inevitable in a multicultural world, where individuals, and groups have differing histories, divergent interests and concerns. There is no, nor can there be universal consensus on what constitutes "ability to read", the meaning of "academic competence" or "authentic achievement" in general terms or within specific academic fields. Experts and nonexperts alike hold plural and often fundamentally contradictory beliefs and values over the meaning of all educational terms. Validating educational tests based on psychometric canons represents a quest for certainty and consensus where certainty is impossible, and agreement is unlikely unless differences are suppressed and consensus is overtly or covertly imposed. Further, as I argue in Chapter 8, the entire concept of "construct validity" on which the scientific credibility of all such tests is rooted is itself internally contradictory and untenable. I also argue that it is possible to develop a system of educational assessment that takes plurality of perspectives and differences in values and beliefs as givens, and treats these differences as assets, rather than obstructions to be overcome.

Assumption 2: The Separability of Ends and Means, and the Moral Neutrality of Technique. Discourse and practice within psychometrics assume that tests, if constructed and interpreted according to accepted standards, are *scientific instruments,* which are value-neutral and capable of being judged solely on their scientific merits. The argument often made in defense of the technology of standardized and criterion-referenced tests is that their development represents an advance over prescientific and subjective forms of assessment, such as grades and teacher-made tests, which intermingle factual observations with the personal, subjective dispositions of the teacher. The basis of the argument for the moral neutrality of tests is that ends and means are separable. Questions such as what constitutes the good or just society, or what is the nature of a good or proper education, because they require moral choices, are not resolvable, and hence lie outside the domain of true science. The choice of means or the best route to a prescribed goal or end, however, is seen as an empirical matter, not a moral question, and hence may be decided scientifically. From this perspective, the job of the assessment expert parallels that of the engineer whose expertise is in the application of the science, not in making judgments about desirability or worth of the enterprise. The role testing expert is limited to dealing with technical or procedural questions within the moral framework set by society.

There are two closely connected assumptions here. First, facts and values, (or what is and what ought to be) are distinct and separable, or they are sufficiently distinct to make possible a non-normative science of educational measurement. What follows from this assumption is that testing experts can make technical decisions without making value judgments. Second, the assessment scientist is best equipped to make judgments about means, that is to develop the ways of assessing educational outcomes and how these are to be properly used and interpreted. Just as it would be the height of irrationality to turn over to a non-engineer the responsibility for designing a bridge or a rocket's guidance system, so too would it be irrational to replace scientific techniques of measurement and the rules of evidence with the opinions and subjective preferences of the non-scientist.

Counterassumption: The Inseparability of Means and Ends. The impossibility of sustaining this fact-value distinction is argued in Chapter 8. In brief, the argument for whether a test measures what it claims to measure rests on the case made for its construct validity, which is considered a technical matter. However, establishing construct validity clearly is not merely a matter of empirics, getting the facts straight and interpreting them according to established rules of evidence. Judgments about an educational test's validity invariably require choices among contradictory values, beliefs and schooling practices (Cherryholmes, 1989; Messick, 1989). In the real world of schooling, separating means and ends is not possible. All assessment procedures have the power to directly or indirectly shape social relationships—how students, teachers, and administrators within a setting interact with one another, what they will or will not say or do in particular situations. Moral questions arise in all social relationships, which can either be resolved by the use of direct or indirect power where the values, beliefs and ideologies of those with the ability to impose their will prevail, or by a process wherein conflicts are acknowledged, and mediated recognizing both differences and commonalties in interests and values. If judgments about assessment procedures and testing are left to experts, then they assume the responsibility for resolving differences over basic moral questions which in a democratic society should be settled by ordinary citizens and/or their democratically elected representatives.

Assumption 3: The Separability of Cognitive from Affective Learning. The psychometric paradigm separates the assessment of learning outcomes and processes into distinct and mutually exclusive categories, separating cognition or academic learning from affect, interests, or attitudes. Sometimes a third category, psychomotor outcomes, is added to the set. Tests of academic achievement, and IQ tests fall into the first category; tests or inventories which solicit a person's beliefs, attitudes, or interests fall into the second; and tests of a person's capacity to perform a hands-on or vocational task (such as auto mechanics or typing) fall into the third. This three-way classification of human learning or capacities divides head, heart, and hand, that is, it separately assesses those areas of human learning and development related to the realm of the intellect, those related to the realm of feelings and values, and those which require manual or physical dexterity. A test of basic educational skills, for instance, purportedly will tell us how well a person knows a particular body of scientific facts or performs a particular set of math tasks. If we want to know the person's interest in math, or whether she is curious about science, we would need to administer a different instrument.

These distinctions are deeply ingrained and institutionalized within the psychometric sciences and are rarely given a second thought. They are legitimated by the Benjamin Bloom's (1956) *Taxonomy of Educational Objectives* which remains the most widely accepted system of classification in the field of education. The distinctions are treated as virtually self-evident and used widely in the everyday discourse of teachers and administrators.

The Counterassumption: The Inseparability of Cognitive, Affective and Conative Learning. As John Raven argues in Chapter 5 and elsewhere (1989), this classification distorts and obstructs efforts to assess significant educational achievements. Raven points out that not only are cognitive and affective outcomes treated as separate categories, but that what he calls the *conative* aspects of human behavior, those concerned with determination, persistence, and will, are inappropriately subsumed under "affective". A person, he points out, can enjoy doing something without being determined to see it through, and he or she can hate doing something, but still be determined to do it. He makes his argument focusing on the "ability to take initiative" which is generally acknowledged as a desirable educational outcome. He argues that taking initiative (which would be categorized as an "affective" outcome in the Bloom Taxonomy) is inseparable from intellectual or cognitive functioning, and from action:

> To take initiative successfully, people must be self-motivated. Self-starting people must be persistent and devote a great deal of time, thought, and effort to the activity. . . . The crucial point to be emphasized in attempting to clarify the nature of competence is that no one does any of these things unless he or she cares about the activity being undertaken. What a person values is therefore central. . . . What follows from this is that it is necessary to know an individual's values, interests, and preoccupations in order to assess his or her competencies. Important abilities demand time, energy, and effort. As a result, *people only display them when they are undertaking activities which are important to them* [Italics added] (Chapter 5, p. 89).

Raven goes on to argue that, if this analysis is correct, it does not make sense to attempt to assess separately cognitive, affective, and conative components of an activity. Affective and conative components are integral to the ability to cognize. "Not only do the three components interpenetrate if the behavior in question—the taking of initiative—is to be successful, these components must be in balance. Determination exercised in the absence of understanding, and the converse, are unlikely to make for a competent performance.''

The proposition that cognitive, affective, and conative aspects of human learning and development are inseparable is in sharp conflict with several accepted canons of traditional psychometry. It runs counter to the widespread practice of using one set of scales to assess values, attitudes, and beliefs and other independent scales to assess knowledge, skills, abilities, or competencies. Raven makes the intriguing suggestion that, if we are to assess such qualities as initiative, instead of trying to develop separate assessments which are difficult if not impossible to interpret, we need to develop indices which unify the cognitive, affective, and conative. He argues that development of all human capacities is highly contingent upon the opportunity structure (the social context), as well as on the learner's will, interest, and knowledge. In Chapter 5, Raven shows that it is technically possible to develop value-based indices that can do more justice both to the complexities of human qualities and capacities, and to how they are fostered and developed.

Assumption 4: The Need for Control from the Center. Testing and assessment procedures are forms of surveillance whose use is the superimposition of a power relationship. Criterion-referenced and standardized tests are sometimes criticized because they shape the school's curriculum and pedagogy. But the *raison d'etre* of *all* evaluative procedures in education, not only standardized and criterion-referenced tests, is to shape the educational process by exerting control over educational administrators, teachers, and/or students. Assessment procedures are inherently political, not only because whoever controls the assessment process shapes the curriculum pedagogy and ultimately the students' life chances, but also because particular forms of assessment promote *particular forms* of social control within the organization, while suppressing others.

My contention here is not that particular forms of organizational management and control inevitably follows from particular forms of assessment. Assessments are only one of many complex factors shaping how schools and school systems are governed. Rather, the claim is that the particular *form* of assessment is a key factor in producing particular forms of social control throughout the organization. In other words, the technology used in the assessment process, will encourage particular forms of management and human relationships within the organization while suppressing others.

The technology of mass administered standardized and criterion-referenced tests produces social relationships and management structures which are largely suited to exercising control from the center, that is, from the central office by local or state educational authorities. Such tests provide virtually no information about what students are capable of doing or where they may need help. These tests produce relative rankings but little substantive information about what students know or can do which is useful to teachers, parents, prospective employers, or to students themselves for making programmatic or individual decisions. The psychometric technology only enables us to classify and rank order students (or teachers), and to constitute individuals as a "case," that is, as belonging to a class or category which possesses a particular set of objective characteristics (*e.g.* high, average, or low achievers, at risk students, etc.).

These tests are used primarily to facilitate what Michael Foucault (1979) calls *le regard,* (the gaze) or visibility to authority. Standardized tests and most criterion-referenced tests are particularly powerful forms of social control because they objectify the subject by reducing all human characteristics to a single number, thereby facilitating comparative rankings, and placing individuals into categories. These ranks and categories allow central office administrators to monitor and manage large numbers of students and teachers. Control exercised by such tests is not direct or overt, their effectiveness, rather, resides in the fact that those who are evaluated internalize or take into themselves the ranks and labels placed on them because these are presumably made by neutral, scientific instruments. Though individuals can and sometimes do resist these valuations of their capacities or achievements, the vast majority succumb because standardized and criterion-referenced test scores are the only educational currency accepted as scientific by the wider society.

Counter assumption: Assessment for Democratic Management Requires Dispersed Control. What should be emphasized for making a case for a contextual paradigm is that intrinsic to the use of standardized and criterion-referenced tests is a form of surveillance and exercise of power which is *unidirectional.* Central office administrators exert power over the everyday life and fate of students, teachers, and parents, who have no way of changing the system of assessment which controls them other than passive resistance or active subversion. While all forms of assessment, including any newer forms we might invent, represent a form of surveillance and constitute a means of control and an exercise of power, it is possible to alter the unidirectionality of control within the assessment system. That is to *re-*form the system of assessment in such a way that it disperses power, vesting it not only in administrative hands but also in the hands of teachers, students, parents and citizens of the community a particular school serves. If we are to have a system of public education supported by public funds, and governed by democratically elected bodies, then oversight by these bodies is essential. Some form of systematic assessment for holding educational institutions and the professionals who work in them accountable for their performance is necessary to monitor expenditures, to insure that that professionals meet their responsibilities, do not exceed their authority, or violate the public trust or students' and parents' rights. But the exercise of power via the assessment process by central administrative authorities at the national, state, or district levels becomes coercive and oppressive without countervailing power over the assessment process exercised by teachers, parents, and students. From both experience and social scientific evidence, it is clear that good schools require a strong measure of autonomy by teachers, other school-level professionals, and participation by the local school-community. Without significant control over the assessment process at the school-level, teacher empowerment and school-based management is an illusion.

In Chapter 6 Elizabeth Adams and Tyrrell Burgess show that a system of assessment can be devised which vests significant power in the hands of central authorities, *and* in the hands of school-level professionals, parents, students, and the local school-community. Drawing upon their experience in the United Kingdom, they show how institutional arrangements and processes can be developed enabling the authorities at all levels to oversee the quality of schooling, to effect system-wide educational policies, and at the same time setting limits on the power of these authorities to trespass on the prerogatives of teachers, school heads, and students. In Chapter 8, I make an effort to extend their argument, and to show how such an effort could be adapted to fit the American experience.

Overview of the Book

A summary of the remaining chapters follows.

Chapter Two. Assessing Mathematics Competence and Achievement, by Thomas A. Romberg, defines and clarifies a conception of authentic achievement in mathematics and examines the validity of the commonly used instruments for assessing mathematics achievement. He concludes with a set of propositions to guide the development of new approaches to mathematics assessment and with an argument for the need to develop new approaches.

Chapter Three. The Assessment of Discourse in Social Studies, by Fred M. Newmann, suggests that a major aspect of social studies assessment should focus on the oral and written discourse that students produce on social topics. He addresses the questions of what discourse is and why it is an important indicator of student achievement in history and social studies. He concludes with his view of what experience and research suggest about the feasibility of this approach to assessment and with a discussion of how the assessment of discourse could provide meaningful and useful comparative indicators of student performance.

Chapter Four. In *The Nature of Authentic Academic Achievement* Fred M. Newmann and Doug A. Archbald argue for a particular view of "authentic" academic achievement, one that challenges the narrow conception of academic learning represented in virtually all current forms of standardized tests. They then examine the problems and implications of their view for assessing achievement.

Chapter Five. A Model of Competence, Motivation, and Behavior, and a Paradigm for Assessment, by John Raven, provides an argument for developing a new assessment paradigm, which is capable of assessing human capabilities and competencies. He proposes a model for measuring human capacities which unifies rather than separates the cognitive, affective, and conative aspects of human learning and development and, drawing upon his research, shows how such a model works in practice.

Chapter Six. In *Recognizing Achievement,* Elizabeth Adams and Tyrrell Burgess, drawing upon their extensive work, summarize an organizational model for a *system* of national assessment, one designed to provide information that enables teachers, students, parents, and public policy-makers to make wise and responsible choices and holds teachers and other professional educators accountable for their performance. Their proposed model, which has been implemented on a modest scale, underlines the interconnections between an assessment system and the way individual schools are structured and governed.

Chapter Seven. In *Approaches to Assessing Academic Achievement,* Doug A. Archbald and Fred M. Newmann include descriptions of efforts to develop alternatives to current forms of standardized and criterion-referenced tests. The efforts they report were generally initiated by school districts or individual schools and were not self-conscious efforts to apply a new theory of assessment. Rather, their development was driven by an effort to find practical ways of overcoming the limitations of conventional standardized and criterion-referenced tests. Though many are initial and partial efforts which would require considerable development before they could be considered for use on a wider scale, they do provide a rich set of possibilities for rethinking and reforming the assessment process.

Chapter Eight. In *Toward the Development of a New Science of Educational Testing and Assessment,* I challenge the basis of the claims that current forms of educational testing are objective or scientific. Drawing from earlier chapters and from several post-modernist and feminist writers, the chapter attempts to reconceptualize the assessment question and advance a case for a contextual paradigm. The chapter concludes with a discussion of the likely objections to the position taken and the prospects for change.

2

Assessing Mathematics Competence and Achievement

Thomas A. Romberg

Introduction

One problem schools face today is that, during the past decade, there has been a radical shift in what the mathematical sciences community considers "authentic" academic mathematical goals for students. In one sense, the shift in emphasis is not new: Many aspects of the reform movement have been under consideration since the turn of the century. However, what is new is the growing consensus on the shift in goals for students and the belief that this vision should be evident in schools today. The dilemma now being addressed is that these goals cannot be achieved by current instructional practices in most schools, nor can school efforts to meet them be assessed using current tests.

To illustrate the need for change, let us examine a stereotype of current classroom practice. A study for the National Science Foundation reported that the sequence of activities in many secondary school mathematics classrooms begins with the more difficult problems from the previous day's assignment worked at the chalkboard by the teacher or a student. This is followed—in some classrooms—by a brief explanation of new material by the teacher, who then assigns exercises for the following day. Almost without exception, the problems are paper-and-pencil exercises taken directly from a textbook or workbook. During the remainder of the class period, students work on the assignment independently while the teacher moves about the room answering questions. The study further noted that "the most noticeable thing about math classes was the repetition of this routine" (Welch 1978, 6).

Although many readers may object to this stereotype of a traditional mathematics class, it is, in fact, all too common. Such an environment fails to foster in students any sense of exploration, curiosity, or excitement. Mathematics is viewed as a vast collection of vaguely related concepts and skills to be mastered in a strict order, with the sole objective of becoming competent at carrying out some algorithmic procedure in order to produce correct answers on sets of stereotyped exercises. Only the work product—and not the process of achieving it or the nature of the task—is evaluated. This fragmentation, emphasis on paper-and-pencil procedural skills, and form of evaluation have effectively separated students from mathematical reality, inquiry, and intellectual growth. In fact, when information is presented in such a fragmented way, it is difficult to remember and to regenerate once forgotten.

It is this picture of mathematics instruction that has been the target of the reform movement. The mathematics education community's response to the current crisis[1] was first to reexamine the basis for such calls for change.[2] The initial consensus was that most students need to learn more, and often different, mathematics in school and that the teaching of mathematics must be significantly improved.

During the past decade, a great deal of activity has been focused on the improvement of mathematics education. Out of the debates and discussions about the crisis in mathematics education has emerged a new vision of the mathematics that it is important for students to know if they are to be productive citizens in the twenty-first century. It is now clear that to provide all students an opportunity to learn the mathematics they will need, the emphases and topics of the present curriculum must be changed. More importantly, the emphasis in structure needs to be on exploration, investigation, reasoning, and communication for all students. In particular, teachers should view their role as guiding and helping students to develop authentic mathematical knowledge. Hence, methods of assessment also should be changed. In fact, the current preoccupation with improved test scores is part of the problem.

The purpose of this chapter is to clarify the meaning of authentic academic achievement in mathematics based on this vision, to examine the validity of commonly used procedures to assess mathematics achievement in light of this meaning of achievement, and to suggest a set of propositions to guide the development of new methods of assessment. The latter is based on the fact that the typical multiple choice, paper-and-pencil mathematics achievement test administered to students does not yield the valid information that is necessary as a basis for making many important educational decisions. Such tests neither assess authentic mathematical outcomes of academic courses nor test the most important mathematical content. This paper concludes that different assessment procedures must be developed.

The Basis for Authentic School Mathematics

The new vision of school mathematics is based on three related concerns. First, current societal and economic expectations make it imperative that more students have an opportunity to learn more mathematics. Second, the mathematical knowledge we should expect students to learn so that they can be productive citizens should reflect the changes taking place in mathematics. Third, research has provided a better understanding of how learning takes place and of how instruction should proceed—information that is critical in instituting the reforms in mathematics education.

Societal Expectations

To understand the nature of the shift in what are considered to be authentic mathematical goals, three societal factors need to be examined: the shift from an "Industrial Society" to an "Information Society," the inadequacy of the current educational system to deal with the implicit shift in the new goals, and the impact of this shift on the uses of mathematics and the expectations of employers.

The Information Age. During the past quarter century, a new technology has evolved that can replace the traditional means of communication (i.e., the printed page) with electronic means by which information can be shared almost instantly by persons anywhere. The shift from an industrial society to an information society is an economic reality, not an intellectual abstraction. And the pace of change will accelerate as the result of continued innovation in communications and computer technology. Furthermore, while the new technologies were originally applied to old industrial tasks, they are now generating totally new processes and products.

This shift from an industrial to an information society has immediate consequences for schooling and, in particular, for the teaching and learning of mathematics:

1. The content and structure of mathematics courses should not be designed to indoctrinate students with past values, but should be derived from visions of the future (Shane and Tabler 1981). Students in schools today will be adults in the twenty-first century. The culture in that era will of necessity be different from that of today. We must attempt to visualize some of the important features of that society if we are to adequately prepare today's children for that world.

2. All students should be taught to reason, to design models, to create, and to solve problems. The most important attribute of the

information economy is that it represents a switch from physical energy to brain power as its driving force, and from concrete products to abstractions in many of its primary outcomes. Instead of training many of our youths to function as cogs in the mechanical systems of factories, we need to train our students in the well-developed thinking skills that are in current demand. This change represents a major shift from the concept of an intellectual elite with the responsibility for innovation while workers take care of production to the new reality of all becoming mathematically literate.

3. In light of rapid economic change, people must anticipate multi-career lives in which they may experience structural unemployment and require reeducation. This highlights the need for a combination of education and training in which students are educated for adaptability and continued learning coupled with on-the-job training for specific tasks.

The Education System. Current goals for school mathematics reflect the priorities of a past era. In the industrial society of the late nineteenth century, it was frugal to educate the populace according to the structure of the economy. A small sector of highly educated elites established public policy, directed the government, managed industry, and advanced the nation's scientific and technological base. The majority of the population, which provided the physical labor for production and services, was educated to the minimum level required for reliable performance. As a result, a dual school system of "high literacy" and "low literacy" evolved (Resnick and Resnick 1977).

Public schools open to the "masses" reflected notions about a literate citizenship appropriate to the new nation. The educational system that evolved during the nineteenth century focused largely on elementary schooling, producing the sharp distinction between elementary and secondary education that persists today. The great majority of children attended school for up to eight years, but few continued on to high school. The curriculum focused on the basic skills of reading, writing, and computation. Teachers in elementary schools were expected to teach all students the entire curriculum. The political conditions under which mass education developed encouraged the routinization of basic skills and standardized teaching. Standardization was a means of insuring that at least minimal curriculum standards would be met, that teachers would be hired on the basis of job competency rather than political or familial affiliation, and that those responsible for the expenditure of public funds could exercise orderly control over the educational process. Such standardization was also a consequence of the notions about the efficiency and effectiveness of routinization that grew out of the Industrial Revolution of the nineteenth century (Bobbitt 1924; Rice 1913).

The consequences of our dual educational system are apparent from recent reviews of the literacy of America's young adults. "Results from the present study show a wide distribution of basic literacy skills, but a severely constrained distribution of higher level ones" (Venezky, Kaestle, and Sum 1987, 3). In other words, we have a "bifurcated work force mirrored by a bifurcated educational system" (p. 52). The educational system of the Industrial Age educated the masses to follow clear and simple directions, to read the newspapers, to perform basic mathematical calculations, and to understand straightforward messages from television. On the other hand, education for thinking has been restricted to a very small, overwhelmingly white minority (Kirsch and Jungeblut 1986). Members of that elite have shared a tradition of scholarly, cultural, and scientific high literacy; they have been prepared for academe and policy-making. This is not to suggest that all of its members were educated to the level of advanced academic study, but it did mean that students were rigorously educated to whatever level they elected, in such a way as to prepare them for that option.

This educational system did not necessarily serve the Industrial Age of the nineteenth and early twentieth centuries very well, and certainly it is no longer adequate. However, the Industrial Age traditions embedded in the dual educational system are hard to change. They include age-graded classrooms, differential schools, tracking at an early age, licensure of general teachers, competence at paper-and-pencil arithmetic, and general mathematics as the terminal course for non-college-bound students. These traditions no longer serve either individual or social needs. In fact, it is not clear that they ever served society well. However, they are obviously inappropriate for the Information Age.

Unfortunately, most proposals for change during the last quarter century have done little more than tinker with changes in one or two features of the system without really challenging the underlying assumptions or traditions of the system itself. This chapter argues that authentic student achievement in mathematics should be based on goals that challenge the industrial assumptions underlying our current dual educational system. Instead, goals should be based on a vision of an educational system appropriate to the Information Age.

The Uses of Mathematics and Employment. The shift in goals for school mathematics is in part the result of pressure from those who represent other disciplines that rely on mathematical knowledge and from business leaders who employ high school graduates. For example, the study of advanced mathematics has tended to be necessary exclusively for the physical sciences and engineering. Today, the computer has made it possible to quantify and use mathematical procedures in an ever-widening variety of disciplines and applications. Furthermore, the mathematical ideas that are important in these new areas of application (e.g., the handling of large sets of data with statistical procedures) are not those that have traditionally been emphasized.

Similarly, the calculation skills needed to be a shopkeeper in the 1920s will not suffice in today's marketplace. Henry Pollak, an applied mathematician, has stated (1987) that industry now seeks employees who have

1. the ability to translate real-world problems into the appropriate mathematical operations for solution,
2. knowledge of a variety of techniques to approach and solve problems,
3. understanding of the underlying mathematical features of a problem,
4. the ability to work with others on problems,
5. the ability to see the applicability of mathematical ideas to common and complex problems,
6. preparation for open-problem situations, since most real problems are not well formulated, and
7. belief in the utility and value of mathematics.

Note how different these skills are from those developed by a student working alone on sets of well-formulated exercises. While mathematics is not taught in schools solely to make students employable, their classroom experiences should not be totally removed from the expectations of employers.

Also disturbing is the fact that the current performance and enrollment picture is bleak for women and most minorities. For example, on the average, black students complete approximately one year less of high school mathematics than their white classmates (Anick, Carpenter, and Smith 1981). Women and most minorities are seriously underrepresented in science and technology careers; only 13 percent of the nation's scientists and engineers are women and only 2 percent are black (National Science Foundation 1982). Furthermore, given that schooling practices are inequitable, this condition is likely to get worse. Affluent suburban school districts already provide their students superior opportunities and resources for the study of mathematics, and they are likely to be the first to react to the current reform movement. These schools already are spending more money on computers, teacher in-service, and the like, thereby widening further the opportunity gap between specific groups of American students.

In summary, schools are social institutions designed to accomplish certain purposes. The problem now being faced by schools is that our culture is changing rapidly. Thus, schools also must change so that students gain confidence in their ability to use the mathematics that will enable them to become productive, employable citizens.

Changes in Mathematics and Its Uses

Even though society is now expecting changes, it would be short-sighted to propose that all students take more school mathematics as it is currently taught. This would be appropriate if mathematics were a static discipline. However, it is not. Rather, it is a dynamic discipline that is growing and expanding. School mathematics needs to reflect both the changes which have been occurring in mathematics in the past century and the changes in how mathematics is used.

Changes in Mathematics. First, consider the picture of the typical mathematics classroom in which students mindlessly carry out repetitive paper-and-pencil calculations. Such mathematics programs fail to reflect the impact of the technological revolution. The low cost and availability of calculators, computers, and related new technology have already dramatically changed the nature of business, industry, government, sciences, and social sciences. Unfortunately, most school children today are not educated to participate in the innovations of this new technological society. Despite the advancements that have made untold computational and graphical power available to the masses, schools invest valuable instructional hours drilling on computational procedures in arithmetic, algebra, statistics, and even calculus; despite the fact that any step-by-step procedure involving the manipulation of mathematical symbols according to a fixed set of rules can be accomplished more rapidly and accurately using a calculator or computer, the majority of our schools do not teach these skills. Some procedures are simple enough that they are best done mentally or by hand, but any that are even slightly complex or take time to do manually should be solved by machine, just as they are outside of the school setting.

The new technology not only has made calculations and graphics easier, but it has changed the nature of the mathematical problems that are posed and, in turn, had changed the discipline itself. Lynn Steen (1986) has recently stated that "major forces are reshaping the nature of mathematics. . . . Most obvious is the increasing importance of algorithmic processes in mathematical methods" (p. 7). Given that computers can perform many calculations quickly, it is no longer adequate to consider one computational procedure. Instead, such questions as *Is this the best procedure? How can we prove it is best? What do we mean by best?* lead to important, unsolved mathematical problems. To reiterate, the computer is changing mathematics and, in turn, it is making certain topics within the discipline more important for school mathematics and others less important.

Another example is the failure of school mathematics to consider changes in collegiate mathematics. For the better part of three decades, the content of the first two years of the college-level mathematics curriculum has remained unchanged. A precalculus course devoted to elementary functions, a two- or three-semester calculus sequence, differential equations and linear algebra, all taught without the use of the computer, provided the standard fare for students pursuing careers in engineering, science, and mathematics. Depending on the background of the students entering the institution, only the entry point and sequencing of these courses might vary. Today, this curriculum is in the process of change. For example, Ralston (1986) argues that although calculus is as important in science and technology as it ever was, the development of computers and computer science has provided calculus with an equal partner called discrete mathematics. While it was once necessary to know calculus in order to comprehend substantive or quantitative concepts in science (Maurer 1985; Roberts 1984), discrete mathematics provides an equally effective window for scientific understanding. In most respects, school mathematics has ignored this fact.

In summary, these changes in the discipline of mathematics need to be reflected in the school curriculum. If such changes are not made, we will continue to train shopkeepers whose mathematical skills are limited to the basic procedures that are now so easily and rapidly accomplished by the calculators and computers we find everywhere in society—except in the schools.

Changes in the Uses of Mathematics. Complementing the influence of technology is the fact that the use and application of mathematics has dramatically expanded. Quantitative and logical techniques have permeated almost all intellectual disciplines. Change has been particularly great in the social sciences and the life sciences. The computer's ability to organize and apply massive sets of information has made quantification possible in such areas as business, economics, linguistics, medicine, and sociology. Furthermore, the fundamental mathematical ideas used in these areas are not necessarily those studied in the traditional algebra-geometry-precalculus-calculus sequence of the high school curriculum. That sequence was designed with engineering and physical science applications in mind. Thus, the curriculum for all students must include the mathematical topics used in many different fields.

In summary, changes in technology have altered the uses of mathematics. These changes must be echoed by changes in the curriculum so that students have an opportunity to learn the skills and ways of thinking that are expected to be of fundamental importance in their adult lives.

Research-Based Knowledge

Evidence drawn from more than a quarter century of educational research also needs to be taken into account so that the alternate picture of school mathematics envisioned is complete. First, in the typical classroom, the conception of learning is that students are passive absorbers of information, storing it in easily retrievable fragments after repeated practice and reinforcement. Research during the past decade has revealed that learning does not occur by way of such passive absorption (Resnick 1987). Instead, individuals approach each new task with prior knowledge. They assimilate new information and construct their own meanings. For example, before young children are taught addition and subtraction, they can already solve most addition and subtraction problems using routines such as counting on and counting back (Romberg and Carpenter 1986). As instruction proceeds, they continue to use these routines to solve problems despite their new knowledge of more formal procedures; they will accept new ideas only when it is no longer feasible to use prior routines. Furthermore, ideas are not isolated in memory but are organized in configurations called schemas. Such schemas are associated with one's natural language and the situations one has encountered in the past. This constructive, as opposed to passive, view of the learning process must be reflected in any reform of teaching and learning.

The earlier picture of instruction in the typical mathematics classroom portrayed the teacher transmitting lessons through exposition to a captive audience. This is, of course, a delivery system based on the most cost-effective means of transmitting information to passive groups. On the other hand, research on instruction has demonstrated the efficacy of project work rather than discrete exercises, of discussions about the origin of concepts and how they are related rather than presentation of independent concepts, and of intrinsic motivation rather than extrinsic rewards. Taken together, these revelations provide a picture of classroom activity which is very different from the stereotype: a class where investigation and exploration are valued, where the teacher is a facilitator of students' creation of knowledge. Thus, instruction should focus on activities that allow students to explore problem situations that challenge them to consider new and different ways of representing relationships and building arguments.

Mathematical Literacy

The term *mathematical literacy* has been chosen deliberately to highlight the shift in the characterization of the goals of school mathematics from that of an industrial metaphor underlying the traditional school program to that of an information/communication metaphor.

The industrial metaphor viewed schooling as "an assembly line" with students as the "raw material input" to the system, teachers as workers "passing on" a fixed body of mathematical knowledge by telling students what they must remember and do (in large part, to become proficient at carrying out calculations), and the end product as the "output" of the system as judged by test scores. This metaphor was based on the need to efficiently prepare the majority of students to fit smoothly into a mass-production economy. To accomplish this goal, knowledge was defined as objective information that had to be acquired, teaching as transmission and control, and learning as absorption.

We have discovered that each of these assumptions is false. Society today needs individuals who can continue to learn, adapt to changing circumstance, and produce new knowledge. Knowledge is viewed as personally constructed information, teaching is guiding, and learning occurs through active participation.

The new metaphor views schooling as a process by which students learn to communicate their ideas about problem situations in a community of shared discourse. It is based on two notions: literacy and disciplined inquiry. Kirsch and Jungeblut, in their report of the NAEP study of literacy, have defined the term as "using printed and written information to function in society" (1986, 3). This definition implies an ability to do something, as opposed to simply acquiring a knowledge of something. Therefore, as Venezky, Kaestle, and Sum have stated, "Literacy is not simply reading, or reading plus writing, but an ability to use print for personal and social ends. It is a functional skill in that it requires the application of various skills in common, everyday situations" (1987, 5). The authors continue by noting that "literacy is also a continuum of skills, not an all-or-none ability" (p. 5). Thus, the development of mathematical literacy involves learning the terms, signs, symbols, and rules for use of a language and, simultaneously, learning to read and write messages in that language in order to communicate with others. Furthermore, its origins and development are situation dependent. However, it does not mean acquiring a haphazard familiarity with or exposure to pieces of knowledge. Instead, it means achieving a growing maturity in dealing with the interrelated concepts and procedures in a specific area, an understanding of how those ideas are used, and a capability for inquiry which reflects the work of mathematicians and users of mathematics. It is in this latter sense that growth in literacy should lead to *disciplined inquiry*—the approach to work that mathematicians use to create new knowledge. In particular, it involves moving beyond a knowledge of concepts and procedures produced by others to gathering and interpreting information about open-ended problems, making conjectures, and building arguments to support or reject hypotheses.

To develop notions about authentic academic achievement based on mathematical literacy, we must consider the following questions:

1. What is mathematics about?
2. How does mathematical knowledge grow?

Answers to these two questions can be developed from at least four perspectives about the content of mathematics and the implied types of instructional experiences which would lead to literacy.

Perspective 1: Empirical Concepts and Procedures

Mathematical knowledge arises from rudimentary ideas acquired through the perception of situations in the complex world around us. Several millennia ago, our ancestors planted the seed for the mathematical enterprise by observing certain quantitative and spatial regularities. From these humble beginnings, mathematics has flowered into the impressive body of knowledge we now possess. Thus, from its origins, mathematics was an empirical science. Its fundamental terms, signs, symbols, and rules are abstractions and inventions created to represent properties observed in the physical environment. Numbers were created to represent the numerosity of sets of familiar objects, signs such as " + " were invented to represent the quantity reached by the joining of sets, and terms such as *parallel* and *perpendicular* were introduced to name spatial properties. The purpose of such a language is communication with others; the terms of the language become useful only to the extent that their meanings can be shared. Thus, one perspective on our two questions would suggest that mathematics is at once a language created by human beings and a set of rules for the use of that language. Its origins are to be found in the patterns of the world (regular and even irregular) in which we live. Furthermore, like any language, it grows and changes as a result of empirical investigations. Thus, to be mathematically literate, all students need to confront a rich array of the common problem situations from which the empirical language of mathematics, its notation, and its rules can gradually be built so that they share in the common meaning for those terms.

Perspective 2: Abstract Concepts and Procedures

A good deal of mathematical knowledge has been created by making that empirically based language and set of rules the objects of human investigation. Again, by observing the properties of numbers, operations, and spatial figures, humans have, by abstraction and invention, created another set of terms, signs, symbols, and rules. Some are generalizations of empirical procedures. For example, the creation of computational routines for empirical processes has made mathematics applicable to many seemingly unrelated problem situations. In addition, no longer bound by perceptual reality, we have extended mathematics by asking *"What if . . . "* questions. For example, while the creation of an equation for the shortest distance between two points on a plane surface has empirical origins, the generalization of this formula to two points in *n*-dimensions does not. And, while the multiplication of whole numbers has its roots in the grouping of objects empirically, more abstract multiplication algorithms do not. They grew out of observations about properties of exponents, such as $a^x \cdot a^y = a^{x+y}$ and the fact that any decimal number can be expressed as an exponent through use of powers of ten. Thus, the second perspective on our two questions suggests that mathematics involves the study of abstract systems and their logic that develops as a result of investigations into different problem situations. Hence, to be mathematically literate, all students should have the opportunity to explore the properties of the empirically derived mathematics and come to see for themselves the relationships, rules of transformations, extensions, and structures gained from these investigations.

In summary, the tasks on which students are evaluated should reflect the interrelated concepts and procedures of specific mathematical domains. Thus, the descriptions of the "content to be learned" for both the empirical and the abstract languages of mathematics should be conceived of as semantic networks associated with such domains. Each network consists of a set of closely related signs, symbols, rules, and problem situations. The problem situations are those that have historically given meaning to the signs and symbols being learned—empirical situations for some and abstract for others. Furthermore, because these networks share a common interrelated set of ideas we have often assigned labels to the networks, such as *whole numbers* and *coordinate geometry*. Thus, the content of school mathematics should be identified by the use of these common labels for mathematical domains; however, it should be understood that, in each case, the referent is the network of ideas being identified.

For example, the related mathematical concepts of addition and subtraction of whole numbers comprise one such content domain. The features of a network which characterize this domain include:

1. The symbolic statements (e.g., $a + b = c$ and $a - b = c$; where a, b, and c are natural numbers) that characterize the domain are identified.
2. The implied task (or tasks) to be carried out is (are) specified. For addition and subtraction, this involves describing the situations where two of the numbers a, b, or c in the statements above are known and the third is unknown.
3. The rules (invariants) that can be followed to represent, transform, and carry out procedures to complete the task (e.g., find the unknown number using one or more of such procedures as counting strategies, basic facts, symbolic transformations such as $a + [] = c \Longleftrightarrow °c - a = []$, and computational routines for larger numbers, among others).
4. A set of situations that have been used to bring meaning to the concepts, the relationships between concepts, and the rules (e.g., join-separate, part-part-whole, compare, equalize, fair trading).

Following the above steps yields a map (a tightly connected network) of the domain.

It should be noted, too, that some rules, or calculation routines, for transforming symbols to other symbols are so useful that mastery of them has been considered essential; in fact, mastery of computational routines is considered by many to constitute mathematical knowledge. I do not deny that a knowledge of computational routines is important even at a time when calculators and computers can perform most computations for us, but such knowledge should grow out of the problem situations that have given rise to the need for algorithms. Furthermore, such procedural knowledge should not be the backbone of elementary school mathematics.

In summary, an expert sees mathematical content as a collection of interrelated domains in which the concepts and procedures of each are expressed as semantic networks (i.e., mathematics is truly a plural noun).

Perspective 3: Reasoning

A critical aspect of mathematics is that mathematicians use a set of intellectual methods when developing conjectures, reasoning about phenomena, building abstractions, validating assertions, and solving problems. These thinking skills, or mathematical methods, are a basic part of mathematics. However, in contrast with the previous two perspectives on our questions, these intellectual skills cut across all content networks. For example, no proposition in mathematics is considered as a mathematical product until it has been validated. Initially, justifications may necessarily be built upon empirical evidence since they were based only on empirical perceptions. However, proving an assertion by presenting a rigorous, logical argument has become the hallmark of abstract mathematics. For example, no geometer who had measured the base angles of an isosceles triangle would conclude that they were congruent based on a demonstration, no matter how accurate the measurements, even though such measurements may have formed the basis of a conjecture about their congruence. Mathematicians demand that this result be deduced from the fundamental concepts of geometry. Thus, a third perspective on our questions is that mathematics involves ways of viewing and thinking about the world. Furthermore, the discipline grows by applying these mathematical methods to a wide variety of problem situations. In this regard, mathematically literate students need to be able to make conjectures, abstract properties from problem situations, explain their reasoning, follow arguments, validate assertions, and communicate results in a meaningful form.

Perspective 4: Mathematics in Use

The power of mathematical knowledge is that its terms and rules are generalizable to many problem situations quite removed from those that originally gave rise to the mathematics itself. In fact, as indicated earlier, mathematics has become the foundation discipline for science and is now increasingly so for the social sciences. For example, logarithms, originally

developed to make complex computations involving multiplication and division easier, have recently assumed new and more powerful applications. Even
though learning to do calculations with logarithms is no longer useful because
computers perform such calculations faster and more accurately, logarithms
are a conceptual tool for evaluating algorithms in computer science, biological statistics, and a wide range of other areas. However, while paper-and-
pencil computational algorithms for such tasks as addition and subtraction are
no longer the central focus of applied mathematics, the decision sequence involved in algorithms is an important conceptual tool that helps address structural properties of operations, which has led to the study of operator algebras.
In turn, the study of such operations had made it possible to simulate com-
putationally a vast array of complex problems, such as the flow of blood
through an artificial heart valve, the trajectory of a hurricane as it approaches
a coastline, and tomographic images of the mantle of the earth. In fact, the
building of mathematical models and the computational simulation of complex situations have become commonplace. As the sciences move increasingly
toward computational methods, so too must the mathematics curriculum if it
is to reflect a modern perspective.

Thus, my answer to the two questions above is that mathematics is a
foundation discipline for other disciplines and grows as a result of its utility.
Hence, to be mathematically literate, it is critical that students be confronted
with a variety of problems from other disciplines and have an opportunity to
build mathematical models, structures, and simulations.

This picture of mathematical knowledge, which reflects the four perspectives about what it means to be mathematically literate, is quite different
from the experiences of students in typical classrooms. The important features
of this vision involve specifying domains of mathematical knowledge as interconnected networks of procedures and concepts that grow in response to a
variety of problem situations (empirical, abstract, and in use). Thus, the assessment of students' achievements should be directed toward the maturity of
their methods of inquiry within each mathematical domain.

Instructional Experience

Authentic knowledge is a product of the ways in which students experience mathematics; the results of engagement in specific instructional activities. In considering instruction, two general principles should be followed.
First, based on the view of content expressed above, all instructional activities
should grow out of problematic situations. Note that while a specific lesson
may not be problem-based, a sequence of lessons should be grounded in a
problem situation. And second, student actions will, of necessity, vary de-

pending on the type of problem situation encountered, and the teacher must be prepared to respond accordingly.

Central to this notion of instruction are problem situations. Traditional teaching emphasized practice in notational transformations and calculation routines as necessary precursors to problem-solving and ignores the fact that knowledge emerges from problems in context, rather than the reverse. Thus, students should be presented with situations that challenge them to analyze the problem and to consider alternatives and possibilities. Note that the emphasis here is on the nature of the tasks or problem situations and not on whether students consider them as problems. Even simple tasks may require analysis for some students. Also, such tasks are quite different from the standard "word problems" that are scattered through typical texts.

There is increasing consensus that improving the capability for learning is inseparable from the specific domain of application. Understanding in a complex domain requires familiarity with its connections—"good thinking almost always involves articulation between knowledge and strategies" (Pressley 1986, 144). The purpose for which knowledge was created and the process by which it is acquired are as essential as the formal structure of the ideas because the mathematical meaning is often derived entirely from the context (Lesh 1985). More specifically, learning to solve problems embedded in a situation is important because "effective thinking is the result of conditionalized knowledge—knowledge that becomes associated with the conditions and constraints of its use" (Glaser 1984, 99).

This kind of learning is most likely to result from a problem-solving situation suggesting that, instead of the traditional expectation that skill in computation should precede word problems, experience with problems develops the ability to compute. Thus, present strategies for teaching mathematics by first teaching skills and then exposing students to stylized application problems need to be reversed; concepts and skills should emerge from experience with problematic situations.

The term *situation* is intended here to mean a position with respect to the conditions and circumstances of some context. The situation should be complex enough to offer challenge but not so complex as to be cooperatively insoluble by a group of students. The situation should parallel the kind of phenomena for which mathematical structures have been typically created (Freudenthal 1983; Romberg 1983). Thus, pupils need to experience the phenomena for which such concepts, structures, and ideas were created. In order to teach the mathematizing of situations, teachers need to create suitable contexts; the most abstract mathematics needs the most concrete contexts. Again, these problem situations are not comparable to the typical "word problems."

However, the situated teaching of mathematics involves more than the provision of manipulatives or the use of realistic problems and applications after instruction in the skills that are necessary to problem solution. It requires, by contrast, realistic and complex situations that are susceptible to simplification. Furthermore, the objective of having students deal with problem situations is not just to find answers, but to communicate with others. For example, on a given problem, students should be able to explain how they have viewed a problem, which signs and symbols they have used to represent it (and why), and how they have reasoned or justified steps in a solution process. To do this implies that most instruction should take place in groups.

For example, instead of instructing children in those notations and expressions designed to represent patterns agreed upon by others, without discussing either the "others" or the process of agreement, teachers need to provide situations in which the students themselves create the patterns. As long as the situations are familiar, conceptions are created from objects, events, and relations in which operations and strategies are well understood. This framework of support can be drawn upon in the future, when rules may well have been forgotten but the structure of the situation remains embedded in memory, as a foundation for reconstruction. Situations should be sufficiently simple to be manageable, but sufficiently complex to provide for diversity in approach. They should involve a variety of conceptual domains, and they should be open as to the methods to be used.

In summary, this section described the meaning of authentic mathematical achievement in the context of the Information Age we are now entering. The illustrations were designed to show that current practices are coherent and based on a common set of assumptions and that we now must challenge current practices and consider new views with respect, in light of the social and economic changes occurring around us. The changes also include the way mathematics is conceived, the way it is used, the way it is taught and, in turn, how assessments of student performance are conducted. The criteria for judging level of performance by a student or group of students should be based on the notions of mathematical literacy. This will involve the student's capability—when presented with a problem situation in a specific mathematical domain—of communicating, reasoning, modeling, solving, and verifying propositions. Also, the index or scale developed to measure performance should reflect the student's level of maturity in that domain.

Validity of Current Assessment

This section poses the question: "How valid is the information gathered via a particular assessment procedure?" To examine this issue, let us examine three types of tests commonly used to assess mathematical performance: standardized tests, criterion-referenced tests, and profile tests. Although other procedures (interviews, observations, judgments about work samples) could be used to assess performance, the ease of development, the convenience, and the low cost of these group-testing procedures have made paper-and-pencil testing common in American schools. Two criteria will be applied: the type of decision for which this test form is appropriate, and its validity for assessing authentic achievement.

Standardized Tests

Norm-referenced standardized tests have become an annual ritual in most schools. Such tests are designed to rank-order respondents with respect to a particular type of mental ability or achievement, or to indicate a respondent's position in a population. Scores derived from these tests are used as the basis of selection and placement decisions. Each test is comprised of a set of independent multiple choice questions. The items have necessarily been subjected to a preliminary trial in a representative pupil group so that it is possible to arrange them in the desired manner with respect to difficulty and the degree to which they discriminate among students. Also, the test is accompanied by a chart or table to be used to transform test results into meaningful characterizations of pupil mental ability or achievement (grade-equivalent scores, percentiles, stanines, and other profiles).

Four features of such tests merit comment. First, although each test is designed to order individuals on a single (unidimensional) trait, such as quantitative aptitude, the derived score is not a direct measure of that trait. It is as if one were measuring basketball star Ralph Sampson's height but, instead of reporting that he is 7'4'' tall, what is reported is that he is in the 99th percentile for American men.

Second, because individual scores are compared with those of a norm population, there will always be some high and some low scores. This is true even if the range of scores is small. Thus, high and low scores cannot fairly or accurately be judged as "good" or "bad" with respect to the underlying trait.

Third, test items are assumed to be equivalent to one another. They are selected on the basis of general level of difficulty (p-value) and some index of discrimination (e.g., non-spurious bi-serial correlation). Furthermore, no claim is made that the items are representative of any well-defined domain. For example, in many subtraction-computation standardized tests, items such as that below are common. Because of the "0" in the tens place, such an item requires successive regroupings and discriminates between good and average subtracters. However, if one were to randomly generate three-digit subtraction problems, few of this type would ever appear.

$$
\begin{array}{ll}
304 & \text{A) } 272 \\
\underline{-\,176} & \text{B) } 138 \\
 & \text{C) } 238 \\
 & \text{D) } 128 \\
 & \text{E) } 232
\end{array}
$$

A typical three-digit subtraction test item.

Finally, such tests have predictive validity. Scores on the Scholastic Aptitude Tests (SATs) are useful because they are reasonable predictors of how well students will do at college (and that alone).

The primary strength of standardized testing is that it does what it was designed to do reasonably well—rank-order individuals. Also, this type of test is relatively easy to develop and is inexpensive and convenient to administer. Furthermore, the results are comprehensible since standard procedures are followed.

The weaknesses of standardized tests are many because they are often used as a basis for decisions that they were not designed to address. In particular, derived scores are invalid indicators of how much one knows. Also, aggregating standardized scores for students in a class (school, district, etc.) to produce a class profile of achievement (class mean) is both a very inefficient method of profiling and a meaningless indicator of achievement. The tests provide too little information in light of the high cost involved. Similarly, the tests are of little value for evaluation or research since the items are not selected as representative of the mathematical domains in the curriculum. Unfortunately, their use appears to be more strongly related to political, rather than educational, purposes. For example, it is claimed that elected officials and educational administrators increasingly use the scores from such tests in comparative ways—to indicate which schools, school districts, and even individual teachers give the appearance of achieving better results (National Coalition of Advocates for Students 1985). Such comparisons are simply misleading. One can only conclude that standardized tests are unwisely overused.

Finally, no claim of validity with respect to authentic mathematical performance can be made. Standardized tests assume that mathematics is a single domain rather than a collection of domains and that all items reflect equivalent but independent concepts and procedures, rather than a network of structured, interdependent ideas. Furthermore, scaling only involves counting the number of correct answers, not the reasoning or strategies used to find an answer.

Criterion-Referenced Tests

These tests are a product of the behavioral objectives movement in the 1960s. They were developed to provide teachers with an objective set of procedures with which to make instructional decisions. Item development was based on the identification of a set of such behavioral objectives as "the subject, when exposed to the conditions described in the antecedent, displays the action specified in the verb in the situation specified by the consequent to some specified criterion" (Romberg 1976, 23). Items randomly selected from a pool designed to represent the antecedent conditions and the same action verb are given to students. From their responses, diagnosis of problems or judgments of mastery of objectives can be made.

Three features of these tests should be mentioned. First, they usually are designed as part of a curriculum to be administered to individuals at the end of some instructional topic. Often, they are given individually, and teachers' judgments are made quickly. For example, they are a part of such elementary mathematics programs as *Individually Prescribed Instruction* (Lipson, Koburt, and Thomas 1967) and *Developing Mathematical Processes* (Romberg, Harvey, Moser, and Montgomery 1974, 1975, 1976). Second, they have occasionally been used in group settings. For example, the comprehensive achievement monitoring scheme (Gorth, Schriber, and O'Reilly 1974) periodically assesses student performances on a set of objectives. Third, decisions about performance are made with respect to *a priori* criteria.

The strengths of objective-referenced tests lie in their usefulness in instruction. As long as instruction on a topic focuses on the acquisition of some specific concept or skill, such tests can be used to indicate whether or not the concept has been learned or the skill mastered. Furthermore, such tests are scored easily and are readily interpretable.

Four weaknesses need to be examined. First, the specification of a set of behavioral objectives fractionates mathematical knowledge. Scores on specific objectives fail to reflect the interrelatedness of concepts and procedures in any domain. Second, objective-referenced tests are costly to construct because hundreds of objectives are included in any instructional program. Third, aggregation across objectives is not reasonable since the objectives are assumed to be independent, not interdependent. Fourth, and most importantly, items for higher-level or complex problem-solving objectives are very difficult to construct and are usually omitted. In fact, as used, these tests reinforce the factory metaphor of schooling and remove judgment from the hands of teachers. They clearly do not reflect how students reason about problem situations, interpret results, or build arguments. Again, there is little match between this method of assessment and the reform vision of mathematical literacy.

Profile Achievement Tests

In contrast to standardized tests, profile achievement tests are designed to yield a variety of scores for groups of students. As early as 1931, Ralph

Tyler outlined a procedure for test construction and validation that clearly articulated the essential dependence of a program of achievement testing on the objectives of instruction and the recognition of forms of pupil behavior indicating attainment of the desired instructional outcomes. Perhaps Tyler, more than any other single test specialist, was responsible for the extension of achievement testing to consideration of the outcomes of instruction. His contributions more than fifty years ago doubtless did much to bring into being the broad modern conception of evaluation in place of the narrower concept of standardized testing. Profile tests are intended to provide information on a variety of topics so that educators (in particular, policy-makers) can compare individuals or groups in terms of those topics.

The current approach to profile testing is to specify a content-by-behavior matrix. For example, to establish a framework for an item domain, a content x behavior grid was developed for each target population for the Second International Mathematics Study (SIMS) (Weinzweig and Wilson 1977). The content dimensions for both Grade 8 and Grade 12 populations were intended to cover all topics likely to be taught in any country. For Grade 8, the content outline contained 133 categories under five broad classifications: arithmetic, algebra, geometry, statistics, and measurement. For Grade 12, the content description was broader, containing 150 categories under seven headings: sets and relations, number systems, algebra, geometry, elementary fractions and calculus, probability and statistics, and finite math.

For each population in the SIMS study, the behavior dimension referred to four levels of cognitive capability expected of students: computation, comprehension, application, and analysis. This classification is adapted from Bloom's (1956) *Taxonomy of Educational Objectives.* The adaptation involved replacing *knowledge* in Bloom's taxonomy with *computation* and eliminating the higher levels of synthesis and evaluation. Both adaptations cause problems. Computation involves knowledge of and ability to carry out a routine algorithm or procedure. However, knowledge of basic concepts does not fit well as either computation or comprehension. Also, eliminating the two higher levels of Bloom's taxonomy is equivalent to admitting that important aspects of problem-solving and developing a logical argument about a conjecture cannot be assessed. The grids were then modified by having each country indicate for each cell its universality (i.e., whether the mathematical skills and knowledge defined by the cell were a curricular element for all, some, or none of the students in the country), and the emphasis and importance the topic or procedure was given in that country's curriculum. In addition, as a check on the comprehensibility of each grid, national centers were requested to supply items they considered appropriate for a sample of cells in each grid. The final International Grid for Grade 12 is reproduced in

TABLE 2.1

International Grid (SIMS)
(from Chang and Ruzicka 1985, 211)

Content Topics	In	Behavioral Categories Computation	Comprehension	Application	Analysis
Arithmetic					
001	Natural and whole numbers	V	V	V	I
002	Common fractions	V	V	I	I
003	Decimal fractions	V	V	V	I
004	Ratio, proportion, percent	V	V	I	I
005	Number theory	I	I	–	–
006	Powers and exponents	I	I	–	–
008	Square roots	I	I	–	–
009	Dimensional analysis	I	I	–	–
Algebra					
101	Integers	V	V	I	I
102	Rationals	I	I	I	I
103	Integer exponents	S	–	–	–
104	Formulas and algebraic expressions	I	I	I	I
105	Polynomials and rational expressions	I	S	–	–
106	Equations and inequations	V	I	I	S
107	Relations and functions	I	I	I	–
110	Finite sets	I	I	I	–
Geometry					
201	Classification of plane figures	I	V	I	S
202	Properties of plane figures	I	V	I	I
203	Congruence of plane figures	I	I	I	S
204	Similarity of plane figures	I	I	I	S
205	Geometric constructions	S	S	S	–
206	Pythagorean triangles	S	S	S	–
207	Coordinates	I	I	I	S
208	Simple deductions	S	I	I	I
209	Transformation (informal)	I	I	I	–
211	Solids	S	S	S	–
212	Spatial visualization	–	S	S	–
215	Transformational geometry	S	S	S	–
Statistics					
301	Data collection	S	I	I	–
302	Organization of data	I	I	I	S
303	Representation of data	I	I	I	S
304	Interp of data (mean, median, mode)	I	I	I	–
306	Outcomes and events	S	–	–	–
Measurement					
401	Standard units	V	V	V	–
402	Estimation	I	I	I	–
403	Approximation	I	I	I	–
404	Determination of measures (areas, volumes, etc.)	V	V	I	I

Note: Topic areas not represented in the Cognitive Item Table have been omitted.
The following rating scale has been used: V = very important; I = important;
S = important for some countries.

Table 2.1. It contains across-country importance ratings of each topic at the four cognitive behavior levels.

FIGURE 2.1

Algebra—Equations and Inequalities. Range of Correct Responses
to the Six items, by Grade (McLean, 1982). © 1982
Reprinted with permission from the Queen's Printer for Ontario.

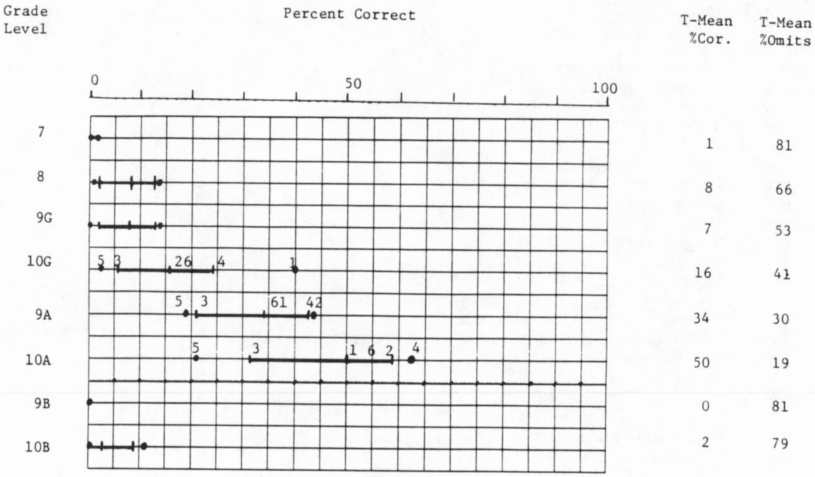

Grade Level	Percent Correct	T-Mean %Cor.	T-Mean %Omits
	0 50 100		
7		1	81
8		8	66
9G		7	53
10G	5 3 26 4 1	16	41
9A	5 3 61 42	34	30
10A	5 3 1 6 2 4	50	19
9B		0	81
10B		2	79

-   this topic is not part of the Grade 7 or Grade 8 program.
-   a surprisingly large number of Grade 10 Advanced students omitted these items.
-   results indicate that, where this skill is needed in Grade 11 and 12, it should be reviewed and practiced then.

Items similar to those in standardized tests are prepared for each cell of the matrix. Data can then be reported in several ways. First, they can be reported in terms of items or cell means. For example, in Figure 2.1 the means are presented for six items on a topic (each given in a different instrument) for different students at different grades in Ontario. Second, item scores can be aggregated by columns to yield cognitive level scores or by rows to yield topic scores (see Figure 2.2).

Profile tests have become very popular alternatives to standardized tests. They have been developed for several major studies of mathematical performance, including the National Longitudinal Study of Mathematical Abilities (NLSMA), National Assessment of Educational Progress (NAEP),

FIGURE 2.2

Percentages. Range of Correct Responses to Topic Group,
by Grade (McLean, 1982, 138). © 1982
Reprinted with permission from the Queen's Printer for Ontario.

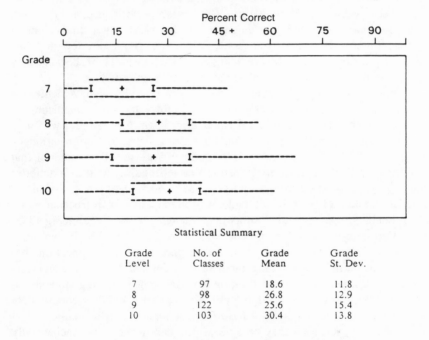

Statistical Summary

Grade Level	No. of Classes	Grade Mean	Grade St. Dev.
7	97	18.6	11.8
8	98	26.8	12.9
9	122	25.6	15.4
10	103	30.4	13.8

First International Mathematics Study (FIMS) Second International Mathematics Study (SIMS), and several different stage assessments.

Four features of profile assessments distinguish them from standardized tests. First, they make no assumption of an underlying single trait; rather, the tests are designed to reflect the multidimensional nature of mathematical content. It must be noted that there often is a temptation to aggregate across topics to achieve a single total score—a score which would be very misleading. Second, the unit of investigation is a group rather than an individual. Matrix sampling is usually used so that a wider variety of items can be included. Third, comparisons between groups are shown graphically on actual scores so that no transformations are needed (see, for example, Figures 2.1 and 2.2). Finally, validity is determined in terms of content and/or curriculum. Mathematicians and teachers are asked to judge whether individual items reflect a content behavior cell in the matrix, and sometimes to indicate whether or not the item represents content that was actually taught.

A strength of profile achievement tests is that they can provide important information about groups and are particularly useful for general evaluations of changed educational policy that directly affects classroom instruction.

However, profile achievement tests are weak in four specific areas. First, because they are designed to reflect group performance, they are not useful for individual ranking or diagnosis. An individual student takes only a sample of items. Second, they are somewhat more costly to develop, and they are harder to administer and score than standardized tests. Third, because they yield a profile of scores, they are often difficult to interpret.

Finally, however, the primary weakness of profile achievement tests centers on the outdated assumptions underlying the two dimensions of content-by-behavior matrices. The content dimension (for example, see Table 2.1) involves a classification of mathematical topics into "informational" categories. As I have argued, " 'Informational knowledge' is material that can be fallen back upon as given, settled, established, assured in a doubtful situation. Clearly, the concepts and processes from some branches of mathematics should be known by all students. The emphasis of instruction, however, should be 'knowing how' rather than 'knowing what' " (Romberg 1983, 122). Furthermore, items in any content category are tested as if they were independent of one another, a practice that ignores the interconnections between ideas within a well-defined mathematical domain. Schoenfeld and Herrmann (1982) cautioned about the problems inherent in testing students on isolated tasks: "If they succeed on those problems, we and they congratulate each other on the fact that they have learned some powerful mathematical techniques. In fact, they may be able to use such techniques mechanically while lacking some rudimentary thinking skills. To allow them, and ourselves, to believe that they understand the mathematics is deceptive and fraudulent" (1982, 29).

Thus, the items should reflect the interdependence (rather than independence) of ideas in a content domain.

The behavior dimension of matrices has always posed problems. All agree that Bloom's *Taxonomy* (1956) has proven useful for low-level behaviors (knowledge, comprehension, and application) but difficult for higher levels (analysis, synthesis, and evaluation). Single-answer, multiple-choice items are not reasonable at those levels. One problem is that the *Taxonomy* suggests that "lower" skills should be taught before "higher" skills; this suggests that the fundamental problem is the *Taxonomy's* failure to reflect current psychological thinking, and that it is based on "the naive psychological principle that individual simple behaviors become integrated to form a more complex behavior" (Collis 1987, 3). In the more than thirty years since Bloom published his *Taxonomy*, our knowledge about learning and how information is processed has changed and expanded dramatically.

In summary, profiling is important, but current profile tests fail to reflect the way mathematical knowledge is structured or how information is processed within mathematical domains.

Summary on Validity

This section has reflected upon current practice and detailed what several of the tests now in common use can and cannot do. The major point to be made is that, while these testing procedures are useful for some purposes and undoubtedly will continue to be used, they are products of an earlier era in educational thought. Like the Model T Ford assembly line, objective tests were considered an example of the application of modern scientific techniques in the 1920s. Today, we are both technologically and intellectually equipped to improve on outdated methods and instruments. The real problem is that all three forms of tests are based on the same set of assumptions—an essentialist view of knowledge, a behavioral absorption theory of learning, and a dispensary approach to teaching. Given the mathematical literacy notions discussed earlier, it should be obvious that new assessment techniques need to be developed which are consistent with this constructivist view of knowledge, learning, and teaching, In fact, if assessment procedures are not changed, continued use of current tests will freeze into place an inappropriate curriculum and be counterproductive with respect to the needed reform in school mathematics.

Assessment of Authentic Mathematical Knowledge

Assuming that a new set of assessment instruments must be developed to gather information about individuals or groups with respect to their mathematical performance, the principles that should be followed include:

Principle 1. A set of specific and important mathematical domains needs to be identified, and the structure and interconnectedness of the procedures, concepts, and problem situations in each of the domains would need to be specified following the steps listed on pages 34–35.

Note that this approach is different from the current approach to specifying the mathematical content of a test in that networks are being defined rather than categories. This means that the interconnections of concepts and prodecures with problem situations are as important as the mastery of any one node (e.g., a specific procedure). For example, consider the following exercise in second grade addition and subtraction:

.

Sue received a box of candy for her birthday. She shared 27 pieces with her friends and now had 37 pieces left. How many pieces of candy were originally in the box?

To solve this exercise, a child would be expected first to represent the quantitative information with the subtraction sentence $[] - 27 = 37$. Second, the sentence should be transformed to the addition sentence $27 + 37 = []$. Then the addition is performed to yield an answer. What is important is that the child must know that separating situations can be represented by subtraction sentences, that subtraction sentences can be transformed into equivalent addition sentences, and that there are procedures for performing additions. Each piece of knowledge, while important, contributes to a solution process or way of reasoning about a situation that is more important than any single concept or process.

Principle 2. A variety of tasks should be constructed that reflect the typical procedures, concepts, and problem situations of that domain.

This is the key principle in that the envisioned tasks are not just a more clever set of paper-and-pencil, multiple-choice test items. Although some typical test items may be appropriate for determining mastery of some specific concept or process, many of the tasks must be different.

For example, some should be exercises that require the student to relate several concepts and procedures, such as the example from addition and subtraction given above. And some should ask students to communicate their understanding of a representation, such as the graphical representation illustrated in Figure 2.3.

Other tasks may emphasize the level of reasoning associated with a set of questions about the same situation, such as the superitem shown in Figure 2.4.

Still other tasks may ask students to carry out a physical process, such as gather data, measure an object, construct a figure, or work in a group to organize a simulation. And still others may be open-ended, like the "carnival problem" depicted in Figure 2.5.

These illustrations demonstrate that there are several different aspects of doing mathematics within any mathematical domain. To be able to assess the level of maturity an individual or a group has achieved in a domain requires that a rich set of tasks be constructed.

Principle 3. Some tasks in a particular domain would be administered to students via tailored testing (and for groups, via matrix sampling as well).

Not all tasks for a domain need to be given to a student or group to determine the level of maturity. Tailored testing involves administering a sample of items following certain rules. The technology is available to systematically

FIGURE 2.3

Example of an Exercise that Asks Students to Communicate Their
Understanding of a Representation (Swan 1987, 12)

The map and the graph below describe a car journey from Nottingham to Crawley
using the M1 and M23 motorways.

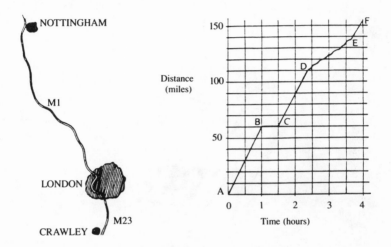

(i) Describe each stage of the journey, making use of the graph and the
map. In particular describe *and* explain what is happening from A to B;
B to C; C to D; D to E and E to F.

vary several aspects of any exercise or problem situation. For example, for the
subtraction exercise under Principle 1, one could vary the situations (join-
separate, part-part-whole, comparison), the size of the numbers, the transformations, and the computational strategies (such as counting, algorithms).
Based on such variations one could accurately judge level of performance
without giving a student every item or the same items as other students.

Principle 4. Based on the tasks administered to a student in a domain, their
complexity, and the student's responses to those tasks, the information should
be logically combined to yield a score for that domain.

Note that this score is not just the number of the correct answers a student has found. Instead, it would involve Boolean combinations of information (such as following inferential rules like "if ___ and ___ , then ___ ").
The intent of the score is that it reflect the degree of maturity the student has
achieved with respect to that domain. Note that this assumes all students are
capable of some knowledge in several domains.

FIGURE 2.4

Example of a Task that Emphasizes the Level of Reasoning Associated with a Set
of Questions (Collis, Romberg and Jurdak 1986, 212)

This is a machine that changes numbers. It adds the number you put in three
times and then adds 2 more. So if you put in 4, it puts out 14.

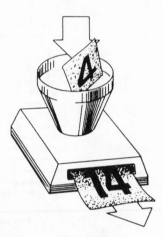

If 14 is put out, what number was put in?
If we put in a 5, what number will the machine put out?
If we got out a 41, what number was put in?
If x is the number that comes out of the machine when the number y is
put in, write down a formula that will give us the value of y whatever the
value of x.

Principle 5. A score vector over the appropriate mathematical domains could
be constructed for each individual or group. Thus, for any individual, one
would have several scores $(X1, X2, \ldots, Xn)$, where Xi is the score for a
particular domain.

Note that this simply reinforces the notion that mathematics is a plural
noun. Mathematics is not a single subject; rather, it encompasses several related domains.

Summary

Awareness of a problem, such as the need for alternative testing procedures for school mathematics, does not mean solutions are easy. It may take
years to replace current testing procedures in schools. Nevertheless, this
should not deter us from exploring plausible alternatives. What is needed are
tasks that provide students an opportunity to reflect, organize, model, repre-

FIGURE 2.5

Typical Carnival Problem (Romberg 1988, pp. 25–28)

sent, argue, and explore within specific domains. Constructing, scoring, scaling, and interpreting responses to such tasks for domains will not be easy, but in the long run it will be worth the effort.

Conclusions

To conclude this chapter, three points should be made.

1. The educational system as a whole, and the teaching and learning of mathematics in particular, need to be changed.

I am concerned that current reform efforts will be no more than a reaction to current weaknesses and that, in order to remedy these weaknesses, we will return to traditional methods of curriculum development, teacher training and, in particular, pupil assessment. Unless changes are made and we get away from traditional practice, we will only contribute to the ongoing difficulties of sterile lessons, further deskilling of teachers, and the inadequate preparation of students. Instead, we need to conceive of curricular structure and of assessments of individual progress in light of mathematical maturity in specific domains.

2. Current testing procedures are unlikely to provide valid information for decisions about the current reform movement.

Current tests reflect the ideas and technology of a different era and world view. They cannot assess how students think or reflect on tasks, nor can they measure interrelationships of ideas.

3.   Work should be initiated to develop new assessment procedures.

Only by having new assessment tools that reflect authentic achievement in specific mathematical domains can we provide educators with appropriate information about how students are performing. Of necessity, this implies that considerable funds be allocated for research and development. Only when new instruments are developed will we be emancipated from old assessment procedures rooted in the traditions of Industrial Age schooling.

The Assessment of Discourse
in Social Studies

Fred M. Newmann

Introduction

This is a position statement which argues that a major aspect of social studies assessment should focus on the oral and written discourse that students produce on social topics. Public attention is most often devoted to comparisons between schools, districts, states, or nations, and this position on assessment is intended to apply to all levels, from the classroom to the nation. To develop the position, several issues will be addressed:

1. What is *discourse?*
2. Why is discourse an important indicator of student achievement in history and social studies?
3. What forms of discourse should be assessed?
4. What does experience and research suggest about the feasibility of this approach to assessment?
5. Will discourse assessment provide meaningful comparative indicators?

The recommendation is not that all traditional indicators be replaced by indicators of discourse, but that discourse should occupy a significant place in a larger scheme of indicators.

What Is Discourse in Social Studies?

We define discourse in social studies as language produced by the student with the intention of providing a narrative, argument, explanation, or analysis. To qualify as discourse, these statements must go beyond the literal reproduction of statements previously produced by teachers, authors of texts, and dictionaries of technical terms, or even notable excerpts from distinguished literary, historical, and scientific works. That is, students should produce language in their own unique ways—not that they must reinvent the wisdom of human culture, but that they should incorporate words, concepts, and phrases used by others into coherent patterns of oral speech and writing to serve purposes unique to tasks of communication in modern times. This is, of course, a tall order, but unless it is kept prominently in mind, we will continue down the rut of fragmented knowledge bits memorized in the short run, easily tested and reported in the media, but rarely used to expand the use of the mind.

In history, social science, or other subjects that compose social studies, intelligent discourse demands familiarity with formal authoritative knowledge (e.g., the structure of government—formal and informal; geography; economic systems; sociological structure; psychological explanations for behavior; philosophical and humanitarian insights on the significance of life and the universe), but these enormous repositories of knowledge pose two difficult problems. The first is the difficulty of selecting a finite core from a virtually infinite universe of content, all of which is "worth knowing" in some sense.[1] The second is the pedagogical challenge of organizing or translating whatever may be taught into a curriculum which "lives," that is, which gives power and meaning to the enormous diversity of subcultures within the United States and which also responds to changing conditions of domestic and global life. In short, the "core" must be static enough to provide comparative indicators, but at the same time it must be a "moving target" that touches the personal lives and emotions of students, inviting them to assimilate and to accommodate knowledge to resolve the puzzles and dilemmas of citizenship.

Thus, discourse that indicates knowledge of social studies content requires the student to integrate relevant formal knowledge of the field into one's own language by referring to proper names and authoritative explanations or interpretations. But these must be produced as responses to novel, contextualized problems that challenge the student to use knowledge in new ways. In short, the questions must invite the production of contextualized knowledge by the student rather than the mechanistic reproduction of isolated knowledge bits removed from social context.[2] Here are some hypothetical examples of student discourse in social studies:

1. The Boston Tea Party before the American Revolution was a violent protest against the many restrictions on the colonists' trade imposed by the English Parliament. Although it was "violent," it really didn't hurt people—physically. It did do violence to property rights, because all that tea was destroyed by people who didn't own it. Still,

I think the protest was justified, because the colonists had taken just about all the peaceful means they could to try to get Parliament to revise some very unjust laws.

2. We got into the Great Depression, because people lost faith in the economy. When people lost faith that prices of stock would rise, they rushed to sell. This lowered prices, people panicked, prices fell further, more panic, etc. As companies lost assets, they laid off workers. The workers as consumers couldn't afford to buy, so companies had to lower prices. This reduced their income further which led to further layoffs, failure to pay bank loans, etc. As people needed their savings, they rushed to the banks. Banks couldn't pay and they failed, which further undercut investment in business. The fear of economic failure made it fail.

Conceivably, statements like these might merely reproduce reports of material presented in texts or teacher lectures, but assuming that they are reasonably original translations in students' own words, they stand in stark contrast to the forms of expression usually required in conventional assessment tasks. Most tasks on standardized tests and in National Assessment of Educational Progress (NAEP) exercises, for example, do not require students to make narrative or interpretive statements. Instead, they typically require students to read a question that can be answered only by the student's choosing the best answer from among four alternatives previously constructed by the test-maker. Such questions fail to generate discourse, because they demand only that the student recognize the language of others.

As commonly understood, discourse involves a reciprocal relationship: a writer (speaker) trying to communicate with a reader (listener) so as to produce a particular reaction from the reader. Presumably the writer's anticipation of the reader's reaction determines, in large measure, how the writer produces language. As Nystrand (1977, 1986) has argued, this process has significance beyond the mere sending of messages between people. In short, it transforms those who produce and who receive the language.

Asking students to go beyond multiple choice tests and to write extended statements will, from a technical point of view, produce discourse, but to decide whether the discourse is educationally worthwhile we must inquire further into the way particular writing tasks are likely to "transform" the writers and readers.

If a student's major purpose in writing is to receive a high grade from the teacher, and the teacher has shown that high grades are given primarily for reproduction of text in proper grammatical form, then, in writing toward these ends, the student becomes only a compliant messenger. This, of course, should not necessarily be considered always a simple or demeaning task, for it can involve committing much to memory and making complex predictions about the actual expectations of the teacher. In turn, the teacher who distributes grades only according to the success with which students accurately transmit predetermined messages functions only as an auditor—a checker to see whether unambiguous criteria have been met.

In contrast, if grades are given for detailed expression of the students' personal reactions to content (for example, in position papers), and if the teacher's response concentrates on how the student might make the statement more persuasive (perhaps to audiences who may not share the student's point of view), the student and teacher are transformed into more autonomous writers, each with something unique to say to the other. The mutual interest between writer and reader in the content of what is said, in contrast to a primarily evaluative judgment, is what makes discourse authentic.[3]

Writing and speaking primarily to summarize texts that have been produced by others has important educational benefits, but in school it is often emphasized so much that student writing becomes inauthentic. Such enormous effort is placed on conformity to formal conventions of writing and speech that students must consistently communicate about topics that have little relevance to their personal lives and to the people who are interested only in whether the form and content matches what teachers and test scorers already know. From the student's perspective this sort of discourse is inauthentic, because it offers no possibility of influencing the reader except on the limited matter of whether the student is competent to write on questions with predetermined answers.

To increase student engagement in the production of language, we should aim for more authentic writing and speaking tasks, and this can be promoted by emphasizing two main purposes for language expression. Authentic discourse (1) provides an opportunity for the student to relate the formal subject of study to personal interests and public concerns, and (2) includes information that has the potential for influencing the reader about issues beyond the judgment of the student's writing competence, for example, to discover new facets of history (through original student research) or to develop new insights on policy and value issues (through student writing of position papers).

If, for example, students are asked to write a personal position paper on the justification for the colonists' revolt against England, they have the opportunity to connect themselves to history and also the possibility of making novel points that might influence the teacher's views of the revolution. If, however, they are asked only to describe three main causes of the revolution, there is little prospect that the teacher will be genuinely interested in what they have to say or that they might influence the teacher's ideas on the topic. Later we discuss in more detail the particular forms of discourse that could provide more authentic assessments.

Why Is Discourse an Important Indicator of Student Achievement in History and Social Studies?

The case for the assessment of discourse rests on several points. It will (1) facilitate the learning of content in social studies, (2) reinforce development of social perspectives considered fundamental to democratic citizenship, especially tolerance or taking the role of the other, and (3) promote higher order thinking. Highlighting these points, however, should not obscure the most significant reason for assessing discourse: The most meaningful indicator of educational success in social studies (and other subjects as well) is the quality of conversational and written statements that students make in social intercourse beyond school. Each of the three points will be discussed in turn.

Explaining in writing or speech what one knows should be seen not simply as a demonstration or a performance, but also as process that enhances learning itself. Even in the taking of notes intended only for communication with self, as in a learning log, writing narratives and explanations enlarges understanding (Nystrand and Wiederspiel 1977). In social studies, writing might address questions such as *What was the central point of the politician's speech? Do I really understand how interest rates affect employment? How would I worship if I were a Moslem?* and *Why did Lincoln try so hard to save the Union?* In this sense, the effort to produce coherent language to answer such questions helps to teach the content of social studies.

Ultimately, however, discourse is oriented toward communication with others, and it thereby leads students to take the role of the other (Nystrand 1986). To be effective, the speaker must construe one's own purposes, thoughts, and language in terms of the anticipated purposes, thoughts, and language meanings of others. Productive discourse thus requires reciprocal thinking—which can be seen as a foundation of tolerance. The persistent effort to anticipate the role of the other does more than facilitate communication; it is the essence of moral sensitivity.

As we have defined discourse for social studies, it entails the production of language that goes beyond the information given to produce an original summary, interpretation, analysis, or evaluation. As such, discourse is, in most instances, likely to stimulate higher-order thinking (Applebe 1984; Newmann 1990), an educational goal emphasized (at least in rhetoric) both within and beyond social studies, especially for its connection to democratic citizenship. That is, critical thinking problem-solving on social issues has been considered crucial to the preservation of democratic values: consent of the governed, individual liberty, the public good and, most recently, to national economic prosperity within the world economy.[4]

Higher-order thinking has been tested through traditional multiple choice items, but these have been thoroughly criticized (McPeck 1981;

Frederiksen 1984, 1988) because they offer little information about how students integrate knowledge to solve problems. In contrast, when students are asked to formulate a problem and to produce language that reveals a chain of reasoning, we learn far more about the workings of their minds than when they simply select choices from predetermined alternatives. Traditional tests may tap some aspects of higher-order thought, and not all forms of discourse can be considered sufficient indicators of higher-order thinking, but discourse exercises would substantially expand our knowledge of student progress on this objective, especially with regard to thinking about the ill-structured problems so common in history and social studies.

Authorities in history and social studies differ on the particular forms of knowledge that students should learn and on the kinds of problems to which they should apply their minds. Thus, choosing unequivocal indicators for achievement in social studies will always be problematic. At the same time, there is consensus that the teaching of required courses in history or social studies in US public schools should be grounded in a theory of citizenship that celebrates the promotion of open and critical discourse on public affairs. Those rationales responsive to scholarship in educational philosophy and democratic political theory (e.g., Giroux and McLaren 1986; Hunt and Metcalf 1968; Lazerson et al. 1985; Newmann 1975; Oliver and Shaver 1966) make a persuasive case that the ultimate indicators of the quality of citizenship are the statements that people make, whether orally or in writing, which indicate their understanding of society, institutions, history, and the relationship of citizens to one another and to the state. In short, we should look to discourse as the most significant indicator because our ultimate educational objective is discourse itself.

If the scheduling of instruction permitted more attention to students' oral and written discourse in schools, and if teachers felt they could use criteria for assessment consistent with their best professional judgment, without being challenged to prove the "scientific objectivity" of their judgments, many say they would rely far more heavily on discourse as the most meaningful indicator of students' understanding. The power of discourse (rather than short-answer responses) as an indicator of understanding is further illustrated by the emphasis placed in higher education on the writing of papers, essays, and the culminating challenge of the oral examinations. Recent analysts of high school reform (e.g., Adler 1982; Boyer 1983; Sizer 1984) consistently emphasize discourse as the ultimate indicator of an educated person. This seems so apparent that it leads one to wonder why it has *not* been so used.

Our failure to establish discourse as a key indicator of social knowledge is not simply an oversight or an easily correctable error. It stems from complex problems and dilemmas. Intelligent conversation cannot be conducted without specific knowledge of the topic at hand. A storehouse of isolated bits of knowledge possessed by a student (e.g., those suggested in the cultural literacy curriculum of Hirsch 1987) can thus be seen as an indicator of the student's potential for conducting intelligent discourse. Responses to multiple choice and fill-in-the-blank items are, therefore, considered reasonable indicators of a student's familiarity with the raw material that must be used to produce intelligent conversation. We may agree with the importance of knowledge of a common body of content and vocabulary, but there are, nevertheless, several problems in using as the main indicators of this knowledge students' choices among predetermined alternatives of their production of short answers to stem questions.

First, there is no absolute sense in which knowledge can be tested. The judgment as to whether a student has a particular unit of knowledge in memory and can apply it appropriately as needed is always dependent upon the task chosen as an indicator of the competence. Each of the following, for example, might be an indicator of whether a student can identify US presidents in the twentieth century:

1. Which of the following presidents served in the twentieth century?
   a. Lincoln
   b. Wilson
   c. Hoover
   d. Truman
2. Name three US presidents who served in the twentieth century.

Suppose a student passed question 1 but failed question 2. What would we conclude about his or her knowledge of twentieth century US presidents?

Second, we question the assumption that the acquisition, storage, and retrieval of isolated knowledge bits must occur *prior* to the application, interpretation, and synthesis of knowledge that occurs in authentic discourse. The fact that intelligent discourse about a problem displays or reveals specific content knowledge does not justify the inference that such knowledge be learned (or tested) first in the form of isolated bits. The belief that we first engage in the simple process of acquiring knowledge bits and later learn the more complex process of using them has been increasingly challenged by cognitive science. Instead, acquisition, storage, retrieval, application, and synthesis can be seen as simultaneous, interactive processes.[5]

Third is the seductive trap that ensnares most of our teaching. In the effort to adequately prepare students for discourse, we spend so much time transmitting knowledge that students rarely have an opportunity in school to produce discourse. Research indicates that retention of isolated knowledge bits is short-lived unless the items are frequently put to use. To the extent that tests focus almost exclusively on student reproduction of these knowledge bits, the tests provide unreliable indicators. Student performance after the testing date will depend, primarily, not on test performance but on the extent to which students have occasion to use the knowledge bits. Since most of the tasks on conventional test are unlikely to be performed beyond the infrequent testing situations, student knowledge evaporates quickly.

The well-publicized surveys on citizen ignorance (or forgetting what was taught) is often attributed to lack of rigor in teaching or insufficient "time on task," but its persistence leads one to suspect a more fundamental cause. If educators and the public continue to conceive of knowledge itself primarily as retrieval of isolated knowledge bits rather than as the conduct of intelligent discourse, most students will continue to forget what they have studied, even though they may have earned respectable scores on unit tests or final exams.

Test-makers might accept these criticisms of the tendency to test for isolated knowledge bits, and they might show much enthusiasm for discourse as a potentially more powerful indicator of knowledge. Their reluctance to promote discourse assessment may be based on other issues such as problems of validity, reliability, comparability, and the costs of discourse assessments. These issues will be addressed later.

How Should Discourse Be Assessed and Why?

Having argued for discourse as a major indicator of knowledge in history and social studies and criticized common beliefs that stand in the way, we now consider more specifically the ways in which discourse might be assessed.[6] Within history and social studies what, more precisely, should we expect students to speak about intelligently? This raises questions of both form and substance. Since the latter is especially complicated, we begin with the somewhat more straightforward issue of form, but to give the discussion more concrete meaning we first present several illustrative tasks for assessing discourse.

Illustrative Tasks for Assessing Student Discourse

The tasks below call for knowledge in U.S. history, world history, social science, geography, and civics.

1. The eighteenth century is considered one of the most important periods in the history of the United States. Discuss some reasons why that century is considered so important. In expressing your ideas, describe key events, people, general trends, and ideas that seemed to take hold of people, and explain why these would be considered important.

2. A person from outer space (who speaks English) arrives on the planet and asks, "What kind of government does the United States have?" How would you answer the visitor who has never been exposed to democratic institutions? Include an explanation of how laws are passed, enforced, and judged, and what rights and responsibilities the citizens have.

3. Americans have been accused of being ignorant of other parts of the world and isolated from other cultures. Show that you are innocent of this charge by describing a society, culture, or country outside of the United States. Discuss as much as possible its history, geography, economy, culture, and critical issues it faces today.

4. What do you think of the following statement: "Americans owe most of their main beliefs, values, and institutions to the Western European tradition." Explain how much you agree or disagree with this statement, and provide evidence for your position.

5. Joe is 25 years old and out of work. He graduated from high school and has worked most of his life in construction, but he lives in a region where construction workers have been laid off by the thousands. He asks why there aren't more jobs. He is told only that "We're in a recession," or "Interest rates are too high," or "Demand is depressed." Joe never studied economics and finds these statements hard to understand. Explain to Joe, in language he is likely to understand, several possible reasons why the economy may not be providing more jobs for construction workers.

6. A friend is coming to town by car to visit you. He phones from the highway on the outskirts of the city, asking for directions on how to find your home. Use the map below to give verbal directions on the shortest way to travel from his arrival point to your home. [The map would include a variety of streets and landmarks, with several possible routes.]

7. The table below gives information on population and age distribution trends in different parts of the United States, economic production, unemployment, employment in different vocations, and educational attainment [insert an appropriate table]. Using this information, describe major changes that occurred in the United States between 1900 and 1960 and also describe the variables, if any, that have remained relatively stable for long periods of time. Wherever possible, explain the reasons for change and stability.

8. Traveling in a foreign country, you meet a person who asks you, in a friendly way, to explain why there is so much violence in America, why there has been so much racial discrimination, why there are such large differences in wealth between families, why politicians

are often exposed as corrupt, why so few people vote, why there
seems to be increasing use of drugs, and other social problems.
Choose two of these topics to explain, using your knowledge of history and contemporary affairs.

Form: Written and Oral

Students should be able to produce intelligent language on social topics
both orally and in writing. Each form is necessary for effective citizenship in
a democracy. In either type of exercise, students can be presented with a topic,
a general question, a problem, a provocative quotation, vignette, or excerpt
from a published work and asked to make a reasonably extended statement
(e.g., about 300 words) in response. The response should indicate that the
student can use knowledge to develop an explanation, an idea, a proposal, an
argument, a narrative; and that various parts of the statement are organized
into a coherent whole. The precise nature of these tasks and more specific
criteria for assessing success on these general criteria must be developed.

Teachers may often assign tasks similar to those suggested, but since
previous national assessments have not focused on writing unique to social
studies, substantial development of format and evaluative criteria may be necessary. Previous experience in the assessment of writing will be helpful, but
new work on the evaluation of knowledge expressed through discourse will be
necessary.

Assessment of oral discourse should also be pursued. Oral dialogue is
the form in which we most frequently share social knowledge with others.
More importantly, it is the prime currency in which we express the concerns
of citizenship. At first glance, it seems to raise two major problems. Teachers
rarely emphasize the production oral discourse as the central goal of instruction. Thus, students are unaccustomed to developing extended oral statements
as indicators of what they have learned. Assessing oral discourse can also
pose logistical problems in the recording and assessment of statements.
Audiotape-recording followed by manual transcription or, perhaps in the future, by computerized voice-to-print transcription could be used. The more
fundamental problem, also relevant to written discourse, may be promoting
this form of competence as a serious objective in social studies classrooms.

Substance: Common and Elective Topics

What in history and social studies should students be able to talk about
intelligently? A minimally acceptable, virtually indisputable answer, is that
every student should be able to conduct discourse on at least one topic of
social-historical significance. Beyond this, however, we face a morass of issues. The first involves the organizational or political unit for which indicators
are intended, which range from the teacher's individual classroom to a set of

classes within a department, to departments within a school, to schools within districts, to districts within states, to states within nations, and to nations across the globe. Indicators may be desired to compare performance of units at particular levels (e.g., between states or nations), but curriculum objectives at different levels can vary substantially for legitimate reasons.

Defining critical topics, or a "core," is further complicated by the vast range and specialization of knowledge in history, geography, economics, political science, psychology, sociology, anthropology, and several other emerging bodies of knowledge (e.g., area studies, ethnic studies, environmental studies, global education, law-related education). Within and between fields, scholars and practitioners disagree about the critical topics on which students should be able to write or speak.

Cultural pluralism poses a further challenge to the selection of content. In contrast to subjects such as math or science, which also experience controversy over selection of the central topics to be taught, social studies is especially interested in helping students to become productive citizens within the communities to which they belong. To the extent that different racial, ethnic, gender, and socioeconomic groups experience different problems in the exercise of citizenship, it becomes increasingly difficult to define a single or common set of topics likely to maximize constructive democratic citizenship for all students in the nation.

Meaningful indicators, however, need not rest entirely on the identification of specific content common to all schools, districts, or states. As a matter of principle and as a matter of necessity, it is unwise to prescribe that all or most of the instruction in social studies be based in a national common curriculum. A case might be that *part* of a national assessment would include student discourse on a limited number of very general topics (e.g., democracy, industrialization, US involvement in war), but these should not be confused with testing of the highly specific terms provided, for example, by Hirsch (1987).[7] To converse well about general ideas requires student use of extensive background knowledge, but there are at least two reasons why the background knowledge itself should not be prescribed as the core to be tested. First, intelligent discourse on such general topics can involve an enormous and unpredictable variety of background knowledge unique to the particular question(s) addressed under the topic. Second, if such background knowledge is prescribed, it, rather than discourse, is likely to become the end. Hirsch himself defines the extensive background knowledge required for cultural literacy as only a vague and hazy understanding of terms. In contrast, we argue that the ultimate goal of discourse must be in-depth understanding.

If part of the assessment presents a few general topics and elective topics for all to discuss, students should also have ample opportunity to demonstrate competence beyond areas that may be chosen as state or national priorities. Students devote significant energy to the study of some topics emphasized in *their* schools but not emphasized in other schools. This body of "uncommon" knowledge, either required uniquely by some schools or studies by students as electives, will also influence the texture of citizen discourse in the nation, and we should examine the quality of discourse on these indicators as well.

Further discussion of the selection of common topics and elective topics may well lead to specification of a set of areas across which some portion of the elective topics would be distributed. It may be decided, for example, that each student should be able to produce discourse on a topic in the history of the United States, on a topic in the history of another nation or culture, and on an elective topic from a broader set of possibilities.

Degree of Specificity in Content

The task of selecting general topics or elective topics should not include specification of discrete bits of knowledge, particular concepts, theories, or explanations characteristic of conventional assessments. Since the goal here is intelligent discourse (not the recall or application of atomized knowledge), and since discourse on these topics can reasonably touch upon a variety of issues and rely upon a variety of specific knowledge, the assessment must provide wide latitude for students to invoke knowledge of diverse sorts. The identification of topics, rather than highly specific terms and knowledge, is necessary not only to remain faithful to discourse as the ultimate objective, but also to recognize (even celebrate) the fact different schools may teach different knowledge as they study the "core" topics.

This is not to minimize the importance of substantive content in the evaluation of discourse. Intelligent discourse in history and social studies demands that students address and incorporate authoritative knowledge in their effort to construct meaningful statements about social life. Thus, discourse in social studies entails not simply the use of general language or thinking skills, but the production of domain-specific knowledge in the students' language. To evaluate student success in social studies discourse, it will be necessary, therefore, to develop general criteria for the content or knowledge that ought to emerge in the discussion of specific topics. Content guidelines, however, must be flexible enough to allow for variation in the content that students use to illuminate topics.

What Does Experience and Research Suggest Regarding the Feasibility of this Approach to Assessment?

Further support for the assessment of discourse can be found in recent reviews of testing that advocate departures from traditional multiple choice formats in fields beyond social studies. In mathematics and science, for example, experts have called for techniques that allow students more opportunity to explain their approaches to the solution of problems, rather than simply choosing from among predefined solutions.[8] In the United Kingdom, innovative assessment efforts in mathematics, science, foreign language, and "oracy" have all stimulated greater opportunities for students to converse, to produce language, and to complete more holistic tasks than conventional tests have permitted (Burstall 1986).

In the NAEP 1981–82 assessment of citizenship and social studies, twenty-five of the sixty-four released exercises were open-ended, requiring students to write answers. Most of these exercises, however, called for short, one-or-two sentence answers, or the making of lists; for example: *Give two things you could do to find out why each candidate thinks as he does,* and *Name as many reasons as you can why laws are needed.* A few items asked students to explain a course of action and provided enough space to suggest that more extended discourse was called for. High reliability in scoring was obtained, but the criteria emphasized primarily whether correct information was included in the answer, with little attention to the form or sophistication of the argument. For the most part, the exercises were focused on specific terms, offering little opportunity for students to define a problem and to organize information from several sources to discuss it.[9] In developing more elaborate procedures for assessing discourse, however, we should build upon NAEP's previous experience with open-ended items.

The assessment of writing probably offers the most extensive experience on which to develop discourse assessment in social studies.[10] Recent research on assessment in English (Greenberg, Wiener, and Donovan 1986; Tyler 1983; White 1986) supports the efficacy, reliability, and validity of writing samples to assess students' skills in composition. The use of writing samples for multiple purposes, including placement in English composition classes, determination of proficiency or minimal competency, and diagnosis is supported by the work of the National Testing Network in Writing, the National Assessment of Educational Progress, and the National Writing Project.

These projects have led to the development of both holistic and primary-trait scoring methods (Applebee, Langer and Mullis 1986; Myers 1980), the assessment of distinct writing tasks (informative, persuasive, and imaginative) by more than 100,000 students, the training of about 70,000 teachers annually to assess student writing at more than 200 sites in the United States and abroad, and survey data indicating that many teachers prefer locally developed, holistically scored writing samples over any other sort of test, regardless of test purpose.

Despite the extensive experience, some debate remains concerning the use of direct writing samples as opposed to multiple choice assessment.

According to White (1986) and others (Fader 1986; Greenburg, Wiener, and Donovan 1986) multiple choice tests do measure some of the skills assessed through the collection and scoring of writing samples, including students' abilities to recognize conventions of grammar, sentence structure, and mechanics, and their ability to correctly choose from several stylistic options. However, multiple choice tests do not directly measure those skills consistently identified by writing teachers as critical to effective composition. These skills include the invention, revision, and editing of ideas to serve particular audiences with appropriate stylistic, mechanical, and grammatical structures.

Until recently, advocates of multiple choice, indirect measures of assessing writing cited the high cost and low reliability of scoring writing samples. But this concern has been revisited due to the high development costs of multiple choice testing, the need for continuous item revision, costs of assuring security in monitoring, questions concerning the validity of indirect measures, and the potential negative effect upon curricula due to lack of attention to actual writing (White 1986).

Holistic scoring and primary-trait scoring predominate as forms of direct assessment of students' writing skills. Holistic or general-impression scoring focuses on a writer's general fluency in responding to a writing task, as well as attending to organization, quality of content, spelling, punctuation, and vocabulary choice. Holistic evaluation is usually conducted by teams of trained readers using scoring guides describing desired features of the writing and identifying high-, medium-, and low-quality levels for each feature. Primary-trait scoring focuses on the specific features necessary to accomplish a particular writing task, as well as the author's understanding of audience (Applebee Langer, and Mullis 1986). Primary trait evaluation is done in a similar manner with teams of trained readers using scoring guides which define and give examples of the particular features sought in each writing task. Both types of scoring are widely accepted as producing reliable scores at acceptable costs.

Estimates of the rate of papers scored by individual readers vary from two minutes per paper (Cooper 1977) to 20 or more papers per hour for complex essays written in 45-minute periods (White 1986) to 20-minute essays read at a rate of 38 per hour (Conlan 1986). Cooper and Tyler argue that scoring reliability as high as .90 for individual writers can be achieved with this method. Standards of reliability are maintained through the development of good scoring guides accompanied by illustrative papers at each level, as well as by the development of a sense of community and a consensus to use the guides among readers (White 1986).

The greatest cost of such assessment is the fee paid to readers. Members of the Wisconsin Writing Project regularly conduct such scoring for a fee of

$50.00 for a four-hour scoring session. Some school districts provide summer employment in scoring for interested faculty members, while other schools assign such tasks to an administrative team headed by a reading or language arts specialist.

In summary, direct assessment of students' writing skills is a widely accepted and regularly practiced process yielding data for multiple purposes, including student placement, determination of proficiency or minimal competency, and diagnosis.

A major challenge of discourse assessment in social studies will be to devise scoring schemes that evaluate not simply the skills of written and oral communication, but students' accurate, relevant, logical, and imaginative incorporation of social studies knowledge into the language they produce. The final indicator should be a measure of student success in integrating historical and social knowledge into one's use of language.

Will Discourse Assessment Provide Meaningful Comparative Indicators?

Teachers concerned mainly with the progress of students in their own classes may have little interest in devising methods of assessment that facilitate comparison with student achievement in other classes, schools, districts, or states. Understandably, teachers may concentrate their attention on assessing how well the student performs on tasks unique to the teacher's goals for the class (itself often seen as special) or to the student's personal history. The teacher's professional autonomy in assessment must be respected. At the same time, the public is entitled to some indicators that offer a basis for comparison. In what ways, if any, might the assessment of discourse in social studies offer meaningful comparative indicators?

Let us assume that feasibility problems in administration and scoring can be solved such that, for any given discourse task, it will be possible to assign a proficiency score that represents the student's success in integrating significant social studies knowledge into a coherent statement. While we have offered a detailed rationale for discourse assessment in social studies, have recognized successful analogous work in the assessment of writing and speaking, and have proposed some illustrative applications for social studies, we do not mean to minimize the problem of arriving at valid and fair proficiency scores.

The social knowledge to be tested and the standards applied to students' language are themselves socially constructed conventions, loaded with ideological, in contrast to "value-free," "objective," or "scientific," content. In this sense, the standards used to arrive at scores will pose persistent problems of equity: how to avoid perpetuation of inequality due to race, gender, and social class discrimination.[11] As comparative indicators are applied to increasing corners of the globe, the more dramatic the effect of dominant interests will be. At the same time, it is possible to minimize unfair consequences of ideological bias through procedures for review of the content and procedures of assessment, along with appeal of assessment decisions. To the extent that the same tasks are given to students in different schools, regions, or states, proficiency rates can be meaningfully compared.[12]

Some might object that proficiency scores are so vague that they fail to allow comparison of precisely which items of knowledge students demonstrate in their discourse. There are two answers to this objection. First, if one is interested primarily in testing student familiarity with a set of standardized, highly precise units of knowledge, this can be accomplished through traditional measures; discourse assessment should not be expected to bear that burden. Second, some discourse tasks may legitimately require students to demonstrate relatively specific knowledge, but this can be indicated in the directions for the task and included in scoring criteria. For example, illustrative task #2 (p.61) might stipulate that students demonstrate knowledge of three branches of government, of at least two provisions of the Bill of Rights, and of election procedures for Congress. Such stipulations would offer more precise standards for the content that intelligent discourse must manifest, but to avoid the regression of discourse assessment back into conventional exercises of recall and recognition, such stipulations must be kept to a minimum.

Discourse assessment does have troublesome implications for comparisons across age groups, but not because of the format of discourse assessment. The problem here is lack of consensus on a sequential curriculum. History and social studies have never been able to establish a sequence of curriculum knowledge sufficiently convincing to scholars, teachers, and diverse communities to prescribe what social knowledge ought to be demonstrated by students at different ages. Our illustrations were written with high school seniors in mind. For these illustrations, we assumed the year of high school graduation and asked, "What forms of discourse on social topics should be demonstrated by young adults about to assume full responsibilities of citizenship?" It might be possible to identify an earlier transition point, perhaps eighth grade, and to identify more elementary discourse tasks, on which the final tasks might build. Of course, there is no reason to insist upon cross-age comparisons on all indicators of social studies knowledge. Discourse on social topics might be one of those tasks assessed only toward the end of secondary school.

International comparisons will also be difficult, but again, not because of the discourse format. What makes these comparisons problematic is the fact that nations differ in the forms of history and social science knowledge they intend for their youth. Perhaps a survey of nations would reveal some commonalities, but I suspect these will be rare. Each nation attempts to teach students something of its own cultural heritage. Thus, specific content tested might be different in each nation. It is conceivable, however, that each nation might produce an index of youth understanding of its own history. Such indicators could be compared, but their interpretation would be difficult. Unless nations can agree on the need for discourse assessment and some common criteria for success for discourse in social studies, there will be no solid basis of comparison. Hopefully, the argument presented here establishes the case for discourse assessment as useful within the United States, regardless of its potential for international comparison.

Conclusion

Conventional methods of standardized and competency testing in history and social studies tend to trivialize social knowledge and to undermine its constructive use because they ask students only to reproduce the language of others. If we wish students to use social knowledge to comprehend and to act with greater understanding in social affairs, we must invite them instead to produce their own language in ways that incorporate formal knowledge from history and other social disciplines. The assessment of discourse is necessary to support this new curricular emphasis. Greater attention to student discourse will facilitate the learning of content, the development of sensitivity to take the role of the other, the promotion of higher-order thinking, and most importantly, intelligent written and oral conversation.

Our failure to emphasize discourse is rooted in such problems as the apparent prior need to transmit to students the knowledge that intelligent discourse requires, the lack of time for teachers to respond in detail to students' written and oral statements, the lack of consensus on curriculum in history and social studies, and the peculiar evolution of educational testing that aims toward standardized numerical indicators.

However, recent research and development in cognitive science, in the assessment of writing and speaking, and in curriculum theory on subjects as diverse as mathematics and social studies suggest possibilities for discourse assessment which, if vigorously pursued, may eventually empower students to actually converse about social topics in ways that invigorate democratic citizenship.

4

The Nature of Authentic Academic Achievement

Fred M. Newmann and Doug A. Archbald

Introduction

The education reform movement of the 1980s cast a critical spotlight on American high schools and brought mounting pressures for accountability.[1] Students, teachers, schools, districts, and states are increasingly pressured to demonstrate their achievements. But what kinds of achievements should be promoted and how should they be assessed? Recent critiques of schooling propose more emphasis on teaching for understanding of sophisticated academic content and higher-order thinking (e.g., Elmore and Associates 1990). Current indicators of mastery, such as school grades, credits, scores on competency tests and norm-referenced standardized tests, are criticized not only for neglecting to assess such qualities, but also for their failure to provide specific information about what students actually know and can do.

Our concern here is not mainly with the technical problem of designing assessments that measure more validly what schools try to teach. Instead we consider the more fundamental question of what general forms of achievement *ought* to be promoted and assessed. Our inquiry arises in response to what we see as widespread disillusionment with the kinds of accomplishments that schools promote and assess. What counts for success in school is often considered trivial, meaningless, and contrived—by students and adults alike. This can depress student engagement in learning, teacher commitment to their work, and public support for the schools. In contrast, the cultivation and documentation of authentic achievement can invigorate teaching, learning, and public support. Ultimately then, the quality and utility of assessment rest upon the extent to which the outcomes measured represent appropriate, meaningful, significant, and worthwhile forms of human accomplishment. We synthesize these qualities into one idea: authenticity. Our purposes in this chapter are to propose specific criteria for authentic academic achievement and to discuss implications of the criteria for curriculum, for the environments in which students work, and for assessment.

Criteria for Authentic Academic Achievement

What criteria help us to recognize authentic forms of academic achievement? This complicated matter involves controversial educational values, it has not received extensive scholarly study, and it beckons for interdisciplinary analysis of the relationship between formal attempts to educate and the ways that human competence is expressed in non-educational settings. The conception proposed here relies in part upon the work of Resnick (1987), Wiggins (1989), and Raven in chapter 5.

Let us consider the kinds of mastery demonstrated by successful adults—scientists, musicians, business entrepreneurs, politicians, craftspeople, attorneys, novelists, physicians, designers. We will try to clarify characteristics of their work that justify calling their accomplishments authentic instead of contrived and trivial. We will also try to identify key distinctions between these "real" accomplishments and the work that students complete in school.

Production of Knowledge

Persons in the diverse fields named above face the primary challenge of *producing,* rather than reproducing, knowledge. They express this knowledge in the form of discourse, things, and performances; that is, through production of original conversation and writing, through repairing and building of physical objects, through artistic, musical, and athletic performance. We do not expect children to attain levels of competence comparable to skilled adults, but we do want students to develop in that direction. To progress on this journey, students should set their sights on authentic expressions of knowledge and should hone their skills through guided practice in discourse, in manipulating objects, and in preparing for artistic and musical performances. In contrast, the conventional curriculum asks students only to identify the discourse, things, and performances that others have produced (for example,by recognizing the difference between verbs and nouns, between socialism and capitalism; by matching authors with their works; by correctly labeling rocks and body parts). As will be emphasized below, the production of knowledge must be based upon understanding of prior knowledge, but the mere reproduction of that knowledge does not constitute authentic academic achievement.

Disciplined Inquiry

A second defining feature of authentic academic achievement is its reliance upon a particular type of cognitive work which can be summarized as *disciplined inquiry*. Disciplined inquiry, in turn, seems to consist of three features: use of a prior knowledge base; in-depth understanding rather than superficial awareness; and production of knowledge in integrated rather than fragmented form.

Prior Knowledge Base. For new knowledge to be significant and valid, it must be based on substantive and procedural knowledge that has been accumulated through previous workers in a field who establish facts, vocabularies, concepts, theories, algorithms, and conventions for the conduct and expression of inquiry itself. Reliance upon a prior knowledge base does not, however, always entail linear development of and agreement with intellectual traditions. The ultimate point of disciplined inquiry is to move beyond former knowledge—through criticism and development of new paradigms which themselves are stimulated by the foundations of prior knowledge. Most of the cognitive work of school consists in transmitting prior knowledge to students and asking them to reproduce it, rather than helping them to use it to produce knowledge.

In-Depth Understanding. Disciplined inquiry tries to develop in-depth understanding of a problem, rather than only passing familiarity with or exposure to pieces of knowledge. Prior knowledge is mastered, therefore, not primarily to become literate about a broad survey of topics, but to facilitate complex understanding on relatively limited, special problems. Such detailed understanding is particularly necessary for production of new knowledge. In contrast, many of the cognitive tasks of school ask students to show only superficial awareness of a vast number of topics.[2]

Integration. To produce knowledge one must assemble and interpret information, formulate ideas, and make critiques which cannot be easily retrieved from the existing knowledge base—all of which require the ability to organize, synthesize, and integrate information in new ways. Success in such tasks is unlikely unless students learn to look for, to test, and to create relationships among pieces of knowledge that otherwise appear unconnected.

To understand scientific theories, literary and artistic masterpieces, architectural and mechanical designs, musical compositions, or philosophical arguments, they must ultimately be encountered as wholes, not as collections of knowledge fragments. For example, teaching students only the separate roles of each dramatic character will not develop an authentic understanding of a play. The characters must be studied in the context of the overall pattern of plot, literary technique, historical context, and philosophical position.

Similarly, an authentic understanding of a molecule or atom should integrate the parts into broader conceptions of matter or energy.

Too often tests of achievement ask the student only to show recollection of unrelated knowledge fragments: definitions of terms; short descriptive identifications of people, things, events; or numerical solutions to problems. Students demonstrate proficiency by giving short responses, as in a TV quiz show, where answers bear little relation to one another. Success on these exercises may contribute to production of integrated knowledge, but cannot be considered an indicator of it.

In highlighting the features of disciplined inquiry, we are not suggesting that students be expected to make seminal contributions to the academic disciplines, professions, and arts. The point is that students are capable of engaging in these forms of cognitive work when the work is adapted to their levels of development, and that authenticity of their academic achievement will be enhanced if the tasks on which they are evaluated advance production of knowledge over reproduction and if the process of production approximates these attributes of disciplined inquiry. Assessment in science, for example, could place more emphasis upon the development, execution, and reporting of a single experiment. In history and social studies, intensive research using primary source materials could help students evaluate generalizations stated in their textbooks. In studying a literary work, one might aim toward students' clarifying and defending their own views of alternative interpretations.

Value Beyond Evaluation

The final, and perhaps most critical, distinction between authentic achievement and traditional achievements in schools is that authentic achievements have *aesthetic, utilitarian, or personal value* apart from documenting the competence of the learner. When people write letters, news articles, insurance claims, poems; when they speak a foreign language; when they develop blueprints; when they create a painting, a piece of music, or build a stereo cabinet, they try to communicate ideas, to produce a product, or to have impact on others beyond the simple demonstration that they are competent. Achievements of this sort have special value which is missing in tasks contrived only for the purpose of assessing knowledge (such as spelling quizzes, laboratory exercises, or typical final exams). The cry for "relevance" is, in many cases, simply a less precise expression of this desire that the accomplishment should have value beyond being an indicator of success in school.

The exercises, tests, and papers that students complete to earn grades usually have no use except as evidence of mastery for the student, parent, and school authorities. Examples of activities that have value beyond evaluation would include oral histories analogous to the Foxfire projects (Wigginton, 1985); scientific study of local ecological issues; student literary publications; students' using their knowledge to tutor others; remodeling or building homes; and, of course, public performances involving music, arts, and other exhibitions.

To summarize, this vision of authentic achievement requires students to engage in disciplined inquiry to produce knowledge that has value in their lives beyond simply proving their competence in school. Mastery of this sort is unlikely to be demonstrated in familiar testing and grading exercises. Instead, it is more often expressed in the completion of long-term projects which result in discourse, things, and performances of interest to students, their peers and the public at large.

Why should we aim toward authentic achievement? We find at least two compelling reasons, and these respond to the problems of the conventional curriculum and assessment mentioned earlier. First, participation in authentic tasks is more likely to motivate students and to sustain the hard work that learning requires. Because authentic work has value beyond the demonstration of competence in school and because it permits more comprehensive use of the mind, students will have a greater stake in authentic achievement. Second, authentic academic challenges are more likely to cultivate the kind of higher-order thinking and problem-solving capacities useful both to individuals and to the society. The mastery gained in school is likely to transfer more readily to life beyond school, which increases the efficiency of our investment in schooling.

Implications for Curriculum

Teaching for Discourse, Products, and Performances

In the conventional approach to curriculum planning, educators tend to prescribe a broad range of knowledge, skills, and values that they believe students need to function successfully as adults. These goals are then translated into lists of subject matter to be covered and items to be tested, which represent pieces of knowledge from the main academic disciplines of history, mathematics, sciences, and literature. This tendency to design curriculum in the form of a comprehensive map of all important subjects has led to the "coverage" disease (Newmann 1988): fragmentation in students' intellectual work, sanctification of superficial exposure over critical understanding, and frustration over the well-publicized failure to teach all that is worth knowing.

In contrast, criteria for authentic achievement imply that ultimate curriculum goals be articulated not primarily through lists of knowledge, understandings, appreciations, or abilities that we expect students to acquire, but instead by describing the kinds of *discoure, products,* and *performances* that we expect students to demonstrate. Mastery is defined by successful completion of anticipated activities, and curriculum and teaching are designed to promote student proficiency in those activities. This means that, to be eligible for inclusion in the curriculum, traditional and proposed content must meet a new standard. No longer will it be sufficient to claim simply that recommended knowledge or skills will contribute to vocational success, civic participation, or personal fulfillment. In addition, it must be argued that proposed curriculum content is necessary for production of the discourse, things, and performances which define authentic outcomes. In this sense the curriculum "teaches to the test," and planning the curriculum begins with visions of and criteria for success in those achievements toward which the curriculum will aim.

Will assessment-driven curriculum lead to trivialization and fragmentation of learning, as has been the case with previous applications of competency testing, behavioral objectives, and mastery learning? If the above criteria for authenticity are followed carefully, we foresee no such problems. The criteria of disciplined inquiry to produce knowledge of interest to students, peers, and the public at large offer strong protections against the prospect of teaching toward endless lists of meaningless outcomes.

Our task here is not to recommend specific content for the curriculum, but, regardless of the subject taught, the criteria for authenticity have implications for the kinds of human interaction among teachers and students that seems required for students to produce knowledge of value through disciplined inquiry in academic subjects. A major implication is the need for substantive conversation in instruction—also a dramatic departure from present practice.

Substantive Conversation

When curriculum becomes guided by the goal of authentic achievement (instead of the reproduction of declarative knowledge), new forms of teaching will be necessary. No longer will it be possible for students to succeed in school simply by listening to the teacher and responding to questions that can be answered usually in less than five words. To complete their projects, students will need to formulate and to ask questions, to explain themselves to peers and adults, and to refine their ideas. While many authentic achievements require capacities other than verbal discourse (working with one's hands, mathematical estimations, aesthetic sensitivities), substantive conversation between the learner and some supportive source—teacher, peer critic, or other knowledgeable authority—is usually necessary. We emphasize substantive conversation here, not because it alone is sufficient to develop all forms of authentic achievement, but because it is usually critical for success in authentic tasks, and because conversation is the major medium through which teachers communicate with students.

Substantive conversation is different from conventional classroom talk in which the teacher usually has only two purposes in speaking to the student.[3] Except for dealing with disciplinary issues, the teacher either wants to transmit an item of declarative knowledge (usually a definition or fact) or to determine whether the student can reproduce it. The student's goal (assuming a desire to cooperate) is to give the answer that the teacher is looking for. The teacher maintains control in the sense of knowing, prior to the conversation, what pieces of knowledge will be communicated and what answers will count as adequate.

In a substantive conversation, the purpose for talking is quite different. Each person is trying (1) to express his or her point of view, often in order to persuade the other, (2) to understand how and why the other holds a particular viewpoint or interpretation, or (3) to arrive at a solution to a problem that neither has previously solved. This last purpose is the most difficult to fulfill, but perhaps most likely to render the work authentic. In pursuing any of these ends, the teacher uses talk to integrate subject matter into the student' meaning system, and the student tries to understand how the teacher's messages might empower him/her in the world. In this sense, each is interested in what the other has to say, the course of the conversation is less predictable, and each participant has some sense of ownership. To fulfill these purposes, substantive conversation requires sustained, continuous talk between two or more people. In school as we know it, the two key participants are usually student and teacher, but students can also learn through conversations with peers, other adults, and well-programmed computers. Teacher-student conversation should remain central, but to expand students' opportunities for expression and feedback it will be necessary to rely substantially upon and to support these other sources as well.

What is the connection between substantive conversation and authentic achievement? Begin with our definition: Authentic achievement is expressed in discourse, things, and performances that make reasonably complete, integrated statements and that reflect students' production of in-depth knowledge. Then ask, "How can we instruct students to make such statements?"We can show them models of authentic accomplishments of others, and we can give them critical elements of declarative knowledge on which to build. But how will they learn ultimately to make their own statements? Substantive conversation is the key. It provides the major crucible for practice, for seeking new knowledge responsive to the problem at hand, for trial, feedback, and revision. In short, substantive conversation forces us to transform declarative knowledge into applied, integrated knowledge.

Implications for Educational Environments

Continuing our consideration of the nature of authentic adult work, we find at least four working conditions essential to authentic academic accomplishment: collaboration, access to tools and resources, worker discretion or opportunity for ownership, and flexible use of time. Since each of these entail important changes in students' working life in school, they should be seen as part of the agenda for restructuring education.

Collaboration.   Achievements outside of school often depend upon the opportunity to ask questions of, to receive feedback from, and to count on the help of others, including peers and authorities. In contrast, typical activities in school require the student to work alone. Working together is often prohibited, because it is seen as a form of cheating. It is important, of course, for students to learn to work on their own rather than become overly dependent on others. But if opportunities to cooperate are consistently denied, this violates a critical process that adults, both expert and novice, consistently rely upon for success.

Useful collaboration depends to a great extent on opportunities for substantive conversation, which itself requires special structural conditions. More time will be needed for teachers to talk and write in sustained ways with individual students and for students to talk with one another. Substantive conversation also entails major shifts in the roles of teachers and students. Teachers will function more as mentors and coaches, less as depositories of static knowledge to be reproduced. Students will function more as constructors and producers of knowledge who rely on teachers for help, less as absorbers or consumers of everything the teacher says. Students will also have to take on the new roles of seeking help from and giving help to one another as they learn.

Access to Tools and Rescources.   When competent people complete significant accomplishments—from books to architectural designs, musical compositions, or collective bargaining agreements—they usually depend upon efficient access to a variety of print materials and machines such as telephones, computers, and laboratory equipment. The information required is too vast and changing to commit to memory. Becoming educated in medieval times, before printing, required memorizing the contents of key manuscripts, because future access was unlikely. But today the specialization and explosion of knowledge create a new challenge. Possession of prior knowledge is critical to disciplined inquiry, but it is now impossible to teach students all the relevant information needed to complete authentic tasks. The new challenge is to learn how to use tools and resources to find the appropriate missing knowledge.

Discretion-Ownership.   Rather than always toiling under predetermined routines arbitrarily dictated by authorities, the authors of authentic work need to influence the conception, execution, and evaluation of the work itself. At a minimum this entails flexibility over the pace and procedures of learning, opportunity for students to ask questions and to study topics they consider important, and students' constructing and producing knowledge in their language, rather than merely reproducing the language of others. There are, of course, important limits on the extent to which students should control the learning of academic subjects. Certain facts, definitions, concepts, algorithms, and processes of verification must be assimilated according to standards in the fields of knowledge to be taught. But for this kind of learning to be translated into authentic products, students must enjoy some autonomy and discretion in its application.

Flexible use of time. The significant achievements of disciplined inquiry often cannot be produced within rigidly specified time periods. Adults working to solve complicated problems, to compose effective discourse, or to design products rarely are forced to work within the rigid time constraints imposed on students such as the 50-minute class, or the two-hour examination period.

Standard time schedules that flow from bureaucratic procedures for managing masses of students and diverse course offerings, rather than from the time requirements of disciplined inquiry, can reduce the authenticity of student achievement. Achievements in non-instructional tasks, such as journalistic writing, interior design, or medical care do, of course involve deadlines and time limits, but here the schedules tend to be determined more by the nature of the work than by the requirements of institutional management.

These conditions suggest several changes in students' work. Without trying to be inclusive, here are a few:

1. To stimulate collaboration and the substantive conversation so crucial to it, more time must be allocated to individualized and small-group instruction.
2. Student access to knowledge must be enhanced by greater use of technology (telephones as well as computers) and opportunities to learn from sources outside of school.
3. Students need to exercise discretion and responsibility in the planning, execution, and evaluation of their work, which further underscores the need for individualized and small-group work along with assessment exercises that permit diverse ways of demonstrating competence.
4. Instructional time should be organized to permit more sustained, long-term in-depth investigation, in contrast to fixed time slots designed for survey coverage.
5. New assessment procedures, as described below, will (in some cases) require participants beyond the school to evaluate student performance.

Implications for Assessment

Assessment tasks calling for the production of discourse, things, and performances will also require departures from conventional procedures. In considering the ways in which adult work is assessed, we notice the special importance of criterion-based standards, multiple indicators, and human judgment.

Criterion-Based Standards. The performances of artists, attorneys, or surgeons and the products of journalists, engineers, or computer programmers are usually judged in relation to substantive standards which, at one end, define minimal levels of acceptable quality and, at the other, suggest where the frontiers of distinction begin. Summary judgments can usually be made about whether the performance or product does the job, or whether it is well or poorly received by the interested parties. This is not to suggest that judgments of quality must be categorically good or bad. Competitive divers, musicians, and debate teams receive numerical indicators that vary from high to low. Reviewers show varying degrees of enthusiasm for concerts, films, plays, and books. The point is that criteria can be articulated that explain the difference between high and low quality.

This may seem obvious enough. The reason for stating it here is to accentuate the failure of much school assessment to set specific performance criteria. Standardized norm-referenced achievement tests determine a student's level of success not by requiring any particular level of mastery on a specific task, but instead by reporting the student's overall score in relation to other students' scores. Overall scores represent numbers of items correct, but since the items consist of a set of diverse knowledge fragments, they do not define a central task or accomplishment on which to evaluate proficiency. Success then becomes defined simply as scoring in the higher percentiles of the tested population. When teachers grade on a curve, this also establishes a normed system which, by definition, limits the proportion of students who can succeed (or fail). Since neither standardized test scores nor grades assigned according to the curve reflect standards with substantive meaning, success on them cannot represent authentic forms of human accomplishments.[4]

Multiple Indicators. In making evaluative judgments about individuals or organizations, we often need more than one indicator of quality. Any single indicator such as a percentile rank or a dropout rate limits the amount of information conveyed and is subject to error. In purchasing a car, most of us are interested not only in price or gas mileage, but in many other factors simultaneously: safety record, reliability and service record, resale value, warranty, and special performance criteria such as acceleration and handling. Teachers, after all, assign grades based not on one test, but on several types of student performance (homework, class participation, special projects, quizzes, major tests). Athletes, musicians, journalists, administrators, and politicians all tend to be judged on several criteria of accomplishment.

The quality of an investigative reporter's article, for example, is likely to be judged in terms of the comprehensiveness of information, the extent to which authoritative sources were used, relevance of the issue to public policy, and its organization and logic of argument. The work of a cabinet-maker may be evaluated in terms of durability, efficiency of design, aesthetic qualities of the materials, and finish. The quality of students' skills in oral communication may depend not only upon range of vocabulary, but also upon sensitivity to the perspective of a listener, clarity of explanation, and the asking of appropriate questions.

At times, of course, single indicators may be important. A team wins a game, an essay or photo wins a contest, a candidate is reelected, a school increases attendance, a student completes a conversation in a foreign language. Multiple criteria may be combined and summed (sometimes after assigning different weights) to arrive at a single numerical indicator. However, it seems critical to the evaluation of authentic work that, at some point in making judgments of quality, multiple indicators be distinguished and used.

In making overall assessments about individuals' accomplishments, it is usually necessary to consider not just one performance (even if it is judged on multiple criteria), but instead to characterize a variety of performances over time. Just as it becomes more informative to examine a full portfolio of work, an athlete's record over a whole season, or several tunes in a musician's repertoire, the assessment of students will be more authentic if it permits observation of patterns of strengths and weakness over a sustained period.

Human Judgment. Whether a given performance or demonstration of mastery meets particular criteria is ultimately a matter of human judgment. Because human judgments of the same messages or event can differ dramatically, the task of evaluation poses a serious issue of reliability: Whose judgment should be accepted as the most accurate indicator of quality? Teachers may use different criteria for grading, or they may interpret a common set of criteria differently for different students. To minimize this problem, vast numbers of standardized or competency tests are used. By requiring that students make only unambiguous responses (they are asked only to choose answer a, b, c, or d, but usually are not allowed to explain themselves in sentences) and predetermining the correct answer, the tests try to eliminate the problem of human disagreement on quality of performance. Although teacher judgment is eliminated, human judgment is not; the judgment of the test-constructors continues to determine the difference between high versus low quality responses.

In contrast, consider the process for determining whether Ph.D. candidates have achieved enough mastery to become credentialed researchers in their field. Here the ultimate judgment is made by a committee of professors who determine the quality of the written dissertation and the candidate's oral defense. Other committees also assess the quality of performance in debates, sports competition, and musical and artistic events. We rely on committees to make decisions about whether to publish articles, whether to award grants and contracts, and whether to hire, fire, and promote workers. In many cases, committees use specific procedures to maximize the use of common standards and to minimize personal bias.

Although it would be difficult to imagine how to rate the quality of academic achievement without employing human judgment, the common approach to testing in education seems to suggest that, for purposes of efficiency and objectivity, the human element must be minimized by prespecifying responses and creating exercises that can be scored mechanically. We believe such exercises lose authenticity not only because they offer no opportunity for students to produce knowledge of value through disciplined inquiry, but also because they deny students the opportunity of being evaluated directly by humans entrusted to apply criteria that summarize the quality of student work.

Conclusion

Experienced educators will recognize that our conception of authentic academic achievement and its implications for curriculum, school environments, and assessment involve fundamental shifts in the way we think about education. Will such shifts ever become reflected in education policy and practice? The destiny of these ideas depends upon at least two significant challenges. First, professionals and the public must be convinced that current approaches are so seriously flawed as to require radical redesign. In spite of a flurry of reform reports and activities within the last decade, the lack of widespread support for new visions of curriculum, teaching, and assessment can be taken as evidence that the general public is quite satisfied with schooling (most students do complete high school and increasing proportions go on to higher education). It is possible to demonstrate the tragic failure of the educational system for millions of students, especially the economically disadvantaged and those deprived of personal social support. But it is often difficult to claim general system failure when confronted with the many students for whom formal education seems to have offered the key to success.

A second challenge to the implementation of this new vision is technical. Although it is possible to find scattered examples of more authentic assessments (see Archbald and Newmann 1988 and this volume), we have yet to demonstrate the feasibility of this vision on a district or state-wide basis, or even within a conventional comprehensive high school. A good deal of experimental and development work is needed to deal with several problems: how to establish baseline standards of quality for authentic outcomes, how to achieve reliability in measurements, how to define common standards across schools as well as those unique to particular schools, how to help educators reconceptualize curriculum, and how to finance all of this.

Generating public and professional support for these ideas and engineering them into a feasible, practical form will take time and considerable effort from classroom teachers, school administrators, policy-makers, assessment researchers, as well as district, state, and national assessment committees. Unfortunately, the accountability movement has built up considerable momentum for conventional forms of assessment. Some may worry that even raising new questions about authenticity might derail the train. We suspect, however, that many accountability trains are on the wrong track or heading in the wrong direction. It would be wise to slow down to take stock of where they are taking us and where we want to go.

A Model of Competence, Motivation, and Behavior, and a Paradigm for Assessment

John Raven

The Concept of Competence

I begin with observations made in one classroom to illustrate some of the limitations of current assessment approaches and to clarify the concept of "competence" which is central to my argument for the development of a new paradigm for educational assessment. Most of the students in this class were involved in interdisciplinary projects. These projects were very thorough-going. The students as a group carried out original investigations in the environment. Their work inside their classrooms formed an integral part of these investigations. Within these class projects, many students had personal projects, distinctive areas of specialization, and distinctive roles.

In the course of his environmentally based work, one student had become an expert on the distribution of different species of butterfly in the locality, their life cycles, and their relationship to their habitats. Another had become an expert on the history of a particular agricultural implement: He had related changes in the implement to a continuous—and apparently autonomous—series of improvements in the design itself, to changes in steel-making on the one hand and patterns of agriculture on the other. Another student had become an expert on the relationship between improvements in that implement, the pattern of land use it demanded and facilitated, and changes in the social structure of the community. Still another had become expert on the current social structure of the area—who knew whom and what they talked about. Others had studied changes in the architecture and layout of the village and the occupations of its inhabitants.

What was most striking in this class was the teacher's distinctive concerns. She was not preoccupied with covering a syllabus. Her attention focused on the competencies which she hoped to help her students develop through the activities they carried out. These competencies not only included reading, writing, spelling, and counting, but they also included communicating, observing, and finding information needed to achieve goals. Such information was often collected, not only by reading books, but also by observation, talking to people, inventing, persuading, and leading.

The problems that these students' accomplishments pose for conventional measurement paradigms are almost insurmountable. The specialized knowledge the students gained simply would not show up on traditional attainment tests—indeed these students would likely get *low* scores on such tests because they would not have mastered the required knowledge. To do justice to the students, it would be necessary to administer a series of individualized tests to tap each student's specialty.

However, these are the least of the problems this work poses for the measurement paradigm that dominates education and psychology. More important than the unique store of specialist knowledge built up by the first student cited above was the fact that he had developed a number of the *competencies* required to be a scientist. Among other things, he had learned to be sensitive to the cues that reveal an unresolved problem; he had developed the ability to make glimmerings of insight on the fringe of consciousness explicit; he had learned to *invent* ways of making observations; he had learned to notice things which no one had noticed before; he had learned not only how to find information in journals, but also how to use what he did find to stimulate the kind of lateral thinking required to make use of the information obtained; he had learned to solicit and make use of the ideas of fellow students and 'ignorant' people in the community; he had learned to write, to telephone, and to visit university lecturers who were interested in the same problem, and he had spoken to them as equals; he had sharpened up his ideas by sparring with them; he had learned that he had a right to ask new questions and not merely answer other people's; he had learned that he could both ask and answer questions; he had learned to tolerate the frustrations involved in trying to find better ways of thinking about things; and he had learned to invent ways of summarizing his data and communicate it to others—and not just in writing.

The competencies cited in the last paragraph are a subset of the competencies the student developed as he pursued interdisciplinary studies. But he could equally well have developed them as a result of engaging in other activities he valued and was motivated to undertake. It is important to note that the second student mentioned above developed a different subset of competencies, sensitivities, thoughtways, and perceptions in the course of undertaking an original historical study. The third had developed a similar, but by no means identical, selection of the competencies needed to be an excellent sociologist of one kind or another. And so on for the other students.

If our traditional assessment procedures are unable to cope with the problem of idiosyncratic, specialist, high-level, new knowledge, they are even less able to document the growth of the subtle skills, motivated habits, thoughtways, and preoccupations that make up the repertoire of a competent scientist, historian, sociologist, photographer, reporter, cook, or mother.

But even this does not exhaust the assessment problems posed by the educational process cited above. The students had worked in groups, developed specialized roles, and developed the competencies needed to function effectively in those roles. Several students had become good at coordinating the activities of others; others at putting members of their group at ease and smoothing over interpersonal difficulties. Some gained skills as negotiators, others at presenting the results of other people's work to external visitors— communicators rather than original researchers. And so on. In the course of undertaking these activities, all students learned to communicate, to invent, to make their own observations, to work with others, to lead, and to follow.

All these competencies defy conventional measurement. This is of the greatest importance. Without means of assessing these qualities, even students who have come through such educational programs cannot know that they are different from students who have come through other educational programs. Still less can they identify the ways in which they are different from them: They cannot know that they think differently, see things differently, have different priorities, tend to work differently with others, or that they can do different things. Without means of assessing these qualities, teachers cannot in subsequent projects build on the competencies which have been fostered in the course of the previous ones. Students cannot get credit for the talents they have developed when they come to scramble for a job or for entry to courses of further education. Teachers cannot get credit for having fostered these competencies in any form of accountability exercise. At the societal level, we cannot prevent the appointment of people to influential positions who do not possess important high-level concerns and qualities like those mentioned. But perhaps most significant is that the absence of means to assess these qualities limits our conception of what education *is*. In the current scheme of things, even the word "academic" fails to denote activities which lead people to observe, to think, to find better ways of thinking about things, or to communicate effectively.

It is important to note that the fact that the researchers were able to identify the competencies these students had developed demonstrates that the measurement problem is, in principle, solvable. The key features of what the researchers did were (1) they observed students as they were undertaking tasks they cared about (2) they recorded the multiple and substitutable competencies students displayed while undertaking those tasks (3) they made use of a descriptive scientific framework rather than one grounded in "variables", and (4) they distinguished between students in terms of the activities they cared about and the competencies they displayed while undertaking those tasks. The central message here is that our research demonstrated that it is possible to build an alternative measurement paradigm, one which can be used by policy-makers and educators to assess such complex and socially valued competencies.

It is difficult to see how the commonly available tests can be regarded as valid if they fail to document the most important outcomes of an educational process. Failure to assess outcomes which cannot presently be measured with conventional tests, deflects policy discussions away from the educational process and outcomes that are most important and focuses attention on those easiest to measure. The lack of concern with this issue suggests that there is widespread failure to appreciate the implications of *not* finding ways of assessing a wider range of the outcomes of the educational process. Notwithstanding the sentiments echoed in most reports in the United States and the United Kingdom over the last several years, the attention of politicians, school reformers, administrators, teachers, parents, and students is thereby focused entirely on low-level outcomes that are generally of little importance to the individuals concerned or the societies in which they live. The reliance on inadequate and invalid tests in attempts to improve the quality of education directs teachers' attention away from achieving the very goals that are in the long-term interest of both students and society.

I wish to emphasize that this is not a diatribe against testing or assessment. To the contrary, educators *do* need to be able to identify and assess students' interests and talents in order to be able to implement effective educational programs. Teachers *do* need to be able to monitor progress toward their goals so that they can take corrective action when necessary. Students *do* need to be able to identify what they have learned. They *do* need to be able to get credit for their accomplishments. Teachers and administrators *do* need to be able to identify the relative merits of different types of educational programs. They *do* need to be able to find out which aspects of those programs are working well and which are not, and how to improve them. Indeed, educators need a whole range of tools to help them to administer individualized, competency-oriented, educational programs: They need to be able to identify students' interests and talents and devise personalized programs that will enable students to practice a wide variety of competencies, and they need to be able to monitor students' reactions to those programs. In addition, teachers need to be able to diagnose learning difficulties in ways that enable them to prescribe appropriate remedial action. Traditional tests of educational achievement are not suitable for any of these purposes. Clearly, a new measurement paradigm is required.

The Inseparability of Competence, Values, and Interests

A place to begin to build an alternative *measurement* paradigm is with the question: "What is the connection between competence and initiative (or motivation)?" We read almost anywhere that initiative is a quality which educators should foster. To take initiative successfully, people must be self-motivated. Self-starting people must be persistent and devote a great deal of time, thought, and effort to the activity. They need to initiate innovative action, monitor the effects of that action, and learn from those effects more about the problem they are trying to tackle, the social, political and environmental context in which it is situated, and what is effective and ineffective about the strategies they are using. To succeed, they must anticipate obstacles in the future and invent ways of circumventing or overcoming them. They will need to build up their own unique set of *specialist* knowledge. Often, they will need help from others. This may require the ability to organize coalitions with others to deal with social and political forces that would otherwise deflect them from their goals.

The crucial point to be emphasized in attempting to clarify the nature of competence is that *no one does any of these things unless he or she cares about the activity being undertaken.* What a person *values* is, therefore, central.[1] In practice, that which is valued may be a particular *outcome* (such as stopping a factory from polluting a river) or it may be a particular *style of behavior* (such as getting people to work together effectively). What follows from this is that it is necessary to know an individual's values, interests, and preoccupations in order to assess his or her competencies. Important abilities demand time, energy, and effort. As a result, people only display them when they are undertaking activities which are important to them. It is meaningless to attempt to assess a person's abilities except in relation to their valued goals.

The above analysis of the nature of initiative also implies that it does not make sense to attempt to assess separately the cognitive, affective, and conative[2] components of an activity. One cannot meaningfully assess "the ability to develop better ways of thinking about things" independently of the pleasure the person derives from doing so, and of his or her determination to make glimmering insights explicit. *These affective and conative components are an integral part of what we mean by the ability to cognize.*[3] Not only do the three components interpenetrate, but if the behavior in question—the initiative—is to be successful, these components must be in balance. Both determination exercised in the absence of understanding, and the converse, are unlikely to make for success.

These observations are in sharp conflict with many traditional canons of psychometry. I have argued that one cannot assess abilities independently of values. This means that it is essential to adopt a two-stage approach when assessing competence. We must first find out which types of behavior someone values, and then, and *only* then, assess his or her ability to bring to bear a wide range of potentially important cognitive, affective, and conative behaviors to undertake the activity effectively.

It is important to emphasize that the widely accepted convention within psychometrics that one can use one set of scales to assess values and another set of scales to assess knowledge, skills, abilities, or competencies simply does not make sense. The latter will only be developed and displayed in relation to the former.[4] Furthermore, since people generally do not know what their distinctive preoccupations and concerns are (since they do not know what other people's are), one of the best ways of finding out what people care about is to ask the question: "In the course of pursuing what kinds of activity does this person display multiple and high-level competencies?"

This analysis of the integral relationship between initiative and competence also highlights another way the dominant measurement paradigm in psychology and education fail. Conventional psychometric theory places great stress on internal consistency (or, to use the technical term, *factorial purity*). Scores, derived from tests composed of items which do not correlate with each other, are said to be meaningless. Yet it would seem from this analysis that this assertion is incorrect. People's initiatives are more likely to be successful the *more* independent and different things they do in the course of pursuing their goals. For example, they are more likely to be successful if they reconceptualize the problem, obtain the help of others, persist over a long period of time, and so on. Yet their inclination and ability to do any one of these things in pursuit of their goals is unlikely to be closely related to their inclination and ability to do others. Furthermore, if they do any of them them particularly well it will, to some extent, compensate for their failure to do others.

It follows from the argument made in the last paragraph that, if we are to assess such qualities as initiative, instead of trying to develop measurement tools that are as internally consistent as possible we need to try to develop *indices* made up of items that are as little correlated with each other as possible. (This is actually not so heretical as it appears at first sight because it is standard practice to make use of multiple regression equations which involve summing-over maximally independent variables to obtain the best prediction.)

In summary: If we are to find ways of assessing important human traits, we will need to abandon our desire to develop value-free, internally consistent measures.

The Inseparability of Social Context from the Assessment Process

This is an appropriate point to introduce one more proposition that has emerged in the course of our work: value-based cognitions of social processes are central to competent behavior and need to be documented in any meaningful assessments of competence.

Behavior is very much determined by such things as people's beliefs about how things *should* be done, who should relate to whom, and about what. Their actions are very much influenced by their perceptions or roles— by what they think it is appropriate for someone in their position to do, by what they think other people expect them to do, and by how they think other people will react to their behavior. Their performance is shaped by their understanding of what is meant by terms like *management, participation, majority decision-taking, managerial responsibility, wealth, and democracy.*

Because this conclusion raises the spectre of social control and teachers brainwashing children, it is necessary to reinforce it by saying that we initially came upon it from exactly the opposite starting point: When we compared more competent with less competent farmers, teachers, bus drivers, blacksmiths, managers, and military officers we found that, in each case, it was the nature of the political behavior (with a small *p*) the more effective people were engaged in that was most important. Put the other way round, the most important source of incompetent occupational behavior in modern society is the inability and unwillingness to do something about the wider, social, institutional, and political context outside one's job—because it is this context that overwhelmingly determines what one *can* do within it.

Because the ways people define the situations they find themselves in has a marked effect on their behavior, that context has other direct and indirect effects. It influences their behavior directly through the constraints it places on what they can do, and it influences it indirectly through the concepts, understandings, and competencies people are able to practice and develop. It therefore follows that, if one wishes to assess competence, it is necessary to assess both the perceived and the actual institutional context in which it occurs. It is either meaningless or wildly prejudicial to say that people lack the ability to do something they have never had the opportunity to practice doing. The only solution is to make a description of the context part of the assessment of the individual. To summarize: *The need to describe the situation or context in which individuals find themselves must be an integral to the assessment process.*

Although satisfactory measures of competence must be value-based and include the wider social and civic perceptions and understandings just mentioned, one unfortunately cannot discover these simply by asking people to identify the behaviors they value, their beliefs about how society works, and their role in it. Because they do not do not know much about the values, preoccupations, and thoughtways of others, they cannot perceive, much less identify, the ways they themselves are distinctive.

Not only are people unable to perceive and identify their own distinctive values and beliefs but some of the most important value-based social cognitions are shared by all members of a cultural group. For this reason, even an observer from that group who was able to see into the heads of his peers would be unlikely to notice and report them.

Recapitulation and Reinstatement

In the course of these remarks I have introduced some ideas which my colleagues and I have taken many years to stumble upon and make explicit—and which contrast sharply with many traditional assumptions in psychological and educational measurement. For this reason, it may be helpful to represent the same ideas in a different way. I do this, making use of a three-dimensional diagram proposed by Ron Johnson and shown in Figure 5.1. Johnson argues that behavior is a resultant of three sets of variables: skills and abilities, motivation, and the situation in which people find themselves. For our purposes we substitute *components of competence* for skills and abilities and *values* for motivation.

So far so good. But I have also argued that:

1. Components of competence will only be developed and displayed while those concerned are undertaking tasks they care about. They cannot be abstracted in the way suggested by the diagram and assessed independently of motivation. Stated differently, *motivation is an integral part of competence.*
2. Effective performance—the resultant—is much more dependent on the number of independent and substitutable competencies brought to bear in a wide variety of situations in order to reach a goal than it is on the level of competence or ability displayed in relation to any one of them in a particular situation. It *is the total number of competencies individuals display in many situations over a long period of time in order to reach their valued goals that we need to assess,* not their level of ability in relation to any of them. An *overall* index of a person's "ability" or "motivation" is virtually meaningless.
3. The situation in which an individual is placed influences the values that are aroused and the competencies that are practiced and devel-

FIGURE 5.1

Johnson's Model

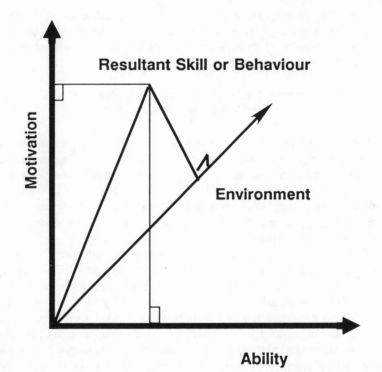

oped. Not only do environments have the power to transform people, people actively select themselves into, and attend and respond to different features of, particular environments. Johnson's diagram does not recognize this. It gives the impression that a change in some feature of the environment will lead to an increase (or decrease) in the quality or frequency of a particular behavior, with the motivation and ability of the actor remaining unchanged.

Despite these limitations, Johnson's diagram is useful because it emphasizes (1) that it is important to assess all three sets of variables, (2) that behavior is a product of all three sets of variables, (3) that the components of competence can only be assessed in relation to a task the individual cares about, (4) that behavior is influenced by people's perceptions of the situation in which they find themselves, their understandings of the way the organization works, and the reactions they expect from others, and (5) that people will only display the levels of competence they are capable of if they define the situation in which they are placed as one that will enable them to undertake activities they care about.

Above all, the diagram emphasizes that the competence people apply to perform tasks they are given—the resultant—cannot, on its own, be treated as a meaningful index of their current competence to perform that task, let alone an index of the competencies they possess.[5]

A Formal Model of Competence, Motivation, and Behavior, and its Assessment

I now turn to the task of elaborating a model of competence and the way its components may be assessed. I have argued that it is meaningless to assess the self-motivated competencies that make for effective behavior except in relation to the activities the person in question cares about. We have also seen that there is a large number of components of competence, that many of them are relatively independent of each other, and that these competencies are cumulative and substitutable.

This way of thinking about competence may be made more concrete by reference to Grid 5.1. On it, some of the types of behavior different people value have been listed across the top. These behaviors are grouped into three clusters (achievement, affiliation, power) identified by McClelland in 1958[6] and confirmed empirically in our own previous work.[7] Down the side are listed a number of components of effective behavior that, if present, are likely to result in the overall activity being successful. These components of competence include cognitive activities (e.g., making plans and thinking about obstacles to goal achievement), affective activities (e.g., enjoying the activity or wishing that a necessary, but distasteful, task was completed), and conative activities (e.g., determination and persistence). However, also listed are a number of other factors that contribute to successful performance—such as having the support of others and believing that one's behavior is consistent with both one's own and others' views of what is appropriate for someone in one's position to do.[8]

The importance of separating these value and efficacy components in assessment can be reemphasized by taking another example. An individual who values success at football may show a great deal of initiative in relation to football, be very sensitive to feedback from the environment, seek the help of others to improve performance, monitor and continuously improve his or her style, seek out new techniques and ideas, be sensitive to minor cues which suggest ways to improve, be sensitive to the approval or disapproval of his or her peers, have the will-power to persist in the face of difficulty, and be able and willing to persuade local politicians to provide a pitch or field. Never-

GRID 5.1

A Model of Competence

Valued styles of behavior

Components of effective behavior	Achievement				Affiliation				Power		
	Doing things which have not been done before.	Inventing things.	Doing things move efficiently than they have been done before.	Finding better ways of thinking about things.	Providing support and facilitation for someone concerned with achievement.	Ensuring that a group works without conflict.	Establishing warm, convivial relationships with others.	Establishing effective group discussion procedures.	Ensuring that group members share their knowledge so that good decisions can be taken.	Articulating group goals and releasing the energies of others in pursuit of them.	Ensuring effective compliance with one's demands.
Cognitive											
Thinking about what is to be achieved and how it is to be achieved.											
Anticipating obstacles to achievement and taking steps to avoid them.											
Monitoring the effects of one's actions to discover what they have to tell one about the nature of the situation with which one is dealing.											
Making one's value conflicts explicit and trying to solve them.											
Having an appropriate understanding of how society works.											
Believing that other people whose opinion one values will expect one to engage in activity.											
Believing one's actions to be in the best interests of mankind.											
Affective											
Turning one's emotions into the task.											
Selecting tasks one enjoys and facing up to the need to complete necessary but unpleasant tasks.											
Anticipating the delights of success and the misery of failure.											
Conative											
Putting in extra effort to reduce the amount of risk involved in the activity.											
Summoning up energy, determination and will-power.											
Persisting in the face of difficulties.											
Habits and Experience											
A range of appropriate routine, but flexibly contingent, behaviors each triggered by cues which one may not be able to articulate and which may be imperceptible to others.											
Experience of the satisfactions which have come from having accomplished similar tasks in the past.											

theless, if the ability of this same person to engage in these complex, cognitive, affective, social and conative activities is assessed in relation to performance at mathematics—a goal, for the sake of argument, we may assume this individual does not value—then one might erroneously conclude that he or she is unable (and not just unmotivated) to engage in the activities mentioned. Teachers, psychologists, and managers have, in the past, too frequently been guilty of drawing such erroneous conclusions.

Attention should be drawn to the fact that, while this model is readily comprehended as a model designed to help us to understand and assess motivation—the styles of behavior someone values and his or ability to pursue those goals effectively—it is, in reality, a model of competence.

Relationship Between Descriptive Statements and Profiles. In principle, Grid 5.1 can be used to identify the behaviors people value and the components of competence they tend to display in pursuit of them. For any one person, an assessor could, after having made relevant observations, enter checks in the appropriate cells under the behaviors the person values. By adding up the checks in any one column, the assessor can obtain an index of how likely it is that the person concerned will undertake that kind of behavior effectively. By summing the scores obtained in adjacent columns under each of the overall headings, scores which indicate the probability that a person will reach achievement, affiliation, and power goals can be obtained. This yields profiles directly comparable with those published by McClelland, and which he (in the present context, misleadingly) refers to as motivation profiles.

Heterogeneous Indices or Internally Consistent Factor Scores? Not only must values be assessed as an integral part of the assessment of competence, but the components of competence we have identified cannot be meaningfully analyzed or identified in factorial or dimensional terms. The scores obtained by summing down the columns in Grid 5.1 are, quite obviously, not "unidimensional". Indeed, the more independent and heterogeneous the competencies that are composited the better—provided, of course, each relates to goal achievement.

Overall Indices versus Detailed Descriptive Statements. In practice, a description of the types of behavior that people value and the competencies they display in the course of trying to reach them provides much more useful information than a single total score. Such a description is radically different from a profile of scores across a series of factorially independent dimensions. The assumption behind a factorial profile are that behavior is best described and understood in terms of people's relative scores on a small number of dimensions. The assumption behind the model developed here is that behavior is best understood by identifying people's values, perceptions, and expectations, and the components of competence they tend to display spontaneously in pursuit of their valued goals.

"Atomic" vs "Variable" Models. The difference between factorial profiles and descriptive statements can be illustrated by taking examples from physics and chemistry.

Physicists have shown that the behavior of a projectile is best described by the equation:

$$s = ut + \tfrac{1}{2}ft^2$$

(the distance traveled at a particular time is determined by the initial velocity multiplied by the time elapsed plus half the acceleration multiplied by the square of the elapsed time).

The factor analysts' model is analogous. For example, it may assert that the degree of leadership displayed is a function of the person's scores on a number of other variables, such as extroversion and intelligence.

Unlike physicists, chemists use a quite different type of equation in their work. They argue that substances and the environments where they are placed are best described by listing the elements of which they are composed and the relationship between these elements. The descriptors (elements) are drawn from a large set known to all chemists. The elements that are not present do not need to be listed. The behavior of the substance in a particular environment is then described by equations that make it possible to describe transformations as well as monotonic combination:

$$Cu + 2H_2SO_4 = CuSO_4 + 2H_2O + SO_2$$

(copper plus sulphuric acid yields copper sulphate, water and sulphur dioxide).

It is argued here that human beings might better be described and understood by adopting a model that has more in common with that used by chemists than that used by classical physicists. Such a model would enable us to indicate people's values and the components of competence they tend to display spontaneously, together with relevant and significant features of their environments, without restricting us to the small number of variables that characterize factor-analytic models.[9]

I will push the analogy to chemistry a little further. Following this model we might find ourselves writing a *summary* description of an individual and the environment where he or she lives and works. This might take the following form (the symbols used are exemplary only and should in no way be taken to suggest that we have developed even a preliminary version of a table of "human elements"):

$$Ach_4Pow_3;Auth_4PartCit_2;NuP_4HostP_3;DP(T)_1$$

Such a statement might be interpreted to mean that the individual shows a spontaneous tendency to display four components of competence in pursuit of achievement goals, and three in pursuit of power goals. Four items contributing to the set dealing with participatory citizenship were endorsed. Four aspects of the environment were supportive of the individual's goals: the manager modeled achievement behavior but did not delegate, encourage participation, nor create developmental tasks for his subordinates. There was "hostile press" from other people in the individual's environment. Concern with efficiency and effective leadership were scorned. The task assigned to the individual had little developmental potential: it was a routine task that prevented the person concerned from developing perceptions and expectations appropriate to innovation.

If the equation were written in some way which permitted movement, one would conclude that the individual would be likely to become frustrated and lose motivation to engage in achievement and leadership behaviors.

In fact, of course, such summary statements could be filled out in a great more detail, and very usefully, too. One could identify exactly what type of achievement or power behavior the individual thought it was important to engage in; one could identify exactly which competencies were brought to bear in pursuit of each; one could identify the particular perceptions and expectations that encouraged or prevented the person concerned from engaging in such behavior; one could say more about the role models to whom he or she was exposed by managers, colleagues, and subordinates; and one could say more about the tasks set and their probable effects on the person's future development and motivation.

Before leaving this discussion it is worth reiterating that such *statements* about people *and the environments* where they are placed *enable us to handle the transformational processes which occur in homes, schools, and workplaces.* They also enable us to handle the problem that the same competencies exercised in different contexts take on a different form. Greeno and his colleagues apparently take the position that, because competencies may take a different form in different contexts, they are not generalizable.[10] But this is not necessarily the case. The same qualities may look different in different contexts—indeed copper looks and behaves very differently when it is combined with oxygen instead of sulphur. But it does not cease to be copper.

It is important, for the sake of clarity, to note what I have argued in the course of this discussion. First, I noted that people's areas of competence could be described by putting checks in the cells of a two-dimensional grid. I then noted that summary scores which could be derived were conceptually identical to McClelland's "motivation" profiles. However, I also noted that since Grid 5.1 was only an illustrative sample drawn from a much larger grid, one could achieve the effect we obtained by writing chemist-type descriptive statements about people. These would identify the student's values and the competencies they displayed when pursuing them. Such a procedure would enable us to describe the environments where people live and work—and this would both enable us to model transformational developmental processes and the problems discussed by Greeno and his associates.

One final observation may be made about the methodology advocated here. The crucial component in what we have been doing is that we have been mapping and sampling relevant *domains* of beliefs and expectations. This is no routine handle-cranking concurrent-validity-driven activity. Quite the opposite: It can only be carried out effectively in the light of a thorough understanding of the area one is dealing with. The need is, therefore, not so much for a new *methodology* as for a clear expectation that scientists should devote time to what is, after all, the crucial phase of any scientific enquiry worth the name.

Implementing Competence Assessments

In this part of my chapter I summarize work using the model developed above. In the course of so doing, the methodologies we have employed to operationalize the model will be illustrated. However, if the reader is not to be disappointed with what is to follow, it is important to approach the material with realistic expectations. Virtually all the work on which this chapter has been based has been carried out in "spare time," on an unfunded basis.[11] It has proved possible to use the measurement model outlined above without difficulty in program evaluation. It was used in both our evaluation of the Lothian Region Educational Home Visiting Project[12] and in our evaluation of the links established between primary schools and agencies of nonformal education, such as zoos and museums.[13] In both cases, it enabled us to show that, contrary to the received wisdom, adults (whether parents or teachers) had, for better of worse, dramatic effects both on children's and adults' values and on their competence to undertake valued activities effectively. It has also been employed without difficulty when assessing what might loosely be called national and organizational climates and patterns of competence associated with economic and social development and decline.[14]

We have had more difficulty using it for *individual* assessment purposes. However, even here, one set of procedures (Behavior Event Interviewing and Records) provides relevant and useful information in an elegant and cost-effective way. Other procedures (based on value-expectancy methodology) have shown considerable potential. The remainder of this part of my chapter will summarize these procedures.

Statements

There are two essential prerequisites to obtaining meaningful external assessments of competence. First, assessors should be thoroughly familiar with the conceptual framework summarized above and developed more fully in *Competence in Modern Society.*[15] Second, they, like good mothers[16] and managers,[17] should both have gone out of their way to pay attention to what students say and do (including the meanings of their gestures and innuendoes) and thereafter have created situations where students can enthusiastically pursue activities they care about, growing in confidence and competence in the process. If they have done these things, teachers and lecturers will, if they are good observers, find it relatively easy to put checks in the cells of an extended version of Grid 5.1 to indicate which activities students value and the competencies they display spontaneously in pursuit of them. An alternative is for teachers simply to list, after the manner of a chemist (or doctor, when writing a prescription), the behavior students value and the competencies they display while pursuing valued activities. The lists of values and components of competence published in *Competence in Modern Society* may be used as *aides-mémoires* for this purpose. If this approach is adopted, teachers can also usefully describe the situations in which students have worked, using the framework presented for describing classroom climates (in terms of the motives they tend to arouse and the behaviors they tend to encourage) presented in *Education, Values and Society.*

It is important to note that, whereas most external assessments of people take the form or *ratings,* what one gets by following the procedures described above is a series of *statements* about people and the environments where they have been observed. These are analogous to chemical descriptions of substances and the environments in which they are placed.

It will be readily apparent that this procedure requires one to be thoroughly familiar with the ideas summarized above and then to devote a considerable amount of time to the process of (1) studying students' interests and talents, and (2) creating situations where those talents can be expressed. (If teachers have failed to create appropriate individualized developmental environments, or failed to make their observations in such environments, any statements made about—or ratings made of—high-level competencies will be meaningless.) Because of the time required, the use of rating systems—such as those often found in staff appraisal systems—are not a feasible or sensible proposition in many settings. On the other hand, familiarity with (indeed, day-to-day use of) the framework is crucial to the development, release and effective deployment of human resources. It is therefore essential that teachers develop the habit of thinking more carefully about their student's talents and how best they can be developed and deployed. This objective might best achieved, however, not by pitching them directly into assessing these qualities, but by encouraging them to use the results of the more student-based assessment procedures and climate surveys to be described below.

In the past we have experimented with, indeed advocated the use of, Behaviourally Anchored Rating Scales.[18] In essence, this procedure requires raters to agree on, for example, precisely what level of initiative is indicated by a specific behavior of a particular ratee. At first, the approach appeared to be very promising. However, we encountered serious difficulties when trying to implement the necessary procedures. The reason for this took some time to emerge. Although it was obvious from our earliest trials that behavior one teacher described as "initiative" would be described by another as "the student trying to ingratiate himself with his teacher," it was not until we had recognized the centrality of values to the assessment of competence that we were able to appreciate that this problem could not be resolved without first finding out what the *student's* values were—and then respecting those values, whatever they were. That done, we could begin to get some agreement about what was meant by such qualities as "initiative" *in relation to the student's own priorities*. But, even then, if one wished to assess his or her competence, one had to develop behaviorally anchored scales for *all* competencies listed in *Competence in Modern Society* in relation to all possible goals. The task became even more cumbersome than putting checks in an extended version of Grid 5.1. We backed off.

Behavioral Event Interviews

Behavioral event interviews[19] require teachers and lecturers to share more of the responsibility for assessment with students. Students are asked to think of—or keep records of—times when things went particularly well and particularly badly for them; they are asked to report both the events they were particularly pleased about and the events that led them to feel frustrated and uncomfortable. They are asked to record what happened, what led up to the situation, and what the outcome was. They are asked to say what they were trying to do or accomplish. (In this connection care has to be taken to reassure them that it is both appropriate and important to record "unacceptable" goals—such as passing the time as pleasantly as possible in warm friendly conversation—because workplaces and society need people who value such behavior and do it well.) They are asked to describe their thoughts and feelings while they were engaged in the activity. And they are asked to say what others did, what they did, and how others reacted.

These records are then scored by the teacher or lecturer, or by an external agency, using a variant of Grid 5.1. The student's values and the competencies displayed when pursuing them are very apparent to anyone familiar with the conceptual framework developed above. The basic interview or record sheets remain available should students wish to challenge the overall statements made about their values and pattern of competence. If the interviewing and scoring are carried out jointly by student and teacher—and possibly the students' peers—a wealth of information is available to guide future placement and development. The methodology is elegant and, provided all concerned are prepared to take personal development seriously, it has the potential to progressively initiate both staff and students into ways of thinking about human resources and their development and utilization that are essential to the future development both of the educational system and society.

Variants of the methodology have been developed independently by Stansbury[20] and by Burgess and Adams.[21] Their work is important for two reasons. On the one hand it indicates that it is feasible to envisage that such assessments might be much more widely employed in schools. On the other, it alerts prospective users to the amount of time which is required if students are to be offered the guidance and counseling that is required as a basis for effective competency-oriented education, itself a prequisite to meaningful assessments of multiple talents.

The Assessment of Competence Using Value-Expectancy Methods

Value-expectancy methodology is designed to get inside people's heads, assess the (reinterpreted) three dimensions in Johnson's diagram, and compute the resultant(s). The methodology enables us to assess people's values, their perceptions of relevant features of their environment, what they expect the effects of their actions to be, and how much importance they attach to each of the anticipated consequences. The consequences examined include those arising from the individual's own competence (or the lack of it) and consequences that follow from other people's reactions to his or her behavior. If appropriate, people's confidence in their ability to deal with the reactions they expect from others is also documented. The methodology enables the assessor to combine these bits of information together in order to calculate the strength of the resultant disposition to undertake different kinds of tasks effectively in particular kinds of situations.

It is easiest to introduce the theoretical basis of value-expectancy-instrumentality methodology by reference to the work of Fishbein. In the late 1960s, Fishbein[22] simulated a paradigm shift, in the then-quiescent areas of "attitude" measurement, by emphasizing, and finding an elegant way of handling, something everyone had always known—but had not taken into account in the theories or practice of attitude measurement current at the time (and something that is still neglected in the measurement of personality and abilities). This is that behavior—such as buying biscuits or using contraceptives—is primarily determined by multiple beliefs and feelings that come into play in particular situations rather than by a single underlying "attitude" or personality variable.[23]

Fishbein made two fundamental contributions to our ability to think about, and handle, these issues. First, he focused attention on something repeatedly emphasized in this chapter, namely, it is important to assess the respondent's attitude toward, or valuation of *the behavior in question*—and not his or her value for the object of the behavior. One should study the respondent's attitude toward *using* those contraceptives—rather than his or her attitude toward the contraceptives. Second, he found a means of tying together three well-established, empirically based, theoretical viewpoints about behavior.

The first of these traditions holds that people will be inclined to engage in an activity if they are relatively certain that the activity will lead to satisfactions they value. The second holds that they will be more likely to do something if they feel that the behavior is consistent with their self-images— with the sort of person they want to be. The third viewpoint it that people will be more likely to engage in a behavior the more certain they are that other people expect them to do so, and the more dependent they are on a favorable reaction from those other people.

There is considerable evidence[24] to support each of these viewpoints taken individually. The predictive validity of measures based on any one of them is typically of the order of .4. The beauty of Fishbein's work was that, for the first time, it enabled us to assess each of variables more systematically and then to tie the three sets of variables together. The method of combining and weighting the component parts is itself supported by a considerable body of empirical research. The effect of these developments is that predictive validities of .8 and .9 are not uncommon.

Before moving on, attention may be drawn to the way in which Fishbein's model parallels that developed above in connection with Grid 5.1. There we argued that the capacity to undertake a valued activity effectively was multiply determined; it was dependent on bringing to bear a number of relatively independent—but substitutable—competencies, each having cognitive, affective, and conative components. It was argued that effective behavior depends on having an appropriate self-image, on perceiving oneself as having the support of relevant reference groups, and on having an appropriate institutional framework in which to work (i.e., on *shared* beliefs about priorities, relationships, and ways of doing things).

In nontechnical language, what the Fishbein version of value-expectancy-instrumentality theory does is ask people what they think the consequences would be if they engaged in any particular behavior and then to weight those consequences with the importance attached to each. Three domains of possible consequences are systematically studied. These may be loosely called *personal* consequences, *self-image* consequences, and *reference groups' reactions.*

The personal consequences which may be studied include a person's response to such statements as *"I would enjoy doing this"*; *"It would take up a great deal of time which I would prefer to devote to other things"*; and *"If I did this, I would have a lot less money for other things"*. The self-image (or, more correctly, personal normative belief) consequences would include responses to such statements as *No self respecting person would to this; It is my duty to do this;* and *I would be working for the long-term good of mankind if I did this.* The reference group consequences include statements as *My grandmother would object to my doing this; My workmates would encourage me to do this;* and *God will punish me if I do this.*

Each of these perceived consequences has to be weighted by the importance persons attach to them or their motivation to comply. What my grandmother thinks won't have much influence on my behavior if I don't *care* what she thinks. So, to apply the model fully, we first have to find out how *certain* the people we are assessing are that, if they engaged in the behavior, each consequence would follow—and then how important each of those consequences is to them. We then multiply the certainty ratings by the probability ratings and sum the resulting products.

To use the value-expectancy-instrumentality theory to index the likelihood people will display selected competencies in the course of undertaking tasks they care about, we first identify, in practice, tasks they "feel a need" to carry out by asking them to complete a *Quality of Life* questionnaire (see Figure 5.2a). On this questionnaire they are first asked to indicate how *important* various features of the environment are to them, and how important they think it is to be able to do various things at work. Thereafter, they are asked to say how *satisfied* they are with each of these same features of the environment and with their opportunity to do each of the things they have said they would like to do. Their responses are then examined, and an item they have rated both important and unsatisfactory is selected.

The *Consequences* questionnaire is then used to explore their perceptions of the consequences of trying to do something about this discrepancy. What do they think would happen if they tried to persuade other people to do something about it? What would happen if they tried to do something about it themselves? The consequences studied cover the domains identified in Fishbein's model: They include such things as conflict with other values, whether doing it would enable them to be the sort of person they want to be, and their perceptions of how their reference groups would react.

The process may be illustrated by taking an example. Suppose we are interested in exploring the consequences that students expect to follow from trying to persuade their fellows to behave more responsibly. The students

FIGURE 5.2a

The Assessment of the Components of Competence
An Illustration from the Edinburgh Questionnaires

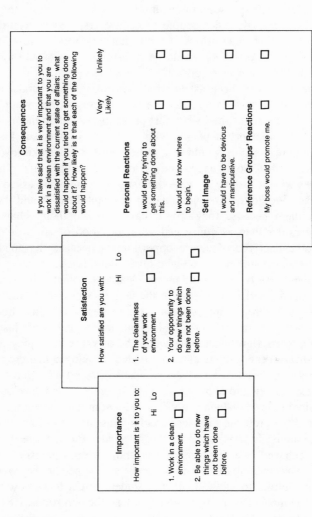

Note: This is a schematic representation only; it does not bear a direct relationship to the questionnaires.

would first be asked what they thought the personal consequences would be. They often think that trying to do this would make them uncomfortable and unhappy, leave less time for other activities they value, and demand abilities they feel they do not possess. In the absence of these abilities, any attempt on their part to persuade other people to behave responsibly would demand a great deal of effort, lead others to think that they were getting above themselves, and the whole thing would be a disaster. They would look, in their own eyes and in the eyes of others, very foolish indeed.

After they have been asked what they think the general consequences would be, they are asked whether the sort of person they would like to be would do these things—and what sort of person *would* do them. They sometimes feel that the sort of person who would try to persuade his fellows to behave more responsibly would be a rather pious, priggish killjoy, and that to be successful, they would have to be devious and manipulative. They may not themselves wish to be any of these things. Finally, they are asked how others would react: Would their friends support or reject them, would their teachers condemn them because they would have exposed their behavior as self-interested rather than as concerned with the good of all, would they, like Socrates, be deprived of career opportunities because they had identified themselves as the sort of person who takes moral issues seriously? If one cumulated these results, one would have a clear assessment of the strength of the student's disinclination to engage in the activity (see Figure 5.2b)!

By going through the process we have described, one obtains a great deal more useful information than this single index. In the case just described, one would learn a great deal that would be of value in helping to devise an individualized, generic-competency-oriented, developmental program to help the student concerned, if he or she so wished, to resolve value conflicts and thus release energy into chosen tasks, and to practice and develop competencies required to reach valued goals. The student might, for example, pay more attention to the probable long-term social consequences of not behaving in a socially responsible way. He or she might be encouraged to meet other people who had behaved in a responsible way and not been punished or forced to behave in ways incompatible with being the sort of person they want to be. As a result of getting to know them, the student might learn how to persuade other people more effectively without having to be obnoxious. He or she could be helped to practice the skills required to obtain the cooperation of others.

Classroom Climate Measures

Not only would the information obtained by using the above procedure be of value in making it possible to design an *individual* program of development for this particular student, the data collected from all students in a class would be of value in enabling the teacher (or an external accrediting

FIGURE 5.2b

Flow Chart (oversimplified and schematic)

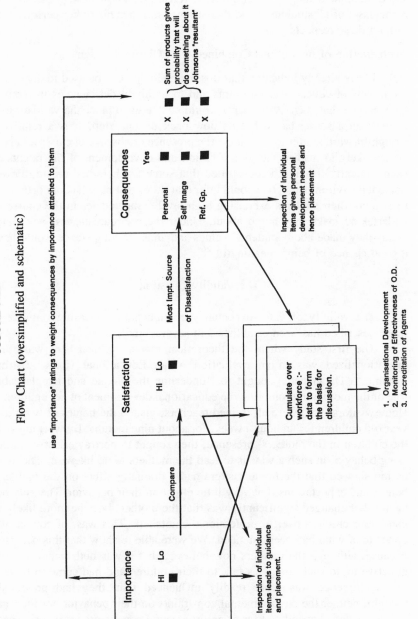

use "Importance" ratings to weight consequences by importance attached to them

Importance

Hi ■   Lo

Inspection of individual
items leads to guidance
and placement.

Compare

Satisfaction

HI   Lo ■

Most Impt. Source
of Dissatisfaction

Consequences

Yes

Personal ■

Self Image ■

Ref. Gp. ■

X ■
X ■
X ■

Sum of products gives
probability that will
do something about it
Johnsons "resultant"

Inspection of Individual
Items gives personal
development needs and
hence placement

Cumulate over
workforce :-
data to form
the basis for
discussion.

1. Organisational Development
2. Monitoring of Effectiveness of O.D.
3. Accreditation of Agents

agency) to assess the quality of the teacher's overall program of placement and development and his or her ability to release the know-how, goodwill, and enthusiasm of all students—and thereafter to improve his or her performance in both these respects.

Accreditation of Institutions Combined with Observer Judgments

I have already indicated that this methodology can be used to document the effects of educational programs and to highlight deficiencies in them. I have argued that such assessments would enable us to place the validation of courses on a sound basis. Let us now back up one step. It is a relatively straightforward matter to determine the presence or absence of classroom processes likely to lead to the identification and development of the talents of each student.[25] Having demonstrated that some teachers had created developmental environments, one could infer that they must have had opportunities to *observe* their students exercising high-level competencies in the course of undertaking tasks they cared about. Under these circumstances, any statements they made about students' values and areas of competence would have a good chance of being meaningful.[26]

The Validity Question

The validity of value-expectancy-instrumentality measures similar to those described has been established in several studies.

The first study where the theoretical model outlined here was fully operationalized was in an evaluation of an Educational Home Visiting Scheme.[27] The Scheme sought to "underline the unique and irreplaceable role of the mother in promoting the educational development of her children." Home visitors, who were all trained teachers, visited the homes of two-three year old children for an hour a week, for about nine months. By working with the children in the mothers' presence, they sought to portray effective mothering behavior in such a way as to lead the mothers to do likewise. The evaluation showed that the home visitors had a dramatic effect on the mothers' beliefs and expectations, but very little effect on their behavior. The only behavior that changed significantly was that the mothers became more likely to hand their children over to professional caretakers. This was, of course, the opposite of what had been intended. We were able to show that this occurred because, although the mothers now believed that it was both important and effective to do such things as talk to their children and had come to believe that intelligence was more readily influenced than they had previously thought, neither the environmental constraints on their behavior nor their basic values had changed. As far as environmental constraints were concerned, for example, they still lacked the time needed to do the things they had always believed they should do and now recognized to be even more important than they had imagined. As far as their values were concerned, they would still have preferred their children to be dependent on, rather than independent of, them. Thus, despite the fact that they now believed, even more strongly than before, that the behaviors the home visitors modeled were both important and efficacious, they were still prevented from practicing them by environmental constraints and value conflicts. They resolved this dilemma by handing their children over to professionals—whose competence they respected. They ended up feeling even more guilty than before about not doing things they already knew they should be doing.

It emerged that, if the program was to be effective, the home visitors would, among other things, have to *influence* the mothers' values. They would also have to help them, as a central objective of the project, to develop the competencies they needed to gain more control over their own lives—and especially to influence public provision. This, naturally, posed serious dilemmas for the home visitors. Our interest here is, of course, methodological rather than substantive. The point is that the value-expectancy measures we developed proved to be sensitive to the effects of the educational program; enabled us to identify what worked and what did not, and the reasons why; helped us to understand counterintuitive effects of the intervention; and enabled us to identify the (often unexpected) remedial actions that were necessary.

In another project[28] we used the methodology to study the effects of different types of educational program on elementary school students. We found that, contrary to common assertion, different teachers had dramatically different effects on students' concerns, priorities in education, priorities in life, behavior, and patterns of competence. Thus, some teachers led their pupils to feel that it was important to select tasks that were socially important and to obtain the cooperation of others to carry out those tasks effectively. The students learned how to tackle such tasks and how to win each others' cooperation. That they had learned to do these things could be demonstrated by examining the consequences they anticipated—one did not need to observe their behavior. They understood how the local democracy and bureaucracy worked, how to identify leverage points within it, and how to influence it. They knew the strengths of their fellow students. Students in other classes did not think it was important to do these things, did not think it was important to learn how to do them, and (rightly) anticipated disastrous consequences should they try to do them. One of the most striking results of the project was the discovery that, contrary to common assertion, what teachers did reflected (even if it did not match) their priorities,[29] and the patterns of educational activity they created were in turn reflected in their students' values and patterns of competence. Once again, the methodology enabled us to document teachers' concerns and patterns of competence—and it also enabled us to develop measures of program outcomes sensitive to the effects of the educational programs students were offered. These measures in turn enabled us to pinpoint strengths and deficiencies in the programs.

The objective of the work reported in *Competence in Modern Society* was to develop a set of tools (The Edinburgh Questionnaires) that would be useful in staff guidance placement and development and in organizational development.[30] The work showed, somewhat unexpectedly, that the "British Disease" (i.e., low quality and productivity) stemmed from a lack of interest in doing such things as finding better ways of doing things, finding new things to do, finding better ways of thinking about things, working at a task that would, in the long run, benefit the whole organization or society, or getting people to work together effectively. Surprisingly, the anticipated negative consequences, should they decide to do any of these things, were not a significant deterrent to undertaking these activities. They simply did not think it was important to do them. The Edinburgh Questionnaires have since been used in Samoa, Tonga, Japan, China, Hong Kong, Singapore, the Philippines, Canada, and the United States.[31] Whereas some people had reacted to the Scottish data by saying, "Of course, could it be otherwise?", the cross-cultural data make it transparently obvious that things not only *could* be otherwise but *are* dramatically otherwise (in Japan and Singapore) and have the consequences with which we are all familiar.

Taken together, these studies suggest that the methodology has considerable validity in that it enables us to understand, predict, and influence behavior. It has enabled people to gain more control over their own lives and organizations.[32]

Barriers to Further Work

How Is the Necessary R&D to Be Organized?

In this chapter I have argued that new forms of assessment are required, at both the school and system levels, to administer educational programs. I have also argued that new forms of assessment are required to credential the outcomes of the educational process and to enable people to identify, develop, get recognition for, and utilize their talents at work and in society. I have also indicated that new forms of assessment are required for research purposes—to study, among other things, the social and economic consequences (at individual, group, and societal levels) of educational programs that foster different preoccupations and talents.

I have shown that it is possible to both reconceptualize the nature of competence and its assessment and, without further basic research, to operationalize an alternative measurement paradigm in such a way as to generate useful information.

The use of this paradigm and the procedures I have described has not been undertaken on a wide scale. The objection often given is that such procedures would be prohibitively expensive. In my view, implementing such procedures more widely and developing the administrative procedures re-quired to make them less cumbersome for individual assessment would cost but a small fraction of what is currently spent on testing and evaluation. Peters[33] and Flanagan,[34] among others, have underlined the costs to society of not implementing more effective procedures for ensuring that people's talents are identified and developed. Finally, I have shown that, if there is a need to caution against unrealistic expectations in this area, there is also a need for wider recognition of the limitations of the tests currently available and the damaging personal and social consequences which stem from their use.

I will add a few observations about the barriers that have inhibited de-velopment of a new assessment paradigm and the steps needed if more progress is to be made in the future.

At first sight, it is extraordinary that the vast sums spent on educational and personnel evaluation and testing have contributed so little to the neces-sary developments. By and large, we are still working with models of ability and assessment developed in the first decades of the twentieth century. In re-ferring to the vast sums that have been spent, I include not just the huge fed-eral contracts awarded for the evaluation of Headstart and similar experimental programs and for the identification of the "variables" which make for school effectiveness. I also have in mind (1) current expenditures on the seemingly innumberable bureaus of research and accountability located in almost every school system in the country, (2) the budgets of organizations, such as ETS, that develop and market tests, whether for the diagnosis of spe-cial educational needs or for assessing scholastic aptitude or achievement, (3) the vast pool of school psychologists and others who administer, score, and interpret such tests, (4) the student- and teacher-time devoted to assessment over and beyond that needed to diagnose learning difficulties and to prescribe appropriate developmental experiences (the latter being conspicuous by its absence[35]) and (5) military expenditures on personnel assessment.

Given the scale of this testing and evaluation enterprise, it seems re-markable that the developments I have summarized should have had to be based on the work of perhaps half a dozen people—such as David McClelland and Calvin Taylor—who have made these contributions only as a result of extraordinary personal commitment to research and to society, and without significant public funding.

The institutions which might have been expected to promote the rele-vant R&D include the sponsors of educational research and evaluation, test agencies, the military, consortia of bureaus of research and accountability, and the universities. However, I will argue that we should focus our attention on the reasons why the universities—the educational institutions—have not offered more leadership. The lack of sponsorship from *official* agencies is not too remarkable. The conventional wisdom is that one cannot expect research customers to commission research to solve problems they themselves have not noticed or to find ways of achieving goals that have not crossed their minds—or even goals that *have* crossed their minds but are goals they do not know how to reach. Nor can consortia of bureaus of research be expected to press their case effectively. The classical entrepreneurial problem is people are not generally aware of their needs until someone puts a solution in front of them.

What I believe is remarkable is that the researchers who have had the most day-to-day contact with testing, evaluation, the problems of education, and the psychometric and educational research literature have neither emphasized the need for these developments nor gone out of their way to contribute to the new thinking required. It is also remarkable is that there is no reference, either to the need for more broadly based assessment procedures or to the need for a new measurement paradigm, in the papers presented to ETS's invitational conference on The Redesign of Testing for the 21st Century.[36] There is not, for example, in that collection of papers or in the special issue of *Applied Psychology* dealing with computerised psychological testing, edited by Eyde, a single reference to the possibility of using computers to implement psychometric models that could not be implemented using a paper-and-pencil format. There is also no reference to the problems I have sought to address here in the Joint Committee's *Standards for the Evaluation of Educational Programs, Projects and Materials*,[37] in the *Handbook of Research on Teaching*,[38] the 1982 AERA *Encyclopedia of Educational Research*,[39] or in the ten-volume *International Encyclopedia of Education*.[40]

Why have the test agencies not promoted the necessary research and development? They have, after all, assumed the mantle of the classical entrepreneur. In theory, their *raison d'être* is to identify previously unverbalized needs, invent ways of meeting those needs, and place the appropriate produce on the market. Unfortunately, as McClelland[41] and others[42] have shown, the classical theory is wrong. The necessary activities are too long-term and too risky; the original inventor rarely profits. Perhaps as serious is the problem that as with so many of the tools and procedures we badly need in modern society, the necessary products will not be hard and marketable. Then again, despite the theory, commercial organizations are not noted for their enthusiasm to introduce new products when these will upset their existing market. I suspect, however, that the real problem is that the attention of those who control the flow of development funds in these organizations has not been drawn to the unmet needs and the possibility of satisfying them because they do not have the "parallel organization" structure described by Kanter.[43] The time needed to notice the needs, question basic assumptions, and undertake the necessary development work will not have been available—and, indeed, it is an extraordinary fact that the time required to do these things is often deleted from contracts for evaluation activity.

These reflections suggest that there is a central problem at the university level. Those responsible for research and educational policies need to think more carefully about the ways scientific jobs are defined, the responsibilities of scientists, the competencies they need, and the qualities required by those who become researchers. It has not been ignorance of established scientific knowledge (as implied in the writings of those, like Lerner,[44] who emphasize routine testing) which has led to the failures to advance understanding and capitalize upon the discoveries—but a lack of scientific competence of the kind described at the beginning of this chapter. We need to rethink the training we offer prospective researchers.[45] We need to involve our prospective scientists—and others—in more project-based educational programs of the kind described in the beginning of this chapter and by Winter, McClelland, and Stewart.[46] We need to disseminate more appropriate understandings of the research process so that research sponsors cease to accept inappropriate beliefs about the nature of science and the research process and become, as a result, more willing to fund the adventurous research required to advance understanding and lead to the development of the tools and procedures which are sorely needed.

And so we come a full circle—for we are once again discussing the nature of (occupational) competence, the role educational institutions could, and should, be playing in fostering it, the institutional arrangements our educational organizations lead people to accept as appropriate, and the type of people whom our assessment procedures lead us to appoint to influential positions in society. In seeking to identify what has prevented the application of a significant proportion of the funds devoted to testing to development work in this area, we find ourselves discussing why the universities have been unable to undertake the necessary research, change their own offerings, and foster in students the necessary adaptability, conceptual ability, and beliefs about the research process, society, and its operation.

The problem is not simply the usual (and not inconsiderable) one of scientists discarding outworn theories, paradigms of measurement, science, and teaching. The reasons why the universities have been unable to foster scientific competence, adaptability, and willingness to draw attention to research needs include the now familiar facts that they do not foster these qualities, and that students cannot get credit for possessing them or professors for fostering them. But they are also structural. As Schon[47] has emphasized, the universities have developed highly fragmented "disciplinary" structures. These fragmented specialist-knowledge-based "disciplinary" structures serve to minimize competition both within the universities and among the "professionals" they "train." The sociological functions performed by those divisions are, therefore, of considerable importance. However, the effect is that students are forced to "master" (temporarily) vast quantities of information rather than develop the generic competencies common to the advancement of a number of disciplines—and to nondisciplinary professional competence as well. Still less are they generally encouraged to study the workings of society and take responsibility for doing something about the problems they notice. The effects of these oversights show up only when those concerned start working for test and evaluation agencies, school systems, and government departments.[48] University faculty and administrators themselves have the greatest difficulty in branching out into new areas; they have, at least, to behave as if they accept the conventional wisdom on how science advances in order to secure the research contracts on which their careers and the prestige of their departments depend. They have to teach the received wisdom to get their courses accepted by professional bodies whose main sociological function is to protect their members' interests. University faculty and administrators staff are generally not encouraged to reflect on, or spell out, more appropriate institutional arrangements because the framework in which they work is itself often dysfunctional and difficult to influence because of the sociological functions it performs.

It is tempting to revert to a discussion of the professional and civic activities needed if we are to do anything about this depressing situation, the nature of the civic understandings and competencies we need, and the steps we personally could take to influence the future. However, this is not the place to do so. Relevant discussions will be found elsewhere.[49] Here it is sufficient to say that, to run modern society effectively, we need nothing less than new concepts of wealth, democracy, citizenship, the public service, and the role of the public servant. Dissatisfaction with current arrangements is endemic: The most important sources of dissatisfaction with life in modern society are relationships with politicians and bureaucrats. Perhaps the most important single activity required if the necessary civic activities are to be released is for someone to write a book entitled *The New Wealth of Nations*. This would reorient thinking about the modern *politico*-economy as effectively—and appropriately—as did Smith's *Wealth of Nations* two centuries ago. It would, in particular, articulate things people already "know" and legitimize things already happening. It would specifically legitimize the socially participative activities required to produce modern wealth.

Implications for the Process of Education

In this chapter I have spelled out the implications *for assessment* of our research into the nature of competence. However, I began the chapter by describing some outstanding educational activities. I must now set what we have since learned about the nature of competence and its assessment in an educational context. Historically, we began the work summarized here with a study of the goals of education and the perceived barriers to achieving them.[50] In the course of this study (and its replications) we discovered (1) that the wider goals of general education—i.e., its goals beyond the basic numeracy and literacy—were extremely unclear, (2) that the methods to be used to reach these wider goals were still more unclear, (3) that there were major nonobvious, and previously unidentified, barriers to reaching these goals, and (4) that assessment played a major role in deflecting schools from these goals. Accordingly, I sought to initiate—and in a less than perfect way in due course succeeded in undertaking—further work in areas 1, 2, and 3. By and large, it was the simultaneous pursuit of research in these three areas which led to the model of competence and its assessment summarized here. However, the work on *assessment* proved to be unexpectedly important. It led all concerned to become clearer about the *nature* of the qualities to be fostered, and thus clearer about *how* they were to be fostered. Some readers may be particularly interested in the insights we have developed into the educational process while we were engaged in this work. Unfortunately, a summary of these insights would occupy at least another chapter.[51]

Despite the availability of these discussions, it may nevertheless be useful to highlight, very briefly, a number of conclusions which have already been mentioned in passing. One is that any meaningful form of competency-oriented education must be grounded in the students' values. Teachers must therefore be able to identify, and be willing to respect (rather than feel they have to change), individual students' values. They have not always been noted for their ability or willingness to do either of these things. Another is that it is necessary to foster different competencies in different students and foster the same competencies in different students in different ways. This does not fit easily with the current focus on standardized, age-determined, national curricula. Although many reports[52] talk of individualization, at the same time they emphasize the need to prescribe curricula. Prescriptive curricula debase the meaning of the word individualization.

More basically, as Dore[53] has also argued, the kind of individualization needed is fundamentally at odds with our preoccupation with efforts underway in the United Kingdom and the United States to standardize public education—standardization in this context meaning a common curriculum. Other conclusions follow from our view that social and civic competence is central to competent behavior in modern society.

Many elite private primary and secondary schools have recognized the importance of value-laden and political education, and inculcate social values and political beliefs without the slightest qualms. Those who do not accept what a particular school teaches can, of course, always go elsewhere. What I am suggesting here is that, if public schools are to provide effective education, it will be necessary for them to offer students many more options embodying different value positions, encouraging them to choose among them. If public schools are to do this, among teachers' and administrators' first priorities (apart from commissioning the necessary R&D) must be developing *adult* education programs that engage the public in a general reconsideration of beliefs about how society works and should work—and, in particular, beliefs about equality in public provision.

In my view it is necessary for all concerned—the public, professionals, and students—to reconsider what is *meant* by political education. Instead of inculcating political, social, and civic beliefs, teachers will need to foster student motivation and the competencies required to examine the workings of society, and take action on the basis of those observations.

The final conclusion is that any move toward effective education—i.e., toward competency-oriented education—involves a major change in the teachers' role. It implies a shift from the concept of teaching as telling to the concept of teaching as facilitating growth. It implies a shift from teachers being the center of attention and the source of wisdom to teachers being managers of growth and development. Teachers will be required to possess managerial, not merely didactic, competence to do their jobs effectively, and managerial competence above all includes the ability to influence the wider social forces that severely limit what one can do in one's job.

In conclusion, then, effective education requires fundamental changes in assessment. But it involves more: unexpected changes in beliefs about the nature of public provision, unexpected changes in the teachers' role, and new patterns of competence among teachers. Above all, basic changes in assessment practices threaten a wide range of established interests in fundamental ways. Paradoxically, the long-term interests of almost all groups would be best served by such changes. But, disturbingly, human beings often have great difficulty acting in their own long-term interests.

6

Recognizing Achievement

Elizabeth Adams and Tyrrell Burgess

Introduction

This chapter offers the experience, from two pilot projects in England, of the means of gaining external recognition and general currency for individual student achievement and of enabling teachers to take command of their own professional development. The means employed is common to both: it is a personal record of achievement whose probity and reliability is externally guaranteed. By this means the important outcomes of education in the achievements of students and its critical input, the quality of teachers, are measured otherwise than by tests and examinations.

What happens in most areas of the world where there is an established education system is that children and young people are registered in classes in the charge of a teacher responsible for inculcating in them the habit of disciplined classroom behavior and the acceptance of bodies of knowledge to be learned in sequence. The grouping of students may be by sex, age, capability, or parental influence, but it rarely reflects the young person's own preference. Similarly, the curriculum, divided for them into gobbets of predigested subject matter, is for most students less related to their own ideas of what they think they want to learn than to what they are persuaded they need to master to achieve some test standard—which may in turn form the precondition to some further step up the educational ladder.

Young people may think that their teachers exert considerable power, but most teachers in their turn have to accept the tasks and the students allocated to them. In primary or elementary schools a teacher may spend a large proportion of the total school week with the same group or class; in secondary or high schools the need for a recognized level of subject expertise has usually required the teacher to share his discipline with a number of different classes. Fortunately in almost any school, public or private, secondary or elementary, individual teachers attain rapport with some students, individuals, or whole classes. In few schools, however, is such mutual appreciation seriously encouraged. Its immense benefits to the motivation of students and to the successful management of the school are normally discounted.

In general, the organization of schools is based on the timetabling of class contact hours devoted to subjects. No separate provision is made for discussion between teacher and student or between student and student. The outcome is often that students complain that nobody ever listens to them, while a widespread complaint among good teachers is that their entire time at school is absorbed in teaching and testing the required curriculum.

In most schools individual students are not called upon to reflect on their work, to recognize their own abilities, or to identify those weaknesses which could reduce their chances of fulfilling their own purposes. After they have left school, perhaps with scant or irrelevant qualifications, many young people regret their failure to give attention to areas or modes of study which their schools could have made available. At school some of these students seemed apathetic, others hostile to the system, the subject, or the teacher. These students might have been more successful in another school or with different teachers. Since, however, children have to attend the school of their parents' choice or acquiescence, there is no possibility of pairing student and teacher.

What could be done much more generally than appears to be the case at present, however, is to provide timetable space for the discussion and clarification of individual student purposes in relation to educational opportunities. Once the student appreciates that his point of view is being taken into account, he may try to formulate it more fully and is likely to bring greater motivation to his agreed school tasks. These benefits seen so worthwhile that it is a pity that so many young people in all parts of the world complete their required span of years of attendance without them. The main difficulty is to introduce teachers to the art of listening, because long-established traditions exclude it.

Schools the world over are staffed by teachers who achieved their professional status by assiduous conformity to required forms of study and behavior. They cleared whatever hurdles were presented by examinations, conditions for entry to college, and whatever written and practical teaching tests were the condition of attaining qualified status. During their years of preparation for teaching they had little experience of being listened to and still less training in receiving messages from students or colleagues. Throughout they were at the receiving end of instruction and advice from college staff who were not held accountable for their subsequent performance as teachers.

FIGURE 6.1

The Balance of Power Between Teachers and Students

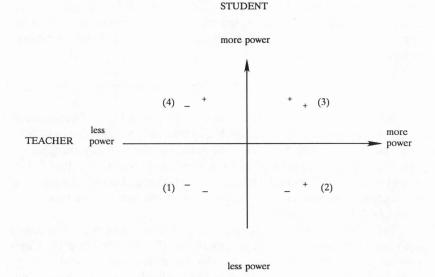

Once accepted into the profession, teachers have little option except to conform to its traditions and to the expectations of the institution in which they serve.

It is not easy to summarize how power is balanced in education, but an attempt is made in Figure 6.1 to illustrate the issue crudely. The two axes represent teachers and the students respectively, with each axis showing a range from very little to quite considerable power or influence on the content, processes and records of educational achievement. The most traditional position is in the bottom left (quadrant 1) where neither teachers nor students have much power of decision, and all are assumed to be doing what they are told. This position is associated with centralized local or national control. In the next quadrant, the bottom right (quadrant 2), teachers are exercising power as far as it lies within their competence: they take trouble to decide what is good for students, but students themselves have no place in the decision-making process. The top right quadrant (quadrant 3) suggests the balance that the authors are encouraging schools to use: it represents teachers and students working together to influence what is done in school time. The last quadrant, the top left one (quadrant 4), shows teachers withholding the exercise of their authority in favor of student choice. This pattern operates in a few select institutions but not, to our knowledge, in any state-supported schools.

Such considerations suggested to us that the need to recognize achieve-ment was the most pressing in education today. We believe it to be more im-portant and potentially more fruitful than changes to the curriculum, national testing, or the appraisal of teachers. The achievement to be recognized is pri-marily that of students in schools, but this in turn leads to recognition of the support of parents, the professional work of teachers, and the educational management of schools.

Justification for a New Form of Assessment

It has long been accepted that there are two main kinds of achievement that can be recognized, those measurable by tests and examinations, and those not so measurable. The former are the academic skills of acquiring knowl-edge, organizing it, reproducing it on demand, and exercising critical judge-ment upon it. The latter are the outcomes of creation and action, management and enterprise, service and leadership—and so on. Schools are used to re-cording both kinds of achievements.

In England, experience with the results of tests and examinations comes partly from public examinations at ages 16 and 18, controlled largely by uni-versities; partly from procedures for selection at age 11, operated until re-cently by local authorities; and partly from schools' own internal testing. There have been large changes here through the new General Certificate of Secondary Education (GCSE) at age 16, and there will be even more arising from the tests at ages 7, 11, 14, and 16, which are to accompany the "national curriculum", provided for in the Education Reform Act 1988. The GCSE has been the product of years of well-funded study, the biggest educational re-search project ever mounted in England and Wales. The new national tests will be based on recommendations of an official Task Group on Assessment and Testing.

The school's experience of recording other achievements until recently has been more local and individual: it has included general statements in the traditional school reports sent at intervals to parents and, in some areas, the use of recording systems developed by local authorities. More recently, schools and other agencies have developed what are variously called records, profiles, portfolios, reports, and leaving certificates, relating to experience and achievement.

Official reports, like Newsom in 1963 and Beloe in 1960, have advo-cated general reporting and recording systems for school leavers, and in 1983 the Secretary of State for Education set in hand the production of such a sys-tem. A draft statement of that year was followed in 1984 by an official policy for a national system of records of achievement. Since then, experience here too has been extensively accumulated. A Records of Achievement National

Steering Committee (RANSC), assisted by a Pilot Records of Achievement in Schools Evaluation (PRAISE), has monitored dozens of projects, including nine officially funded studies by groups of local authorities, into the practicality of the 1984 proposals. It was hoped that, by 1995 every 16 year old would have a record of achievement.

The importance of the 1984 policy statement is that it clearly distinguished, in many ways, the two kinds of achievement described above and the different ways in which it might be recorded. In this, it reflected a permanent and general unease with the predominance of the academic in education at the expense of creativity and capability—unease increased rather than diminished by the development of the national curriculum. Distinct from any official articulation of unease, a highly prestigious body, the Royal Society of Arts, has sponsored the Education for Capability movement to demonstrate how the connection between arts, science, and commerce can be made successfully in school and in higher education.

The purpose of records, said the policy statement, was fourfold: They should recognize, acknowledge, and give credit for students' achievement—beyond examination results; they should enhance students' development by improving their motivation, offering encouragement and increasing their awareness of strengths, weaknesses, and opportunities; they should help schools to see the potential of students and thus to reconsider their curriculum, teaching, and organization; and they should give a more rounded picture of students which would be valued by employers and other educational institutions.

There are a number of central principles on which a system of records is to be based. The first is that records are to be compiled and kept for all students in secondary schools, and summary documents of records made available to them on leaving. Second, they are to be records of positive achievement, not a statement of qualities and defects nor a prediction for the future. Third, they are to be factual, describing how students have responded to what has been offered them at school and giving concrete examples of what has been achieved and experienced—the Secretary of State for Education has explicitly called for coherent statements and ruled out ticks in boxes or the familiar number or letter gradings of the public examinations. Fourth, the final summary document of records will become the property of the student. Although schools will retain a copy, for convenience, they will not be allowed to supply one to anyone else without the student's (the owner's) permission.

These principles mean that every student keeps a file of evidence of positive personal achievements, and the tutor maintains a register of periodic (perhaps weekly) contacts with each student in the tutor group. These positive achievements are reckoned from the individual base line of each student. For one, regular attendance might constitute a legitimate entry; for another, behaving responsibly in an emergency on a school excursion; for a third, producing a poem or composing a melody. The list is endless. Such examples would be pinned to the facts: a student attended punctually throughout the first semester; another held up a colleague who fell into a stream; the poem was entitled "Growing Up." For the final summary, student and teacher would work together to produce a worthwhile description which could be substantiated in recorded facts.

Two potential problems with records have been resolved through experience since 1984. The first concerns timing, the second the place of examination results. In its final report in 1989, RANSC accepted that the commitment to universality for records meant that the final summary would have to be prepared during the spring term of the last year of compulsory schooling (otherwise the many students that the law allows to leave at Easter would do so without a record), and that in turn implied that examination results, whether GCSE or the tests at age 16 for the national curriculum, would have to be gathered separately and added later. In this way records will stand for those worthwhile achievements of students which are not measurable by tests and examinations, and the two kinds of achievements will be seen as complementary and of comparable importance.

They will also reassert one of the traditional principles of English education, that education is a personal matter and succeeds with individuals and not with systems. The Education Acts still provide that education must be suitable to each individual student's age, ability, and aptitude. It is for this reason that the law lays upon parents the duty to see that their child is suitably educated, and not upon schools or the public authorities. Abilities and aptitudes differ, and the promise of records is that they might reflect individuality and variety. The range of talent which is measurable by tests is too narrow and limited for this purpose. At least as important are the talents which are displayed on the initiative of individuals, not simply as a response to scholastic requirements. The individual record directs attention to what each student has gained from the school and has been able to do with it.

The records are important for the schools, too. Teachers know, quite as well as employers and others, that not everything is measurable by tests, indeed that some of the most important qualities and capacities are to be judged otherwise. The general use of records will gradually make clear, to parents and the public alike, what it is that the schools are doing to foster these qualities and capacities. If recognition of the rounded achievement of students is desirable, public recognition of the rounded achievement of teachers and the schools in which they work is becoming urgent.

It is for all these reasons that we have advocated for more than a decade a general scheme of records of achievement. We also identified the chief obstacle to its successful introduction. The problem related not just to records, but to all unexaminable and untestable achievement: it was how to gain for records an external currency and credibility which might be in any way comparable with that accorded to public examinations.

In developing our proposals, we began with those who learn. In education, the learners—the students—are the greatest resource. They do not come to education empty-handed, and it is only if their characters, capacities, knowledge, energies, and hopes can be harnessed that education can take place at all. Their desire to learn will be enhanced if they can themselves take responsibility for their own learning. In short, we proposed to take the individual promise of the Education Acts seriously.

Hitherto, education has been a matter of classes, forms, sets, and streams. The individual has been overlooked. The balance of schooling has been towards assessment, selection, and grading. It has been least good at valuing and developing the unique contribution that individuals can make. There has been too much acquisition and repetition of inert knowledge, too little development of competence and capacity. A heavy price has been paid for this, in apathy and even lawlessness in school, and in dependence and frustration in adult life.

Both can be minimized by offering all young people greater responsibility for their own learning by encouraging them to think of their education as a solution to the problems they themselves can see and understand. As adults, they will have to manage their own lives and face serious problems. The best preparation for this is managing their own lives at school. We learn throughout life: school can be a relatively safe place to learn where people can learn from their mistakes because the mistakes need not be devastating.

Our object was to offer young people the management of their own learning and show how their achievement at school can be recorded and presented. School records compiled in this way will establish what young people have done and can do, and students who have become used to building up such records will become more skilled in managing their adult lives.

Students are not alone in this. They have the support, first of all, of their parents. As we have seen, the duty to see that children are educated is placed firmly upon parents, and the law asserts the principle (heavily qualified) that children are to be educated in accordance with their parents' wishes. English parents have often tried to use this principle as a basis for insisting on choosing one school rather than another. They have not used it to influence what happens to children in the schools to which they happen to go, even though the courts have held that it is to this that the principle applies, rather than to choice of school. For their part, few schools have made serious arrangements for ascertaining what parents' wishes are. Information and opinion tend to flow from the schools to the parents through reports, open days, and parents' evenings. There is little encouragement for the reverse flow. This is a pity, since it is clear that children do best at school when they have their parents' positive understanding and support for what they are doing. Our proposals give parents responsibility for seeing that their children are suitably educated and how their wishes can be effectively considered. They do so by making the assent of parents a part of the students' self-managed learning.

In terms of time, money, and professional skill the main support for young people in their learning is the school they go to. At present the organization of school is ill-adapted to the learning of individuals. Students are grouped by age and often subdivided by ability. They are taught "subjects" for specified "periods." These periods are typically quite short, and between them the students change teachers and rooms: every 35 minutes or so the school is in motion. Academic organization is based upon these subjects, with senior teachers acting as heads of "departments" or "faculties." Schools are in fact free to deploy their staff and to use school time and accommodation as they see fit. However, the internal organization of nearly all schools responds in the same traditional way to the separate subject requirements of the public examination system. It is hard for teachers to imagine any other kind of organization.

In many schools its weaknesses are known. In England, such schools typically set up a parallel "pastoral" organization to make sure that the individual student is not overlooked and his or her human needs are promptly met. This division of academic and pastoral care is not, however, the best solution to the school's problem.

A Plan for Developing Students' Records of Achievement

In this section we suggest new forms of organization in schools to enhance the responsible learning of young people. Briefly, we propose that every student should have an identified teacher, for whom we use the familiar English word *tutor,* responsible for his educational progress through the school. The tutor's responsibility is educational, not simply pastoral. For this tutorial relationship to be a reality, the tutor and the students in his care must have substantial time to meet and work together so that supervision can be real and effective. We propose also that specialist "subjects" should be organized and presented in ways that make them more accessible to individual students, as part of the students' own programs of work. Such a reorganization would have the effect of ending short periods of instruction, minimizing disruptive movement, and making it possible for students to establish personal and productive relations with individual teachers.

This organization is designed to get the best out of records of achievement, by making the records the outcome of programs of education which the young people have planned themselves. The planning of the program and completion of the record takes place in four stages. The *negotiation stage* will occupy the whole of the school year in which the student reaches the age of 14. The *commitment stage* will be at the beginning of the year in which the student reaches the age of 15, and there will a *review stage* before the completion of that year. The *final stage* will be the year in which the student reaches age 16. The record of achievement at age 16 will be ready for the student in the spring of that year.

It is easy to underestimate the revolution involved in requiring individuals at different levels of the authority hierarchy to speak honestly and to keep on listening to each other until the truth emerges. Schools have the special problem that the clients are all junior to their teachers. Students, moreover, have no choice but to attend school. Unless they are enabled to see the opportunities the school offers them, they may act as though their choice were to take it or leave it, not to make it their own. A similar problem affects teachers. Teachers know their duties and their place in the hierarchy of the school. What most teachers lack, and what we have tried to encourage, is a regular program for talking things over with colleagues and talking things over with students. In many schools, discussion of students is casual and tends to concentrate on the exceptions—the gifted and troublesome students. Most students realize that, as far as their teachers are concerned, they are more or less nonentities; and this unfortunate position seems unlikely to improve until each school establishes a routine for the consideration of each student.

The routine that we propose is this. First, every teacher will accept tutorial responsibility for a group of students and be the second tutor for a quite different group. Second, every student on first attendance at the school will be allocated at random to a tutor group and to a second tutor (to provide for the first tutor's absence) and to remain with these tutors for as long as possible. Third, time will be allocated, perhaps weekly, for tutorials which would occupy all teachers (except perhaps the head and deputy head) and all students simultaneously. Last, arrangements will be made for regular meetings of tutors to discuss students.

To make all this practical in schools of different types and sizes, we see no alternative to committing the whole school (or the whole of one major school site) to tutorials at the same time. In this way students of different ages can meet as a group in the teaching space allocated to their tutor. In schools in England, this means the grouping of perhaps four students in each of the age levels 11, 12, 13, 14, and 15 with a tutor. It is our contention that every teacher, regardless of specialism or experience, should have the opportunity to sit down regularly with a group of students of varied age and characteristics, with the main idea of helping them to formulate their educational purposes, build on their interests, recognize their own achievements, and make the best possible use of their remaining span of school time. The mixed age group should help the tutorial scheme. New entrants to the school may be awed to find themselves sharing a serious procedure with older boys and girls, and the more senior students, in their turn, may be surprised at the business-like manner in which some eleven year olds go about building up their notes and records.

Teachers will also benefit. The proposed tutorial system will give every teacher a chance to meet students across the age and ability range and in a different context from that of their own specialist subject. Having to take re-sponsibility for tutoring a few older students will help many teachers to broaden their knowledge of what schooling, as a whole, means to students. Sixteen year olds will be working on their final summary statements, intended for inclusion in their Record of Achievement at 16, and thinking ahead to-wards the next stage in education, training or employment. Having only very few students of this age, any tutor has a chance of giving support in whatever way is called for. The test for tutors is whether they can hear the call; whether they have built a bond of mutual trust with each student; whether they are able to listen and wait for the full message before giving any guidance. The tutorial system proposed here uses each teacher as a tutor equal to any other tutor, regardless of sex, length of service, or position in the school. In the same way, every student ranks as a student worthy of equal consideration by the staff. Each student has a second tutor to whom he or she can turn in difficulty, without seeking permission.

In small schools, we propose that the whole staff meet at regular inter-vals in their tutorial capacity (and not for other schoolwork) to consider each student and discuss any problems that have arisen. In larger schools, we sug-gest the grouping of tutors in circles of about ten members, the groups being selected randomly or based on convenience of meeting time or place. Such meetings should enable student problems of all kinds to be brought to the no-tice of the staff. It is to be expected that tutors of new students would speak on their behalf, alerting colleagues to relevant facts while avoiding breaking confidences. Attending these meetings would help the head and deputy to pick up clues concerning student problems before they reached any crisis. Of particular concern would be the work of students in their fifth year, preparing materials for their draft records of achievement at age 16. Consideration at tutors' meetings of these students' progress and prospects would help teach-ers, as well as the head and deputy head, to get some measure of the value of the schooling they had together provided.

Validating and Accrediting Students' Records

Unfortunately, many proposals for educational change have faltered in the past because it had not been possible to secure general acceptance and recognition of what has been done. For all their faults, external examinations have this advantage: they are accepted by students, parents, teachers, employers, and society at large as carrying a general "currency." A grade on an external examination carries a general standard. It does not depend upon claims or the reputation of an individual school.

It is important to see that records of achievement, and the educational programs and tutorial support leading to their preparation, quickly gain similar external recognition. In considering this we distinguished three distinct tasks to be performed by three distinct bodies, tasks which would be required if records were to gain the standing and acceptability of examinations. The first concerned the programs of study which the pupils were to undertake, the second the probity and reliability of the records themselves, and the third national currency. Before dealing with each of these in turn, it is worth summarizing the parallels between the stages by which reliable examinations are established in England and those proposed here for records of achievement of comparable credibility:

Public Examinations	*Records of Achievement*
Approval of syllabuses:	Validation of students' courses by Validating Board of lay persons interested in the school
Agreement of mode of examination and standards of marking	Accreditation of records by professional group appointed by the local authority
National establishment of examining boards	National approval of accrediting arrangements by the Accrediting Council for Education.

As everyone recognizes, records cannot be produced suddenly at the end of compulsory schooling. The summary record which is to be available to all at age 16 is what it says it is—a summary. The evidence on which it is based is built up (perhaps in a folder or portfolio) over at least two years and based on experience in the courses, programs, and activities which the school makes available. This experience will have been discussed at around age 14. (In England most secondary schools offer "options" to pupils at about this time, both in subjects and in courses that lead or do not lead to external examinations.) The 1984 policy referred to discussions and dialogue between students and teachers about the process which leads to the records. What is needed here is that students, parents, and teachers should have the assurance that the courses and activities which the school is offering and to which they have committed themselves for the students' last two years at school are worthwhile. They will need to believe that, if their programs are satisfactorily completed, there will be a worthy record of achievement to show for it. The assurance is that the proposed education is valid.

This "validation" is a task for the governing body which every English school has. It is a formalization of their existing statutory responsibilities— indeed, it enhances these by giving the governors a specific task rather than requiring them to take only a general and passive interest. Our first proposal, then, is that the governors of each school establish a validating board, to exercise a general oversight of the school's programs and, particularly, of innovations in curriculum and method.

The probity and reliability of the records themselves can be secured by a formal process of accreditation, the need here being to assure all concerned that the record has been properly prepared and that its claims for achievements or standards are honest and reliable. The record must be accurate and just, and known to be so. This accreditation is a task for the local education authority, which in England is the body with statutory responsibility for the provision of education. Our second proposal, therefore, is that each local authority should establish one or more accrediting boards, composed of professional people with experience in considering educational institutions and programs, to give a public assurance that each school's records have been properly prepared and can be depended upon.

National currency is critical to the success of any general scheme. Even long-established examination boards in England require national approval. A new system, like records of achievement, requires it all the more. Our third proposal is for the establishment of an Accrediting Council for Education, which meets annually and receives reports from the local accrediting boards. If one of these boards should express disquiet about a school, or if the council should find something amiss with a board, it should be for the council to alert the local authority to the need for improvement, with the ultimate sanction that national accreditation might in future be denied. (There could be no question of failing to accredit the records of current students who had been preparing them in good faith).

These three elements—school validating boards, local authority accrediting boards, and the Accrediting Council for Education—formed what we described as a "Framework for Validation and Accreditation" for records of achievement. Their functions and possible procedures were outlined in a book we published in 1985. By then we had been able to establish, with the generous help of the Calouste Gulbenkian Foundation, a pilot project to test the feasibility of our Framework. Our object in establishing it was to create and test a means of recognizing, through records of achievement, the efforts of students and teachers in each school, which respected the individuality of students, the professional responsibility of teachers, the purpose of the schools, and the proper functions of governors and local authorities. We wanted to use existing institutions, not create new structures and cadres, with inflated fees to keep such structures in being. We wanted to be economical of all the participants' time and effort and to ensure that the tasks being performed were intrinsically worthwhile. Above all, we wished to establish the value of a system that directly enhanced performance without standardizing the school curriculum and imposing uniformity in schools and local communities. Students deserve better than to be used as mere occasion for sets of answers to permit comparisons of schools, states and regions. The main components of our developed system, both within and outside the schools, are set out in Figure 6.2.

The proposals which we have tried out and found to be feasible in the United Kingdom are relevant to education elsewhere, including the United States. They do not depend on the nature of school curriculum or on the incidence of local national systems of assessment or examination. Rather, these proposals address themselves to universal problems: how to provide the students and the world at large with reliable statements about achievements other than those measured in academic tests, and how to fulfil these aims of education without incurring such unintended outcomes as the widespread rejection of their educational opportunities by young people. The elements of this framework reflect, but do not depend on, the peculiarities of the English system of education, but could well be established in almost any country—anywhere, that is, where there are children and young people for whom records of achievement should be made; where there are school teachers and schools bearing the chief responsibility for encouraging, recognizing, and recording achievement; where there is a community of parents and other local persons immediately concerned with the quality of schooling; and where there is a public body responsible for the provision of education in schools and other institutions. Beyond these elements, the onus lies on each nation to ensure fair treatment of its young people—many of whom feel themselves to be shortchanged in what they have to show for years of required attendance.

It was fortunate for our proposals that we were able to take advantage of the interest surrounding records of achievement for school students, including the official policy statement *Records of Achievement,* published in 1984, and government-supported pilot schemes intended to establish agreement on the main issues arising.

The Records of Achievement National Steering Committee, whose terms of reference were to prepare draft national guidelines for records of achievement and recording systems, published its report in January 1989. In its *Conclusions and Recommendations,* RANSC used the language of our framework. The procedures it recommended for validation and accreditation were entirely on the lines of our work. Paragraph 8.6 says that a record of

FIGURE 6.2

Components of a Scheme of Records

Activities within the School	*Activities of External Bodies*
Year A Head and staff prepare educational program for 14 and15 year olds.	
Programs presented to school's governing body.	
Governing body establishes Validating Board.	Validating Board considers and agrees to school's proposals.
Year B Negotiation stage Students, in consultation with parents and teachers, plan their own two year programs to begin in the following year	Local education authority appoints Accrediting Board for a number of schools.
Commitment Stage By end of year, students have agreed their two year programs.	
Year C Students follow agreed programs, building up a diary or folder of evidence of achievement	
Review Stage At end of year, students review programs and propose changes as necessary.	
Year D Students follow agreed programs and finalize the contents of their diary or folder.	Accrediting Board undertakes accrediting visits and reports findings to Accrediting Council for Education
Completion Stage The program is complete when students have a summary Record of Achievement in which can be incorporated results of tests and external examinations	Accrediting Council for Education approves the Accrediting Boards' procedures.

achievement validation body should be established by the governing body of each school . . . that the accrediting agent for records of achievement should be the local education authority. In addition, it named an existing national body, the School Examinations and Assessment Council, as suitable to accept responsibility for broad oversight of the accreditation procedures of each accrediting agent and keeping the national guidelines under review. These procedures—the framework of validation and accreditation—were used in our pilot project and in no other. What is important for us, however, is not the formal structure but the overall object and its aptness not just for students but for teachers.

In developing our procedures we have sought to build mutual respect and trust between teacher and student and to find ways of recognizing the educational outcomes. We aimed at involving all the teachers in any school, not just a separate category of "counselors." We wanted to show that all students, regardless of the base from which each had started, could receive proper recognition of their achievements. What we found was that teachers in general think they know what is best for their students but fail to enable the students themselves, as individuals, to appreciate what is on offer. In schools where teachers fail to ensure that students subscribe to the school's program as to the best use of their time, young people lose their educational opportunities through lack of motivation.

Every member of a school, whether teacher, student, or nonprofessional staff, is usually constantly aware of the authority hierarchy in the institution. What is not so often understood, however, is that, for certain purposes, individuals have to meet as equals across the boundaries of established hierarchy. When a problem needs to be probed or solutions considered, those most concerned with the issue or most knowledgeable about the options should feel free to speak and should be listened to. Without such arrangements, the top person in any organization—for instance, the head of the school or the teacher in a class—is isolated, unable to receive ideas or information from those best qualified to give them. In schools where every meeting of staff is conducted on hierarchical lines, teachers tend to replicate that pattern in their classes. Such schools may work very conscientiously to inculcate bodies of knowledge, but the ethos of the school and the attitude of many of the young people is less satisfying than where teachers and students learn to trust each other enough to talk things over as they arise. This led us to a further set of proposals.

In the pilot project reported above, we discovered how few heads and teachers had experience of acting as a sounding board to students or colleagues, how little realization they had of the difficulty of elucidating truth about another person's plans, hopes, or fears. Reflecting on this, we saw that few teachers had learned to judge their own quality and strengths, let alone help students to do the same in work on personal records of achievement. We considered that teachers might bring readier understanding to the task of helping students if they themselves were encouraged to develop more awareness of their own achievements and contributions to their school.

With this in mind, one of us wrote an article for *The [London] Times Educational Supplement* in May 1986 and invited any interested teachers to write to him. About a hundred replies were received, and we decided to call these teachers to a meeting before the end of the summer term. The upshot was that we undertook a project entitled Teachers' Own Records, funded by Education Services of Oxford, initially for two academic years beginning 1986–87 and extended for a third year, 1988–89.

Our new project reflected the principle that the maintenance of personal quality is a professional duty. It recognized that the enhancement of quality is not an abstract affair but a matter of matching two uniques—the individual teacher with the circumstances and problems which he or she meets in school. If teachers are to make themselves better at dealing with the problems they face, they need to develop the means to become more self-aware, self-critical, and self-respecting.

The practical proposal we tested in the project was that heads and teachers should keep a record of their own professional standing and continuing achievements. This plan, tried out by a number of volunteers in different schools, would enable all members of the profession to have an accredited statement, annually updated, describing their educational experiences and summarizing their contributions to the work of the school. These records would be in their own words, would belong to the teacher, and would be for use only at the owner's discretion. The process of completing them is intended to enhance the quality of each teacher's contribution to education, while the possession of a record could serve as an *aide-mémoire* and as evidence of professional performance.

In the Guide accompanying each set of blank forms for Teachers' Own Records, the reasons for heads keeping them were briefly stated as follows:

Keeping a Record should help the Head to fulfil professional commitments, enhance the quality of school life, realise career potential, evaluate his or her own achievements and build up a handy compendium of facts about the school. The record can provide the Head with evidence for use at discretion with, for example, the governors, the employers, local advisers, members of Her Majesty's Inspectorate or any professional visitor empowered to make an appraisal.

What greatly encouraged the authors was that, after working on their own records for a year or two, a number of heads and teachers sent us their written comments on their experience. Their main finding was that these aims, listed in the Guide, had been fulfilled. They had gained more value than they had hoped for when they began.

Most other approaches to improving formal education fail to address the fact of the peculiar relationship of teaching and learning. Ready-made schemes of management appropriate to manufacturing industry are of limited use in a school. Applying the business principle of product testing can give misleading results unless the measurements of both the input and the output relate to the individual pupil's base line. Fortunately or otherwise, children are not just passive receivers of bodies of knowledge. Both pupils and teachers are incalculable and unpredictable human beings. The question in school is how best to enable the adults to help the children to learn. As the old adage has it; teaching has failed—however marvellous the curriculum or the examination system—unless learning takes place.

The Need for Teachers to Develop Their Own Records

Our project coincided with unprecedented official interest in England in proposals for external appraisal of teachers, intended to improve education. However, when any appraisal is completed—at whatever cost in time and money—the initial problem remains: how is quality to be improved? The teachers who have been appraised are unlikely to have gained any help from the experience and may have suffered loss of confidence or standing. Such are the unintended effects of external appraisal. The scheme for Teachers' Own Records, as mooted in our project, is different in very significant ways.

First, the new scheme is within the control of the individual teacher. The Record is the teacher's own property and is not to be shown to anyone else without the teacher's permission. It is not open to abuse or misuse. It is not something to which a teacher may or may not be given "access" or the opportunity to challenge: it will be the Teacher's Own Record.

Second, it is a positive statement of achievement. It records, year by year, a teacher's growing professional development, agreed by the responsible person, the head of the school. It does not list the ways in which teachers are held to fall short. Most schemes of appraisal enter a judgement about qualities and attributes, but do not directly contribute to the problem of improvement. When the appraisal is complete, the question of what is to be done remains unanswered. The identification of a weakness does not itself suggest any specific remedy. Indeed, the process may undermine the confidence needed for improvement to be undertaken. By contrast, the Record comes into play once a problem has been solved and professional development has taken place, the principle being "improve first, record afterwards."

Third, the Record summarizes what a teacher has done in his own unique circumstances. It is based on the real problems which individual teachers face and deal with. It concentrates on the teacher's task. It does not set up a list of qualities and attributes against which teachers are judged and against which all are bound to fail in some degree. There is no sense in discovering that no teacher is ideal. Some of the methods used to discover this, like checking boxes of grades *A* to *F* on a list of some two dozen "criteria," are trivializing and demeaning, both humanly and professionally. The assumption that all good teachers score well on such lists is unjustified. The activity of teaching is more subtle and individual than this.

To summarize: the method proposed in the project is that, in each school, teachers should have, year by year, the means to take stock of their present positions, of the tasks that face them, and of the problems that need to be solved if those tasks are to be successfully completed. They are asked to keep a file of evidence for themselves of significant progress and achievement. At the end of each year, they summarize this achievement for inclusion on their Teachers' Own Records. This completed Record is agreed with the head of the school, and is of developing professional competence.

In all this, the head of the school is critical. Heads must see that the arrangements described above are made and maintained. This is partly an administrative matter, but it is also a personal one. If heads successfully introduce ways in which teachers can enhance their professional quality, heads will themselves evolve a means of enhancing their own performance and for summarizing this on their own Records. Heads who do this will find that they need the same kinds of support as teachers. It must be for the local education authority to make this support possible.

As with the earlier project, many features of this one were drawn from existing experience in many English schools. What is new is an attempt to combine best practice by means of the minimum organizational change. The device proposed is the *Teacher's Own Record*. It is commonplace in England to say that education is at present in crisis, that the morale of teachers is low. Our experience confirmed that teachers possess within themselves the means of their own regeneration. During the whole project we kept in close contact with the heads and teachers in the cooperating schools. They went through the procedures developed during the period, sending us their draft records regularly. We needed this evidence of their participation, without which comment on the scheme of Teachers' Own Records is superficial. The content of these confidential records was not our concern, and we divulged no detail to anyone before destroying them all. What we wanted, and what helped us very greatly, was the frank discussion with heads and teachers when we visited the schools on invitation and the written comments which they sent about their individual experiences in keeping their own Records according to the guidelines we provided.

We found that many of the heads and teachers who voluntarily undertook the pilot project proved to have had no experience of reflecting on their own strengths and achievements, let alone discussing these with colleagues or the head. Most of them recognized the benefit to themselves of fulfilling this requirement; especially, they appreciated having an appointment with their superiors to discuss their draft summaries. There were, however, a number who found it extremely difficult to formulate any estimate of their standing as teachers in their school or institution. They felt that someone else—the head or a visiting inspector or other appraiser—should judge their worth. Nevertheless, they wanted this outsider to get it right. They depended on the outsider to recognize the value of their service and their suitability for promotion. Of course, when such teachers had, in fact, presented themselves at promotion interviews, they had tended to be passed over; they had no ready answers regarding their competencies or achievements. It is to the credit of such frustrated teachers that they were prepared to work with us, looking again at their own professional development as well as at their lost career opportunities. The most frequently voiced comment on participation in the project related to the formal meeting of teacher and head at which the teacher's draft summary of his or her strengths and achievements in the school (over the past year) were discussed. Teachers of all ages and various types of school all found this meeting unexpectedly valuable. Several heads expressed their satisfaction over its usefulness. For instance, one long-experienced head of a highly successful school claimed to have learned a great deal in these meetings—and would allow nothing to interrupt the program. Another head, newly appointed within three months of the end of our project, found the system very valuable in revealing the quality and competencies of all members of his staff—a process which would have taken longer in the ordinary way. Similarly, heads who completed their own records found that the exercise paid off by helping them to see their own inadequacies while seeking to record achievements. Those who met their chief education officer for a discussion of their summaries were much encouraged to find how welcome this move was to their superiors and how much both benefited from it.

The follow-up to this pilot has to be in promoting greater professionalism among teachers. They all know that their duties and responsibilities to their students, their colleagues, and their schools means a great deal of work whose outcomes are not readily measurable. Teaching is work, but not like any other—and teachers resent people outside the profession assuming that the success of teachers can be equated with achievements by students in tests and examinations. As we found, however, and as a number of teachers and heads came to realize during the pilot project, it is not a simple matter to identify other evidence of a teacher's value to the individual student or to the school as an institution.

The keynote to professionalism, whether among teachers or elsewhere, lies in focusing on the client. Lawyers, doctors, architects, psychologists—all have to attend closely to the client's point of view before exercising their expertise. Carl Rogers made the case for client-centerd therapy while he was in charge of the Counseling Center at the University of Chicago during the 1950s; and so-called child-centered education, based on John Dewey's half-understood views, was prevalent in several suburbs at about the same time. While the connotation of such terms may vary, the essence of professionalism remains. There are two main points: those in command of the knowledge use it in response to the client's needs, and whatever the organizational status of the profession, its members do not submit to outside control of their skills.

Situations vary. In England, for instance, many medical doctors work within the national health service while others remain outside in the private sector. All of them, however, would claim to exercise their professional skill untrammeled by external interference. The education system is similar in that most teachers work within the maintained schools, while some belong to the independent sector. Until the present time the main external constraint on schools in England has been the university-controlled system of public examinations at ages 16 and 18. These examinations have strongly influenced the organization of schools and have provided ready-made, often irrelevant, criteria for judgement of students and teachers. By contrast, in medicine, a doctor's success is related to the nature of his clientele—a gerontologist is not blamed if the death rate among his patients is higher than that of a general practitioner. But in teaching, schools tend to be judged by their rate of examination success, regardless of the nature of their intake or the turnover of their population. These public examinations are still in place in England but, in addition, the Education Reform Act of 1988 had established a separate and unprecedented external control over school curriculum and assessment for the eleven years of compulsory education. The authors' projects referred to in this chapter were both undertaken before the 1988 act came into force. In our judgement, their significance is enhanced by the new legal position in the United Kingdom, and they become more obviously relevant to the position in other countries where teachers have accepted external controls of the content and process of education.

Conclusion

What is at stake is the professionalism of the teaching body, which can depend only on itself to sustain client-centered procedures as between the teacher and learner. Our projects have shown the practical contribution towards this end made by teachers' keeping records of their own strengths and achievements and teachers' acting as tutors to help students to recognize their real purposes and to work towards fulfilling them. Whatever the external pressures on schools—and these vary in different countries and in various types of school—total control of the relationship between teacher and student is impossible. By building trust and mutual respect between themselves and their students, individually and as a group, and by working with colleagues, teachers can ensure that education succeeds with most students, whether or not examination success comes their way. In any school, teachers can enable students to have the experience of working together and gaining respect for others; teachers can help each student establish the confidence and competence needed to cope with life, through the practice of discussing their purposes and the discipline of recording their achievements.

7

Approaches to Assessing Academic Achievement

Doug A. Archbald and Fred M. Newmann

Introduction

This chapter describes assessment practices that meet one or more criteria of authentic achievement discussed in Chapter 4. The examples are drawn from individual high schools, local school districts, or state agencies in four countries. They represent a broad spectrum of approaches, from scored writing samples to public exhibitions of diverse competencies.[1]

The examples are classified into three groups: (1) tests of discrete competencies, (2) exhibitions, and (3) portfolios and profiles. The assessments examples in Part 1 of this chapter yield quantitative information intended to describe progress or change in individual students and to enable comparison among groups of students. The competencies assessed include writing, speaking and listening, reading, analysis, and problem-solving. The exhibitions described in Part 2 are public demonstrations of mastery. Exhibitions are intended to demonstrate competence on challenging tasks that do not have single solutions and generally require analysis, creativity, and integration of knowledge. Exhibitions are tangible products of students' work, useful and interesting in their own right. They may include public presentation of a research report or literary production, music recital, exhibition of artwork, or demonstration of an invention. Portfolios and profiles, described in Part 3, are summaries or inventories of individual students' accomplishments.

PART 1: TESTS OF DISCRETE COMPETENCIES

When complicated assessments must be summarized into simple numbers that allow for comparisons, it is often useful to break tasks and competencies into discrete parts. The examples that follow show how competency testing in language performance and analytical problem-solving can produce simple numbers, but also meet some of the criteria for authenticity. Similar procedures can be used to assess mastery of specific curriculum content.

Language Performance

The following approaches are designed to assess verbal competence.

Writing Assessment: Holistic Scoring

Every spring, each ninth grader in the Milwaukee, Wisconsin, public schools writes an essay and a business letter, which are graded using holistic scoring procedures. The assessment identifies students who need extra writing instruction prior to graduation. It also helps to reveal strengths and weaknesses in writing instruction among the district's ninth graders.

At a designated time and day, all ninth graders are given the same set of instructions and 90 minutes to write an essay and a business letter. The great majority finish in this time, but an extra half hour is then given to those needing additional time.

The essay, which counts twice as much as the business letter, stresses writing as expression, more than as an instrument for practical ends. Students are required to produce ideas and to support opinions about familiar topics. Recently students were asked to write about problems with their friends, neighborhood, or schools, and present and support three ideas for improving their school. Examples of the business letter include a job application letter and consumer complaint letter.

Scoring. English teachers score the writing during a week in June. They first develop consensus on standards. A small team of experienced readers selects about thirty-five papers (for each writing task) from the pool of student papers to represent the range of quality of student writing. These are called "benchmark" papers. The benchmark papers are duplicated and a set is given to each of the approximately sixty readers.

The business letters are scored first, because they are easier to grade. Guidelines are handed out with written criteria corresponding to each of four possible scores, from 4 (competent, clear mastery) to 1 (highly flawed, not competent). Specific criteria for each of the scores are indicated in Figure 7.1.

Then, using the benchmark papers, the group grades single papers to reach consensus on standards. When the group achieves consistency in its scoring standards with the benchmark papers, the scoring process is ready to begin.

FIGURE 7.1

Guidelines for Essay

(4) COMPETENT - CLEAR MASTERY

- Main idea clearly communicated and of a fairly mature quality

- Ideas well organized (logically)

- Substantial content, superior development

- Paragraphs have clear organization and are developed in a mature fashion

- Effective paragraph transitions

- Language appropriate for a thoughtful essay (excellent vocabulary)

- Command of sentence structure

- Correct usage

- Correct capitalization, punctuation, and spelling

(3) MINIMALLY COMPETENT - ACCEPTABLE

- Main idea clearly communicated

- Ideas sufficiently organized

- Adequate content and development of ideas

- Paragraphs have clear organization and adequate development

- Some attempt at paragraph transition

- Language appropriate for a thoughtful essay

- Minimal number of sentence errors

- Only occasional usage errors (such as agreement, pronoun misuse, tense)

- Basically correct capitalization, punctuation, and spelling

(2) NOT COMPETENT - UNACCEPTABLE

- Main idea vaguely presented

- Ideas poorly organized

- Insubstantial content; ideas inadequately developed

- Little concept of paragraph development or structure

- Little attempt at paragraph transitions

- Language occasionally inappropriate for thoughtful essay

- Sentence fragments and run-ons; few complete sentences

- Frequent usage errors (such as agreement, pronoun misuse, tense)

- Inconsistent use of capitalization, punctuation, and spelling conventions

(1) NOT COMPETENT - HIGHLY FLAWED

- No clear main idea

- Ideas unorganized

- Little content or development of ideas

- No concept of paragraph development or structure

- No attempt at transitions

- Language generally inappropriate for thoughtful essay

- Sentence fragments and run-ons; few complete sentences

- Frequent usage errors

- Incorrect use of capitalization, punctuation, and spelling conventions

(0) Represents a paper that is illegible or off the point. A non-response is also a 0 paper. From Milwaukee (WI) Public Schools.

Packets of twenty papers are given to each reader (student anonymity preserved) for scoring. After all the papers have been scored once, they are read and scored again by a second reader. The first readers use codes to disguise the scores they assign to papers so that the second readers are not influenced by the first rating. Also, papers are shuffled between packets to randomize the assignment of papers to readers. For each paper, the scores of the two readers are summed to produce the final score for each paper.

A leader and a few master readers coordinate the scoring process to ensure that the packets are exchanged properly, conduct intermittent "benchmarking" sessions to ensure that the standards remain consistent, help readers pace themselves, answer questions during the scoring process, and reread and make a final judgment on all papers with scores differing by more than one point. In Milwaukee's scoring sessions, about 1 percent of papers need to be read a third time.[2]

After the business writing samples are scored, the entire process, including the steps for setting standards, is repeated for the essays. A student's final score for the overall writing task is weighted to give the essay twice the value of the business letter. It takes sixty readers five days to score the approximately fifteen thousand writing samples (two per student).

At a debriefing session, the readers share observations about spelling, punctuation, grammar, and organization and the content of the papers. This provides feedback to teachers and central office coordinators about elements of writing, as well as insights into students' concerns and values. Teachers have described the process as "professionalizing"—an opportunity to seriously "talk shop" and to reflect on educational purpose, standards, and evalution in writing.

The writing test also legitimates teachers' efforts to teach writing as a process in which organization and revision of written ideas are pivotal.[3] Central administrators favor the benefits of staff development and the overall contribution to the clarification of standards in the district's writing program.

Writing Assessment: Analytical Scoring

Adams County School District #12 in Northglenn, Colorado, assesses writing competence at each grade each year using primary trait assessment.

All teachers in the district receive a packet describing the purpose of the test, the days on which the test is to be administered, and how to administer it. Students are provided with lined writing sheets, written instructions, and the question to which they must write a response.

Students complete the writing task in two 45-minute class periods. The first period is for outlining and writing a first draft. The next day, students write and turn in the final product.

Paid readers, English teachers from the district and competent readers from the community, grade the writing samples. Each writing sample has two readers. Reliability checks similar to those described in the holistic scoring process for Milwaukee are used.

Readers score the writing samples according to multiple criteria (as opposed to a single holistic judgment of quality). Each student writing sample is rated 1 to 5 on each of the following criteria:

1. *Organization:* Measures the students' ability to logically organize ideas into paragraphs which develop the students' ideas and to combine paragraphs into well-sequenced essays.
2. *Sentence Structure:* Measures students' ability to write complete sentences and to vary syntax.
3. *Usage:* Measures students' ability to select the correct words to carefully communicate a precise message.
4. *Mechanics:* Measures students ability to capitalize, punctuate, and spell correctly.
5. *Format:* Measures students' ability to form letters and numbers correctly and to use correct margins and letter format when applicable.

Figure 7.2 shows the performance standards and writing criteria for the eleventh grade writing sample. The numbers across the top of the chart represent the 1 to 5 rating range. The numbers in the right-hand column show the weighting scheme. In computing scores, format is the least important trait. Mechanics counts four times as much as format; organization, six times as much as format.

When the scoring is completed, the results are processed by computer. The primary purpose of the writing assessment is for district-level monitoring, but teachers also use the results for diagnostic and placement purposes. Student, classroom, and school results can be compared to district norms using the total score and the individual trait scores.

The Assessment of Speech

In 1977, the Assessment of Performance Unit (APU) was established in the Department of Education and Science in Northern Ireland.[4] Each year, using a variety of measures, the language performance of a large national sample of students was assessed. Initially, reading and writing were assessed on a yearly basis. In 1982, the assessment of oracy, or speaking and listening, began.

The APU's main purpose is to monitor student language performance at a national level, with a rationale similar to that of the National Assessment of Educational Progress in the United States. Recently the APU published a

FIGURE 7.2

A Rating Scheme for Assessing Writing

Essays are scored 1 to 5 on each of five dimensions (Organization through Format). The numbers in the column on the right indicate the relative weight of each dimension in the overall grade. Thus, organization is valued most, and counts about 30 percent of the grade; format counts 5 percent of the grade.

QUALITY: 1 (low)	2	3	4	5 (high)
O	Little or nothing is written. Essay is disorganized and poorly developed. Does not stay on topic	Essay is incomplete. It lacks an intro, well-developed body, or conclusion. Coherence and logic are attempted but inadequate	The essay is well-organized. It is coherent, ordered logically, and fully developed	x6
S	The student writes frequent run-ons or fragments	Occasional errors in sentence structure. Little variety in sentence length structure	Sentences are complete and varied in length and structure	x5
U	Student makes frequent error in word choice and agreement	Student makes occasional errors in word choice and agreement	Usage is correct. Word choice is appropriate	x4
M	Student makes frequent errors in spelling, punctuation, and capitalization	Student makes an occasional error in mechanics	Spelling, Capitalization, and punctuation are correct	x4
F	Format is sloppy. There are no margins or indents. Handwriting is inconsistent	The margins and indents have inconsistencies—no title or inappropriate title	The format is correct. The title is appropriate. The margins and indents are consistent	x1

O = Organization
S = Sentence Structure
U = Usage
M = Mechanics
F = Format

From Adams County Schools, CO.

handbook for practitioners describing the methods of the oracy assessment program. The APU also encourages schools to develop their own programs to assess speaking and listening competencies of students. This project illustrates the importance that can be placed on oral discourse and provides some guidelines for assessing it.

Several principles guide the APU's assessment of oracy:

1. Talk serves many different communicative purposes, thus, assessment should reflect the variety of purposes.
2. Oral communication is relevant across the curriculum.
3. The oral and written modes should be seen as reciprocal and integrated aspects of students' overall communicative ability.
4. Listening and speaking should be considered as reciprocal and integrated aspects of students' oral communicative ability.
5. Spoken language is sensitive to context, and so assessment must be designed to take account of contextual factors.

The tasks used to assess students' oral skills are categorized under five general communicative purposes. These are:

1. Instructing/directing.
2. Giving and interpreting information.
3. Narrating.
4. Describing and specifying.
5. Discussion.

Each of these uses is broken down into a number of more specific purposes which lead to one or two specific assessment tasks.

Specific assessment tasks are designed to be as realistic as possible in order to elicit language of a kind students would be expected to use outside the test situation, to put pupils at ease to encourage spontaneous and unselfconscious speech, and to be stimulating and fun for the participants.

In each task a student is asked to talk with another person or small group to achieve a particular purpose. In most cases the other person is a friend the student selects; sometimes small groups consisting of the friend and other students are the listeners; in some cases the assessor is the listener.

The requirement for a realistic and relaxed setting for the students is balanced against the need for standardization, which entails a pre-scripted instructional protocol that has been carefully developed and rehearsed to sound natural and non-threatening.

Each student's performance is scored in three ways. During the oracy task, students are given a holistic score (1 to 7), as well as an "orientation to the listener'' (eye contact, nonverbal gestures) score (1 to 5). The assessor tapes each student's oracy task, which is also evaluated later by a pair of trained assessors using analytical scoring techniques. For the analytical scoring, the categories are:

1. Sequential structure (organization) [1 to 5].
2. Lexico-grammatical features (lexical selection and syntax) [1 to 5].
3. Performance features (hesitancy/fluency, tempo/pacing, and verbal assertiveness) [1 to 3].

Following are some examples of tasks developed by the APU to assess oracy.

Distinguishing Among Complex Visual Patterns: Bridges. One student (the listener) has a sheet showing pictures of six bridges. Another student (the describer) has a sheet with only two of the pictures. The describer and listener face each other so that neither can see the other's sheet. The describer must describe the two bridges on his sheet so that the listener can identify which two of the six bridges on the listener's sheet the describer is describing.

The describer, after receiving his or her sheet and thinking about the pictures for a minute, is instructed to describe the bridges one at a time and in as much detail as possible. The describer is asked to begin the description of the second bridge when he or she thinks he has given enough description of the first so that the listener can correctly identify the first bridge from the six on his sheet. The listener is told not to identify verbally any bridges until both descriptions are completed. The listener cannot ask questions. This encourages the describer to provide as much detail as possible.

Interpreting for a Listener a Series of Events Depicted in a Set of Drawings: Spider Web. A student listens to a several-minute tape that describes how a garden spider builds its web. While listening, he or she examines and arranges sequentially, in accordance with the recorded description, six picture cards that illustrate different stages in the process. Finally, the listener must recount the stages in the process to another student, using the diagrams as an aid.

Summarizing a Short Recorded Message which Interpets a Diagram: Language and the Brain. A student is given a diagram of the human brain and listens, while taking written notes, to a several-minute tape on ''language and the human brain.'' Afterwards he or she must explain and summarize the contents of the tape to a listener who has not heard the tape.

In each of these tasks only the speaker is assessed. The listener's responses are not a criterion for success. Instead, the main purpose is to assess the speaker's ability to translate visual observations and oral messages into one's own language, demonstrating effective orientation to the listener, good organization, proper lexico-grammatical features, and aspects of speech performance such as fluency and proper timing.

The APU has developed other tasks to assess oracy in different contexts and for different purposes. In some APU tasks students describe to the assessor information unique to the student. For example, after being asked to describe "something you have learned recently" or "a place you know about," students then respond to conversation-style questions on the subject they have chosen. Students are urged to select topics the assessor is unlikely to know much about, which places the student in the position of a knowledgeable authority.

Although oral discourse is rarely assessed systematically, a strong case can be made for its importance as a goal of schooling (Newmann, Chapter 3, this volume). The APU assessment methods, developed from substantial research and classroom experience, illustrate how this goal might be approached.

The Assessment of Reading

Most conventional reading tests assess students' awareness of information. They reflect and, implicitly, purvey a rather narrow conception of "understanding." These tests consist of multiple, short, contrived reading passages followed by questions, with one correct answer, asking for literal comprehension, simple inferences, and the main idea.

The Illinois Reading Assessment departs from common standardized reading tests in its theory-based organization and items. Valencia and Pearson, researchers instrumental in the development of the state assessment, write, "Readers actively use all available resources (i.e., background knowledge, text, reading strategies, situation) to reason and construct meaning from what has been read" (1988). The assessment reflects this, using lengthy narrative or expository passages, questions that often have more than one correct response, and a format that reflects a broader conception of reading and understanding. Because the test requires students to think about an entire story and to probe behind its literal narrative, the test is more consistent with academic authenticity's requirements of integration and depth.

The Illinois test has four sections with the following purposes.

Topic Familiarity. These items assess a student's prior knowledge of a topic before reading about it. Students read a summary of the passage. Then they decide how likely it is that a number of ideas might be included in the reading passage.

For example, students read that the passage (a 1500-word short story) will be about a man who wants to buy a house from an old woman, even though the house is not worth anywhere near the price she is asking. Then they answer *yes, maybe,* or *no,* about the likelihood that in the story:

- The woman agrees to sell for a lower price.
- the woman shows the man around the house.
- the woman gives her house to the man.
- the man mows the lawn.
- etc.

Constructing Meaning. These items can have more than one correct response and are in six categories:

- Vocabulary: What do words and phrases mean in the context in which they are used?
- Characterization: What are characters' key traits/motives based on information in the passage?
- Explicit: What key information is given in the passage?
- Implicit: What assumptions, events, motives, etc., are unstated but can be inferred?
- Application: How can information from the text be applied to new situations?
- Author's purpose/craft/bias: What were the author's purposes, and how do elements of textual style and form relate to those purposes?

An example of an item in the categories "Characterization" and "Implicit" is:

Which of these sentences accurately describe the relationship between Michael and his mother, Mrs. Grimes?

(a) They hated one another.

(b) His early generosity later turned to anger and thoughtlessness.

(c) She remained loyal to him after his cruel treatment of her and even after his death.

(d) He never stopped showing his love for her.

(e) Michael had been difficult for her to deal with after her husband died.

Reading Strategies. These items assess the student's knowledge of strategies to improve reading comprehension. Two problem scenarios are posed to the student. The first, *Problem Solving,* asks students to rate the value of each of a number of different strategies (e.g., "reread the first sentence of every paragraph") in clarifying or answering questions about the passage.

The second scenario, *Centrality/Importance,* asks the student to rate strategies to identify and distinguish the value of different ways of summarizing the text's central messages. For instance, a statement to the student asks him or her to imagine having just read the story and being asked to tell a classmate what the story is mainly about. It is followed by five items, including the following: "It is about a fifty-year-old man who wanted to buy an old house that was for sale. It had been in a flood once and was famous. The man talked to the owner." Students then evaluate the appropriateness of each statement.

Literacy experiences. These items ask students about their literacy experiences in four reading and writing areas: in-school activities, out-of-school activities, strategies used while reading and writing, and various uses of reading and writing. These items provide data on students' reading habits, attitudes, and perceptions of their instructional experiences, and they give teachers and administrators information to guide instructional decisions.

Machine-scoreable multiple choice reading tests are mandated in over 80 percent of the states in this country and will continue to be used for the foreseeable future. The Illinois test advances the technology of large-scale reading assessment by measuring and promoting a broader, more authentic conception of reading. Tests of the future need to address the challenge of efficient assessment of richer, context-based uses of language.

Analytical and Problem-Solving Skills

Essay and Oral Exams

The essays and oral examinations required in graduate programs are often considered the most rigorous and valid tests of academic competence. They are recognized internationally for the depth with which they assess mastery of specific subjects as well as analytical skills. Usually they require integration of knowledge and production of extensive discourse. Given by thousands of separate academic departments, these exams are not standardized according to the tasks presented, testing conditions, and/or criteria for success, but within specific subject fields there is probably substantial consensus on the hallmarks of competent and distinguished performance.

Why aren't essay and oral exams used more frequently in high schools? High school teachers try, within severe time constraints, to assign short essays, but as a rule, when students are asked to express themselves in school, they have few opportunities to write or to speak more than a sentence or two. This is particularly tragic, since most people would probably agree that the best way to determine whether a person understands a subject or a problem is simply to ask him or her to *explain* and to respond to further questions which

FIGURE 7.3

An Essay Question on Acid Rain

Mary is going to hike into a lake in the Oregon Cascades. Fifteen years earlier, Mary had been to the same lake to conduct a study for the Oregon Fish and Wildlife Commission. At that time the lake was a typical high mountain lake surrounded by coniferous trees on three sides and some alders, birches, and maples on the more level, meadow side of the lake. The lake had been a favorite fishing spot for her father and grandfather, producing many shrimp-fed rainbow trout. She learned that crawfish from the lake were good bait for the fish.

Describe the changes you think might have occurred in the plants and animals of this environment if Acid Rain had significantly affected the area. Make specific references to the assigned reading to support your hypotheses.

The following criteria will be used to evaluate your response:

1   point will be given if your response is clear and well organized.

1   point will be given if the response is logically supported by specific references to the background reading.

2   points will be given if the response shows "in-depth" thought, that is, a careful and thorough consideration of the possible effects that acid rain might have had on this environment.

the explanation itself is likely to provoke. Large teaching loads and the technology of testing have perhaps obscured this important principle, but fortunately several leading educators continue to emphasize the use of written and oral language as the coin of academic mastery (e.g., Adler 1982; Boyer 1983; Sizer 1984).

Student writing of essays, especially outside of English courses, is infrequent, but teachers in most subjects have devised thousands of interesting assignments. Figure 7.3 gives an example of an essay question that could follow a science or social studies unit dealing with pollution.

Oral examinations in high school are rare. Students may participate in small-group discussions, and occasionally even in short Socratic discussions, but these are rarely required as significant assessment exercises. To complement the kinds of oracy exercises described above, oral examinations focused on subject matter content can be used. These can take several forms, for example, student debates, teacher examination of student small groups that have researched special topics, teacher examination of individual students, and, as described further in Part 2, individual students being examined by a committee of adults. In these situations students would be expected to explain and to justify their conclusions, first through an initial statement and then by elaboration in response to further questions posed by the examiners. As in writing and oracy assessment, specific criteria for evaluation can be articulated and-probably scored reliably.

Assessment through extended written and oral discourse raises a number of logistical issues that cannot be solved here. Progress in this direction could be made, however, by assessing fewer students at any given time and staging the assessments throughout a course of study. A teacher with five classes per day and 125 students could administer a good essay or oral examination to only three students per class each week. In nine weeks, all 125 students could be tested. If this were to occur in each class in each of the students' four main subjects, once a semester or twice a year (e.g., one major essay and one oral exam), it could make a major impact on students' achievement.

NAEP Exercises

The following test exercises, drawn from the National Assessment of Educational Progress's Pilot Study of Higher-Order Thinking Skills Assessment Techniques in Science and Mathematics (NAEP 1987), illustrate that for some purposes it is possible to assess depth of understanding without requiring student production of extensive written or oral statements.

Triathlon (Interpeting Data). Students are required by this paper-and-pencil task to examine data on five children competing in three athletic events (i.e., frisbee toss, weight lift, and 50-yard dash) and decide which of the five children would be the all-around winner. Students must devise their own approach for computing and interpreting the data and explain why they selected a particular "winner." Students need to be careful in their interpretation, because lower scores in the 50-yard dash are better than higher scores, while the converse is true in the frisbee toss and weight lift:

Student Assessment Sheet

Joe, Sarah, Jose, Zabi, and Kim decided to hold their own Olympics after watching the Olymics on TV. They needed to decide what events to have at their Olympics. Joe and Jose wanted a weight lift and a frisbee toss event. Sarah, Zabi, and Kim thought running a race would be fun. The children decided to have all three events. They also decided to make each event of the same importance.

They held their Olympics one day after school. The chidren's parents were the judges and kept the children's scores on each of the events. The chidren's scores for each of the events are listed in Figure 7.4.

FIGURE 7.4

Triathlon Results

Child's Name	Frisbee Toss	Weight Lift	50-Yard Dash
Joe	40 yards	205 pounds	9.5 seconds
Jose	30 yards	170 pounds	8.0 seconds
Kim	45 yards	130 pounds	9.0 seconds
Sarah	28 yards	120 pounds	7.6 seconds
Zabi	48 yards	140 pounds	8.3 seconds

Record Findings
(A) Who would be the all-around winner?

_____

(B) Explain how you decided who would be the all-around winner. Be sure to show all your work.

Account for Findings_____

_____

_____

Heart Rate and Exercise (Designing an Experiment). Students design an experiment to determine the effects of exercise on heart rate. Students need to identify the variables to be manipulated, specify what needs to be measured, and describe how the measurements should be made to provide reliable results. This exercise can assess students' understanding and planning of scientific investigations when actual experimentation in a classroom or assessment setting is difficult.

Student Assessment Sheet

Usually your heart beats regularly at a normal rate when you are at rest. Suppose someone asks you the following questions: Does your heart rate go up or down when you exercise? How much does your heart rate change when you exercise? How long does the effect last?

Think about what you would do to find answers to the questions above. What type of experiment would you design to answer the questions? Assume that you have the following equipment available to use: an instrument to measure your heart rate (such as a pulse meter), a stop watch, and some graph paper. Briefly describe how you might go about finding answers to these questions:

Describe Experiment _____

_____

_____

The NAEP tasks include criteria for scoring the responses. For instance, in the Heart Rate and Exercise task, performance is rated on a 0-to-6 scale. A 6 is awarded for a description that includes all the essential elements for a successful experiment: a baseline measurement (at-rest heart rate); timed exercise; heart rate measured immediately after exercise; and repeated measurements of heart rate over a set period of time until normal. A 1 is awarded for an irrelevant or meaningless description of an experiment or a very incomplete experiment that does not go beyond a mention of exercise. A 0 is for no response. One additional point is awarded for any indication of a need for repetition of trials in the experiment. Two additional points are awarded for statements indicating the value of repeating the experiment using different durations or intensities of exercise.

The Triathlon is scored in a similar fashion. A 4 is given for an accurate ranking of the children's performance on each event, for citing Zabi as the overall winner, and explaining the results. At the lower end, 1 is given for a selection of an overall winner with irrelevant or non-quantitative calculations or with no explanation; 0 for no response. More specific scoring criteria for each of these assessment tasks are described in NAEP (1987).

Alverno College's In-Basket Exercise

The in-basket exercise of the outcomes-based assessment program at Alverno College in Milwaukee poses a variety of problem-solving tasks that require on-the-spot analysis, synthesis, and evaluation (Loacker et al. 1984).

Typically the in-basket exercise requires students to adopt a professional role (manager, secretary, board member, etc.) and to describe how they would respond in a situation where a decision must be made under realistic time and information constraints. Information is provided in various forms: memos, dossiers, reports; but students must also rely on their prior knowledge about the roles of others involved in the situation.

The students are asked to tell or write about what they would do and also to create or supply whatever written responses (for instance, letters or memos) that might be called for. These products are then assessed according to specific criteria. The following examples illustrate a range of in-basket exercises:

1. The student is vice-chair of a school board subcommittee established to deal with complaints about censorship of curriculum materials. The chair of the committee is out of town on an emergency, and the vice-chair must respond to immediate demands, including requests from a coalition of book-banning community activists to establish a formal textbook reviewing committee, along with a telephone call

from a newspaper reporter and a letter from a state legislator inquiring into the controversy.

2. The student is a teacher with an afternoon devoted to professional activities. The teacher receives a set of communications from the principal instructing him (her) to write a diagnostic report based on test and behavioral information about a student, a lesson plan for a substitute teacher, a communication to a parent with a complaint, and a recommendation to the principal regarding a decision to make rules regulating use of a student commons area.

3. A student is given a brief history and the purposes and programs of an urban cultural center and, as a newly hired publications specialist, is confronted with several tasks: editing an article and reducing its length by one third; handling an irate citizen unhappy with the center's service; writing an editorial in response to a newspaper article which quotes the irate citizen and which identifies him as an important member of a Citizens for Tax Reform group campaigning for cuts in government spending; and preparing an outline for a talk to a college class in technical writing.

These exercises are designed to draw on information and experiences from particular courses the students have taken. Students are expected to integrate previous learning with new information provided in the exercise, to adapt their communications to the perspectives and interests of the relevant audiences, and to develop priorities and make decisions with limited information and time.

Performance on the in-basket exercises is evaluated typically by panels of judges. Community professionals with expertise in the roles to be simulated often participate in the assessment process. Where the in-basket exercise calls for oral presentations, audio and video recordings are used to enhance the reliability and precision of assessment. A taped record also permits students to review and learn from their performance.

The criteria used to assess performance include initiative, adaptability, assertiveness, persuasiveness, problem analysis, decisiveness, and efficiency. Students receive general feedback on their performance, along with statements indicating areas of strength and weakness related to specific criteria. This helps students and their teachers set new learning goals for future work.

Frontenac Secondary School's Assessment of Technical Studies

Students in the Technical Studies Program at Frontenac Secondary School in Kingston, Ontario, spend most of their class hours designing, constructing, and repairing things, and solving practical problems related to auto mechanics, woodworking, machine shop, drafting, and electrical studies. Until recently, however, these skills were assessed only through paper-and-pencil tests, a frustrating contradiction for both students and staff. A new procedure has dramatically improved the validity and usefulness of assessment in the technological studies program.

Half the final exam for each course in the Technological Studies Department is a conventional written test. It assesses knowledge of structural properties of materials, principles of design, mechanical and electrical processes, names of tools and equipment, and safety precautions. In addition to the written final exam, students must demonstrate their ability to use their technical knowledge with hands-on performance. For instance, the written test in electrical studies covers, among other topics, Ohm's law and theories of parallel circuitry. In the demonstrations, students are required to create an electrical device based on a wiring diagram. In a recent exam they had to construct an alarm unit to warn a person that their headlights remain on after the ignition has been turned off.

Assessment tasks are standardized within each shop, but the procedure varies from shop to shop depending upon the contingencies of the task, class size, and the instructional priorities of the shop teacher. For the electrical studies exam, each student is provided with a workspace, a wiring diagram, and a supply of tools and materials. A two-hour time limit is imposed, which approximates actual conditions of employment where one is under some pressure to work at a steady pace. How well the alarm unit functions is the main criterion for success, but students are also graded on neatness and precision of work (soldering, wiring, etc.), speed, and safety (putting on safety goggles, unplugging tools after use).

As another example, a used car is brought into the auto mechanics shop. Each student, acting as a consultant to a hypothetical buyer, must identify mechanical problems and make recommendations. A checklist is used by the instructor to assess the thoroughness and accuracy of the student's diagnosis and recommendations.

In the technological studies program this approach is used mainly to assign course-end grades, but it also has provided useful feedback to teachers and students on the process of teaching and learning these skills.

Assessment in Connecticut's Common Core of Learning

The Connecticut Department of Education's Common Core of Learning (CCL) specifies achievement goals in academic subjects. The department's Bureau of Evaluation and Student Assessment has developed an assessment program designed around two purposes:

- To provide a status report on the condition of science and mathematics.

- To encourage instructional and curricular change in science and mathematics.

Assessment tasks of the first type are administered within schools' math and science courses. They answer questions like: What do students who take [name of course] know and how well can they apply their understandings in extended performance situations? An example from mathematics follows, for which students are given two weeks to do a research project:

Food Market Price Comparison

Many grocery stores claim to have the lowest prices. But what does this really mean? Does it mean that every item in their store is priced lower, or just some of them? *How can you really tell which supermarket will save you the most money?* Your assignment is to design and carry out a study to answer this question.

The task requires both individual and small group work. First, students individually prepare a written research plan to describe which stores and products will be compared, how prices will be recorded and compared, and how data will be analyzed. Second, in two in-class meetings, students collaborate in small groups and develop a written final plan. (Groups should be of mixed ability and set up by the teacher.) The teacher gives feedback on each group's final plan. Third, each group member takes two trips to stores and participates in data analysis. Fourth, the group prepares a final report, and each member individually reports results orally to the class, describing his or her own contribution, analyses, conclusions, and recommendations regarding wise shopping. Each student hands in a written log of their activities and ideas during the project. Fifth, following the group reports, each individual student solves a near-transfer task which applies the same mathematical skills and procedures in a different context.

Five criteria, known in advance by students, are used for scoring both the group and the individual products. These criteria are shown in Figure 7.5. Performance on each criterion is rated "excellent," "good," or "needs improvement" in accordance with pre-specified standards for each criterion. Finally, each student completes a group performance rating form which is reviewed and initialed by the other group members. (Figure 7.5b shows the criteria students use for this task.)

Sample CCL Performance Task in Science: The "Survival" Investigation[5]

Assessment tasks of the second type answer questions like: What does the average graduating senior know about mathematics and science and how well can he or she apply this knowledge in particular performance situations

FIGURE 7.5a

Performance Criteria for Scoring Mathematics Task in Connecticut's
Common Core Assessment Program

1. Students can identify appropriate data to gather to solve a practical research
    problem.
2. Students can select and use an appropriate mathematical approach to solve a
    practical research problem.
3. Students can display the data with charts, graphs, or tables in a way which helps
    illuminate the answer to the research question for the reader.
4. Students can draw, from their data, conclusions which are mathematically cor-
    rect and relevant to the solution of the problem.
5. Students can write their conclusions in clear, correct narrative form.

FIGURE 7.5b

Group Performance Areas

The 8 group performance areas relate to how often students:

1. participated in the group's activities
2. stayed on the topic
3. offered useful ideas
4. were considerate of others
5. involved others
6. communicated clearly
7. found the group experience useful in solving problems
8. found the group experience enjoyable

(e.g., laboratory experiment, writing sample about a scientific issue)? Assessment tasks are administered to a random sample of students under standard conditions and scored using standard criteria. Students do multiple tasks
and are assessed by state-trained assessors.

   An example from science is the "survival" investigation.[5] It requires
setting up and drawing conclusions from an experiment. The student is given
paper and a pencil; containers, lids, and two fabrics of different materials and
sizes; a variety of construction materials (tape, string, etc.); thermometers, a
ruler, and a watch; and paper toweling. The student is then presented with
apparatus and the problem stated below:

Statement of the Problem:

   Imagine you are stranded on a mountainside in cold, dry, windy
   weather. You can choose a jacket made from one of the two fabrics in
   front of you. This is what you have to find out: Which fabric would keep
   you warmer?

An assessor gives prescribed instructions and rates the student's performance using a scoring sheet. The assessor may give the student suggestions for guidance—to use a container filled with warm water (instead of a person), to make "jackets" for the container from the materials, to give each fabric a "fair test," and to clearly record all the steps and conclusions "so that someone else can understand what you have found out."

Selections from the scoring guide for assessing students' performance on the "survival" task are shown in Figure 7.6.

Specific Curriculum Content

The high school curriculum focuses heavily upon knowledge of particular facts, concepts, generalizations, and theories in specific subjects. While the examples above have been organized under the more general competencies of language performance and problem solving skills, it is important to recognize that success on many of these tasks also requires understanding of specific subject matter frequently taught in high schools.

In the examples of the holistic and primary-trait scoring of writing samples and the speech (oracy) exercises, the criteria appear to be "content-free," but this is a misconception. Research has shown that to write or to speak clearly requires extensive conceptual knowledge about the meanings of words shared by one's audience.[6]

Assessments that present students with open-ended communication and problem-solving tasks can evaluate student understanding of topical knowledge in two ways. First, the task itself can be designed to focus on problems unique to particular subjects, as was illustrated in the oracy tasks focused on the garden spider and the human brain, the essay exam on acid rain, the NAEP exercises on empirical inquiry, the Alverno task on censorship (some knowledge of the *Constitution* would be required), and the Frontenac tasks for electrical studies. Similarly, general writing assessments could require writing about particular subjects in the curriculum.

Second, when appropriate, criteria intended to assess understanding of specific content can be added to the scoring process. Such criteria are included in the essay exam on acid rain and the NAEP exercises. All of the examples, however, could require as criteria for success that students incorporate into their responses a set of specific facts, concepts, theories from the subjects studied.

Specific curriculum content can also be assessed through short answer and multiple choice questions. As commonly used, these questions usually fail to assess authentic forms of achievement, but if creatively constructed, they can assess aspects of disciplined inquiry and integration of knowledge.

FIGURE 7.6

Selections from "Survival Experiment Scoring Guide" in
Connecticut's Common Core Assessment Program (sections have been omitted)

Student Familiarity with Activity
  1 = has done almost exact same exercise
  2 = has done similar exercise
  3 = has not done same or similar exercise

Approach Used (If student changed approach, encode the approach used that led to final conclusion.)
  1 = fabric wrapped around hand—qualitative
  2 = fabric around thermometer—qualitative
  3 = fabric around thermometer—set temperature drop: time interval measured

Control - Fabric (size and fastening)
  1 = controlled
  2 = not controlled

Temperature Measurements
  1 = all measurements within 2 degrees of test administrator's readings
  2 = all except one or two measurements within 2 degrees of test administrator's readings
  3 = more than 2 measurements different from test administrator's by more than 2 degrees

Recording of Data
  1 = data organized and recorded clearly enough to permit appropriate interpretation
  2 = data not organized and recorded clearly enough

Conclusion
  1 = conclusion consistent with data
  2 = conclusion not consistent with data
  3 = conclusion not possible because of design or execution

Overall Evaluation of Experiment
  1 = design and execution such that one could "trust" conclusion
  2 = design and execution have minor problems which could create some doubt about conclusion
  3 = design and execution such that one should have no faith in the conclusion at all

Discrete Competencies in Perspective

The movement for accountability has expanded competency testing at the school, district, and state levels. Practitioners and researchers alike recognize the double-edged character of competency testing.[7] There is a recognized need to maintain uniform standards and assure mastery of explicit skills and knowledge, but competency testing can trivialize skills and knowledge, it can produce arbitrary cut-offs between passing and failing and, if overly centralized, it can suppress creative curriculum and teaching.

Although familiar multiple choice and short-answer tests produce quantitative indicators, they cannot assess student production of discourse, things, or performances, and their format militates against the assessment of depth of understanding and integration of knowledge. In contrast, the examples in this section show a range of methods that permit quantitative assessment of discrete competencies under standard conditions that also meet these criteria for authenticity.

PART 2: EXHIBITIONS

Discrete competencies are usually assessed within the confines of schools. In contrast, exhibitions often involve production of discourse, things, and performances for the public. Exhibitions usually also require integration of a broad range of competencies and considerable student initiative and responsibility in carrying out a project. Such projects pose major challenges, consistent with the philosophy of ''Walkabout'' proposed by Gibbons (1974).

The Walkabout is a rite of passage to adulthood for Australian aborigines in which the adolescent must survive alone in the wilderness for several months. Gibbons proposed that this spirit of personal challenge and risk-taking be applied to schooling. Initially he suggested that curriculum and assessment be based on challenges in five main areas: adventure, creativity, service, practical skill, and logical inquiry. Several high schools have adapted these ideas, and Gibbons has developed them further.[8]

''Passages'' at Jefferson County Open High School (JCOHS)

JCOHS is a small public high school in Evergreen, Colorado, west of Denver. It is a typical small high school in terms of per-pupil expenditures, student-staff ratio, and instruction in some traditional academic subjects, but in most respects, the school departs markedly from traditional practice. Daily attendance is not required, except for a nine-week orientation that introduces new students to the responsibilities of self-directed learning and helps them select an advisor (a teacher). There are no required courses, and neither letter grades nor credits are used. In fact, probably the majority of student time is spent outside of classrooms.

The Program

The program is guided by the belief that didactic, classroom instruction is only one source of learning and growth; other sources are manual labor, public service, social interaction, individual reflection, and direct experience with diverse environments. Students learn science, history, algebra, and other traditional academic subjects from teachers, community professionals, and sometimes from other students who have expertise to share. They read, write, and do assignments in study rooms equipped with instructional resources. Students do committee work, participate in school governance, and plan schedules and trips. They work in the cafeteria (including preparing meals), in the administrative offices, on the school grounds, and at other sites.

And they travel. Two large vans owned by the school make 10 to 15 trips throughout North America each year. The trips range from several days to two weeks and have included river expeditions, wilderness backpacking, visits to ancient ruins in Mexico, and underwater exploration in the ocean.

Students at JCOHS are involved in shaping and evaluating their own learning. At the beginning of each year each student, working closely with an advisor, develops an Individual Learning Plan. It states goals, how they will be achieved, and what courses or activities will be pursued. A parent conference follows to insure that clear expectations are shared by the student, the staff, and parents. In biweekly meetings with the advisor, the student discusses and shows evidence of progress; plans can be modified if needed. Formal recognition for completing the Individual Learning Plan is given after the advisor receives written evaluations from the student about each completed activity with a corresponding response by the teacher or other person in charge of the activity.

After completing this phase, which can take from a semester to several years, the student begins the "passages" which, as described below, are the culminating challenges to demonstrate the diverse competencies required for graduation. The final requirement for graduation is a well-organized 20- to 30-page written "transcript" which summarizes and interprets the learning that has been documented through evaluations and passages.

Flexibility in the organization of courses, instruction, and related activities is critical to the program. This is facilitated by the school's small size, about 250 students. Each certified staff member is responsible for 12 to 20 students and spends from one-third to one-half time advising, which fosters the development of close personal knowledge of the abilities, interests, and progress of the advisor's students. Weekly school-wide governance meetings to which all are invited provide an open forum to discuss issues and make decisions. Courses, community experiences, and other learning activities are initially structured in several-week to several-month blocks. But course offer ings and school-sponsored activities can be changed through the gover-nance meetings, and Individual Learning Plans can be changed in consulta-tion with the advisors.

Passages at JCOHS

The "passages" are designed to demonstrate competence in six broad areas: practical skills, creativity, adventure, career exploration, logical in-quiry, and global awareness/volunteer service.

From the time of entry, students learn about the passages through ad-visory groups, participation on passsage committees, and observing others fulfilling their passage requirements. However, students cannot begin their own personal passages until they demonstrate the requisite level of indepen-dence and academic competence to their advisors. A written proposal is pre-pared according to several guidelines:

1. State your proposal as a challenge. Be specific. State the kind of performance and the level of performance you will pursue.
2. Outline the preparation you will need: training, practice, information-gathering, and so on.
3. List the resources you will require—equipment, people, workspace, transportation, materials, money, etc.
4. What is the greatest obstacle you expect to encounter?
5. What positive sources can you draw on to overcome this obstacle?
6. What is your first step in launching the passage?
7. List the other steps that lead to the completion of your passage.
8. What form will your presentation or demonstration take upon com-pletion of the passage?
9. What is your proposed date of completion?

The student discusses the written proposal with the advisor, changes it if necessary, and then presents it to a staff member chosen on the basis of expertise as a passage consultant who may require further modification. The proposal then goes to the student's passages committee, made up of the ad-visor, (a) parent(s), the principal, a student experienced with passages, an-other student, and the passage consultant. When the committee approves, the student begins the passage.

Passages can last from two months to two years. Some examples illus-trate the many different activities on which passages have been built:

- Running the lunch room
- Construction and maintenance work around school

- Helping an elementary physical education teacher, for several months, to supervise the playground and take care of younger children
- Library research on the AIDS disease and work on the Denver AIDS hotline
- Working with a Denver energy cooperative weatherizing homes and helping the poor surmount home energy problems
- Teaching a class at JCOHS
- Working as an apprentice to a chemist involved in research on the effects of carbon dioxide on the atmospheric ozone layer
- Volunteering at the local chapter of the Audubon society and participating in research on wetlands ecology

When the passage is complete, the student writes an extended evaluation of the experience and makes a presentation to his or her passage committee. The purpose of the presentation is to document the effort expended, the resulting achievements, and how the student has benefited intellectually and emotionally. Slides or pictures can be displayed, along with products, testimonial letters, or other evidence. The committee reviews the written evaluation and presentation with the student, and if the documentation is considered acceptable, they celebrate the completion of the passage. Successful completion of all six passages must be demonstrated for graduation.

A final requirement—students have come to call it "the seventh passage"—is a written summative evaluation of their high school experience. This is a reflective discussion on what they have done and learned, and the document is used in place of the traditional type of high school transcript.

Walden III's Rite of Passage Experience (ROPE)

This program uses exhibitions in a major senior year project to guide students through a process of "pulling it all together" and to evaluate their achievement on graduation requirements.

Walden III High School, Racine, Wisconsin, has a graduation requirement called the "Rite of Passage Experience," or ROPE. All seniors must demonstrate mastery in fifteen areas of knowledge and competence by completing a *Portfolio, Project,* and fifteen *Presentations* before a ROPE committee consisting of staff (including the student's homeroom teacher), a student, and an outside adult. Nine of the presentations are based directly on the materials contained in the Portfolio and the Project, the remaining six presentations are developed specially for the presentation process itself.

Procedure

The Portfolio. The Portfolio, developed during the first semester of the senior year, is intended to be "a reflection and analysis of the graduating senior's own life and times."[9] Its requirements are:

1. A written autobiography, descriptive, introspective, and analytical. School records and other indicators of participation may be included.
2. A reflection on work, including an analysis of the significance of the work experiences for the graduating senior's life. A resume can be included.
3. Two letters of recommendation, at minimum, must be included from any sources chosen by the student.
4. A reading record, including a bibliography, annotated if desired, and two mini-book reports. Scores on reading tests may be included.
5. An essay on ethics exhibiting contemplation of the subject and describing the student's own ethical code.
6. (a) An artistic product or a written report on art, and (b) an essay on artistic standards for judging quality in a chosen area of art.
7. A written report analyzing mass media: who or what controls mass media, toward what ends, and with what effects. Evidence of experience with mass media may be included.
8. (a) A written summary and evaluation of the student's coursework in science/technology; (b) a written description of a scientific experiment illustrating the application of the scientific method; (c) an analytical essay (with examples) on social consequences of science and technology; and, (d) an essay on the nature and use of computers in modern society.

The Project. Every graduating senior must write a paper based on library research which analyzes an event, set of events, or theme in American history. A national comparative approach can be used in the analysis. The student must be prepared to field questions on both the paper and an overview of American history during the presentations which are given in the second semester of the senior year.

The Presentations. Each of the above eight components of the Portfolio, plus the Project, must be presented orally and in writing to the ROPE committee.

Six additional oral presentations are also required. However, for these, there are no written reports or new products required by the committee. Supporting documents or other forms of evidence may be used. Assessment of proficiency is based on the demonstration of knowledge and skills during the presentations in each of the following areas:

1. Mathematics knowledge and skills should be demonstrated by a combination of course evaluations, tests results, and worksheets presented before the committee; and by the ability to competently field mathematics questions asked of the graduating senior during the demonstration.

2. Knowledge of American government should be demonstrated by discussion of the purpose of government; the individual's relationship to the state; the ideals, functions, and problems of American political institutions; and selected contemporary issues and political events. Supporting materials can be used.

3. The Personal proficiency demonstration requires the student to think about and organize a presentation on the requirements of adult living in our society in terms of personal fulfillment, social skills, and practical competencies; and the student should discuss his/her own strengths and weaknesses in everyday living skills (health, home economics, mechanics, etc.) and interpersonal relations.

4. Knowledge of geography should be demonstrated in a presentation that covers the basic principles and questions of the discipline; identification of basic landforms, places, and names; and the scientific and social significance of geographical information.

5. Evidence of the graduating senior's successful completion of a Physical Challenge must be presented to the ROPE committee.

6. A demonstration of competency in English (written and spoken) is provided in virtually all the Portfolio and Project requirements. These, and any additional evidence the graduating senior may wish to present to the ROPE committee, fulfill the requirements of the presentation in the English competency area.

Timeline

At the beginning of the senior year, all seniors enroll in a semester-length ROPE class. In consultation with the ROPE supervisor, they select the teachers, outside adult, and student to be their ROPE committee. In the ROPE class, students receive instruction from visiting regular subject-matter teachers, supervision, and guidance in the development of their Portfolio and Project, and they complete a portion of the work for these tasks. The ROPE instructor monitors, advises, reprimmands, and keeps students on schedule. Both the Portfolio and the Project must be completed and handed in to the instructor by the end of first semester.

During the second semester, all seniors make oral presentations to their committees on the tasks of their Portfolio, their Project in American history, and on the other areas in which demonstrations of proficiency are required. Presentations usually last an hour to an hour and a half. The number of presentations students give varies, but most complete the requirements with five to nine separate appearances before their committee (more than one requirement may be completed in a single appearance).

Evaluation

The instructor of the ROPE monitors and insures overall presentability of the Portfolio and Project, but does not grade the students. The ROPE committees evaluate the portfolios and projects on a pass-fail basis, and each of the oral presentations on a grading scale of *A* through *F*. Each committee determines its own standards for grading, but generally both quality and students' seriously applying themselves are important. In addition, the work must be well-organized, grammatically correct, neat, and reflect the English proficiency level of a high school graduate as judged by the student's committee. To earn a diploma, a student must receive a passing grade in at least twelve of the required areas of the ROPE, which also meet district requirements for proficiency in math, government, reading and English.

Community-Based Learning and Learning Contracts at "Learning Unlimited"

This program uses learning contracts to guide and hold students accountable for community-based learning. The contracts provide criteria applied both to exhibitions and to more conventional paper and pencil tests.

At North Central High School in Indianapolis, Indiana, Learning Unlimited is a school-within-a-school that enrolls about 400 students. It has a director who works with student directors and a community education coordinator/secretary. Learning Unlimited offers 22 semester-length academic courses. Students take traditional academic courses, but spend much time learning on their own and participating in the community. Through contractual agreements between student, teacher, and community resource persons, Learning Unlimited strikes a balance between a uniform academic curriculum and an individualized student-directed learning program.

The Curriculum: Courses and Community Work

Each Learning Unlimited course is organized around a set of general curriculum goals and more specific objectives developed by the teachers in the high school. For example, General Goal number 11 for History states that the student must be able to: "(1) cite two reasons for the development of the cold war; (2) define collective security and identify three areas in the world where America is committed to this concept; (3) compare and contrast our involvement in Korea and Viet Nam. . . .

Each student is given a list of the course objectives for the semester and has the option of attending class regularly and following recommended readings and assignments or creating an individualized set of tasks and objectives aimed at the overall course goals and objectives. In either case, a formally signed contract is agreed upon between student and teacher. At the end of every course a required final exam covers the course objectives.

In addition to regular course requirements, all Learning Unlimited students must complete a minimum of 24 hours of community-based learning experiences each semester in both their junior and senior year. Most students also participate in a freshman/sophomore field trip; and all upper-level students are encouraged, but not required, to participate in "intensives"— several-day to several-week trips to other cities or regions.

The Learning Contract

Each student's learning is guided by and assessed according to the individual Learning Contract. A contract covers six weeks. It includes goals, competencies, conference dates with the teacher, activities, a timetable, criteria for evaluation, and signatures of student, teacher, and parent. Each contract is developed through consultation (and negotiation) with the course instructor.

To help students specify academic objectives for their contracts and to provide a common curriculum, Learning Unlimited teachers formulated twelve general academic goals and a more extensive list of specific academic competencies. In developing a contract, a student is free to draw on these competencies. A list of readings and supplementary materials connected to the academic competencies is also available for students to use in the Learning Contracts.

The community-based learning experiences are also incorporated in the contracts. Over one hundred community resource sites participate regularly in the program, and agreements between the student and the community resource person are established in separate contracts. One student volunteered four to five hours a week working with the professional organizers of the Pan American Games in Indianapolis. Other students have worked at the zoo, at businesses, at fire and police stations, and as aides at day care centers, hospitals, and nursing homes.

Students must indicate on their Learning Contract what they will do and what they expect to achieve. Most often the community experiences result in some form of written product; for instance, a journalistic account of a community issue; a sociological or political analysis based on data from participation in a community agency or service; or a personal reflection on an experience presented in a diary-like format. Other forms of documentation are encouraged: slides, physical products, anything that demonstrates thoughtfulness and achievement resulting from the community experience.

A single community project can serve as a resource for more than one Learning Contract. For instance, from the Pan American Games project, the student developed a slide show presentation for his photography class, a paper on the international issues involved in the Pan American Games for his government class, and a journal of his daily experiences and observations for his English class.

Evaluation

Each six weeks, grades are determined in a conference on the contract between the student and the teacher. Final course grades are determined by final exams and student performance in relation to their Learning Contracts.

Students are also evaluated by the community resource person who signs the student's time card and fills out a standard evaluation form. Criteria are dependability, attitude, effort, and extent of fulfillment of community project contract. The form also asks the resource person to assign a letter grade on overall performance and to assess the quality of the overall experience for the student.

This same general contractual process occurs for the shorter field trips and the longer, more in-depth "intensives." That is, students must reflect on their experiences and communicate their thoughts to the class or to some other audiences in accordance with the timeline and quality specifications of the learning contract.

Exhibitions in Perspective

The programs where exhibitions occupy a central role emphasize the student as an independent worker and the teacher as a resource or coach. Teachers and principals in these schools note that students often have difficulty adjusting to the independence. Their struggle can be eased through special preparation courses and regular teacher-student conferences. Teachers may also need special help in becoming less the dispenser of knowledge, more of a coach, advisor, and counselor with a better knowledge of the student's capabilities and interests.

Exhibitions need not be confined to small high schools nor to schools dedicated to nontraditional forms of teaching, learning, and assessment. Within conventional high school courses, teachers can (and do) assign major projects, either as special unit activities or as end-of-course demonstrations, that could qualify as exhibitions (e.g., production of video tapes, public debates, publication of oral histories). Exhibitions within courses can bring special life to instruction.

Since exhibitions do not rely exclusively on traditional tests, and they offer significant recognition for mastery in arts, crafts, academic and innovative endeavors, they have unique potential for engaging otherwise alienated students.

Public exhibitions of mastery can clarify standards of achievement and celebrate the ideal of competence for a broad range of students. More than any other form of assessment, exhibitions of mastery are most likely to fulfill all the criteria for authentic achievement: disciplined inquiry, integration of knowledge, and value beyond evaluation.

This form of assessment requires extra staff work and some changes in the scheduling and structure of courses. It is time-consuming to carefully manage and judge exhibitions. However, on the basis of reports from faculty and students, the high level of student engagement in learning and the clarity of educational purposes fostered by these approaches makes them well worth considering by all high schools.

PART 3: PORTFOLIOS AND PROFILES

Portfolios and profiles furnish a broad, often longitudinal, portrait of individual performance in several dimensions. Each can offer authentic and multiple indicators of achievement. Portfolios are intended to give comprehensive, cumulative portraits, but not necessarily on standardized indicators. Profiles emphasize teachers' ratings on scales of diverse competencies or student characteristics such as perseverance.

Portfolios

A portfolio is a file or folder containing a variety of information that documents a student's experiences and accomplishments. The portfolio can contain summary descriptions of accomplishments, official records, and diary items.

Summarized descriptions of accomplishments can include samples of writing; audio, video and photographic recording of performances and projects; and testimonies from authorities on the quality of student work. Experiential learning that is the grist for exhibitions (described in Part 2) can be summarized. Students in English Schools have described such examples as designing a mechanical device to help a handicapped friend, organizing a talent show, taking the responsibility of arranging meetings with visitors to the school and showing them around, forming a group to grow a garden and selling the produce to earn income, and participating in charity fund-raisers.

A variety of formal records are also usually included: a curriculum transcript, scores on standardized tests or other examinations taken during high school, evidence of membership and participation in school clubs or academic events, a list of awards or any other distinctions, letters of recommendation.

To encourage students to reflect on their learning, they may be required to keep a diary. The portfolio will be enhanced by including excerpts from the diary that illustrate the student's views of his or her intellectual and emotional development.

A portfolio gains legitimacy if its contents are validated by appropriate authorities, such as teachers, guidance counselors, or community representatives. The Learning Contracts of Learning Unlimited required signatures of an adult representative responsible for overseeing the community learning experience, the child's parent or guardian, and the teacher supervising the experience. The Walden III Portfolio, part of the ROPE program to certify graduation, is validated by experts in the disciplines represented in the Portfolio, persons with more general knowledge of the candidate's character and abilities, and a person who officially represents the school.[10]

Portfolios in Vermont's Assessment System

Vermont will assess student achievement of fourth and eleventh graders in writing and mathematics using three methods: a uniform test, a portfolio, and a "best piece." This approach combines newer assessment methods with more traditional means, providing a balanced view of the capabilities of Vermont's students. Vermont will train its teachers in using portfolios and other authentic measures to assess student achievement.

Uniform Test. All fourth and eleventh grade students will take a test that uses equivalent tasks administered under the same conditions and scored uniformly. The mathematics test will include open-ended questions and longer problems. By using test items taken from the National Assessment of Education Progress mathematics test, Vermont will be able to compare the scores of Vermont students with those in the rest of the country.

Portfolio and "Best Piece". Each fourth and eleventh grade student will keep portfolios of his or her work in writing and mathematics. The portfolio will contain the work that the student has done in class over the course of the year. Significant work, papers, poems, extended problems, examples of mathematical reasoning, and work that has challenged or excited the student will be included. In writing, areas to be covered include informative and persuasive writing. In mathematics, reasoning, problem-solving, and communication will be included.

Several times during the year the student will discuss the work in the portfolio with his or her teacher. As the end of the school year draws near, each mathematics student, in consultation with the teacher, will select the "best pieces" from the portfolio, examples of work that the student believes most accurately reflects his or her strengths. In writing, students will select just one "best piece."

Because the portfolio is the result of regular classroom work, the teacher will have assessed each piece already. The teacher will then give the portfolio an overall rating and discuss the rationale with the student.

At the end of the year, teams of Vermont writing and mathemtics teachers trained in evaluating portfolios and "best pieces" will visit every school, selecting a sample of portfolios and evaluating them and the "best pieces" within. Using published criteria, two writing teachers will assess writing portfolios, and two mathematics teachers will assess the mathematics portfolios. The evaluation team will also validate the assessment of the portfolio made by the classroom teacher.

The evaluation teams will write a report that summarizes the results of their review. The report will describe the range of student achievement in the school as reflected in the "best pieces," the curriculum as revealed by the work in the portfolios, and the way students are assessed by their teachers.

Reporting. In the fall, using the results of the uniform tests as well as the portfolio and "best piece" assessment, the school will report the outcomes to the community on School Report Day. In the winter, the commissioner will publish the results.

Portfolios in Arts PROPEL

Pioneering work on portfolios in the teaching and assessment of art is taking place in the Arts PROPEL project, a collaborative effort between Educational Testing Service, Harvard Project Zero, and the Pittsburgh Public Schools that is funded by the Rockefeller Foundation.[11]

In Arts PROPEL, the portfolio is less an instrument of grading and standard-setting than it is an instrument used directly to enhance the quality of learning in visual arts, music, and imaginative writing classrooms. Portfolios are used not just as repositories of finished work. Students also include journals, sketchbooks, or notebooks to work out ideas, draft, intermediate, and final projects, false-starts, and materials the student finds relevant from other sources. The portfolio contains as much information as possible relevant to a student's development in a domain.

General principles rather than a single method guide the use of portfolios in Arts PROPEL. First, when a student enters a class, it is important to obtain a sense of what that individual brings to the situation. The portfolio process begins with a background interview. Teachers frequently learn about student's intense engagement with and understanding of a domain (e.g., music), even though these have not developed in the context of a formal school setting. Teachers then can capitalize on student interest and prior knowledge in helping students develop their portfolio.

A second use of portfolios is to explore the development of a single project in depth. Students keep all work that was produced during the process of completing a project. This includes sketches, drafts, written reflections, and materials from outside sources. Together, teacher and student uncover the types of choices that were made, crucial points in the project's development, and sources of satisfaction or dissatisfaction. Inquiries are made regarding sources of ideas, handling of skills, and directions to pursue.

A third use of portfolios is to explore student development across a range of projects. Discussions around this aspect of portfolios focuses on patterns of student interest and development. This part of the process enables students to transcend the role of "assignment-completer" to one which approximates the role of writer, musician, or artist. This evolution means that students begin to develop a personal voice in their work as well as a sense of artistic identity that serves as a strong motivational source for continued engagement in a domain.

To be most profitable, portfolios must be used in a pedagogy with a project orientation and by teachers and students comfortable with reflecting on their work. Students need to be engaged in long-term projects that bring together skills and understandings that represent the deepest and most central objectives of a curriculum. Portfolios are not of great utility in an educational environment based on decontextualized skill training and evaluation. Second, written reflection, discussion, and critique are integral to assessment with portfolios. This communicates the message that learning is not a passive, receptive process, and that the most successful education occurs when students take responsibility for their own learning. These values are pivotal to the development of a "portfolio culture."

Currently, the Arts PROPEL project is concentrating on two key issues in the portfolio process: the development of a portfolio culture and the building of portfolio collections. Work is also proceeding on the role of portfolios in institutional concerns, such as accountability and standard-setting. The remaining years of the project will try to accommodate these institutional functions while preserving the qualities that make portfolios such an important instructional vehicle.[12]

Profiles

Unlike portfolios, profiles are not created by individual students and do not contain actual samples of work. Rather, profiles are forms that teachers, students, and sometimes parents fill out with ratings and summary judgments or descriptions of achievement.

In England and Scotland profile systems have been developed with several goals in mind: to convey a rich variety of information about the interests, character, accomplishments, and academic proficiency of individual students; to allow comparative judgements across time and peers; and to involve only minimal burdens of record keeping.[13]

Records of Achievement in the Wootton Bassett School

Teachers at the Wootton Bassett School, Swindon, England, needed to develop an assessment system that was both individualized and standardized, and that would provide a more comprehensive picture of student achievement than grades or test scores.

At the end of every unit (before the unit exam is graded), each student's performance is recorded on an assessment card that provides the following information:

Topic	Effort	_____
Name	Presentation	_____
Class	Communication	_____
Date	Research	_____
	Test	_____

Comments: (continuity of work through unit; attitude toward homework; etc.)

Student performance on each of the four major criteria (effort, presentation, communication, research) is scored on a 1 through 4 scale:

Effort: (to be related directly to child, not to quality of work)
1. A constant maximum "try-er" in the unit.
2. Consistently tries hard, needing only occasional encouragement.
3. Inconsistent approach; constant prodding at certain times.
4. An unsettled and lazy approach requiring *constant* prodding.

Presentation:
1. Neat writing; lots of good diagrams.
2. Reasonable writing; adequate number of reasonable diagrams.
3. Poor writing; shoddy but recognizable diagrams.

4. Writing illegible or nearly so; few diagrams of very poor appearance.

Communication:
1. Written work consistently explains the achievements sensibly and in good English.
2. Written work often explains the achievements sensibly and in good English.
3. Written work sometimes explains the achievements sensibly and in good English.
4. Written work is disjointed, making little sense.

Research:
1. Regularly shows originality of thought or action beyond that taught or set.
2. Now and again shows qualities as in 1.
3. Rarely shows qualities as in 1.
4. For their ability they are doing as required, yet have shown no originality or initiative in the topic. (This person could still be top of the class in other respects).

Test: the test score is shown as a mark against the maximum for that text, e.g., 27/50.

Cards for each student go into individual student files, thus providing a detailed and comprehensive record of achievement in individual subjects.

The Scottish Research Council's Pupil Profile System

A national commission of educators and private citizens in Scotland was charged with overseeing the development of an approach to assessment which "would be equally applicable to all pupils; which would gather teachers' knowledge of pupils' many different skills, characteristics, and achievements across the whole range of the curriculum, both formal and informal; which would, with a minimum of clerical demands, provide a basis for continuing in-school guidance, culminating in a relevant and useful school-leaving report for all pupils." The reference for this is Patricia Broadfoot "The Scottish Pupil Profile System,"pages 56–71 in Burgess and Adams. The following approach was developed by the Scottish Council for Research in Education working with teachers in a variety of comprehensive high schools over a three-year period.

The assessment system has three parts:

Class Assessment Sheet. Each teacher in the school fills in a Class Assessment Sheet (Figure 7.7a) for each class at the end of the course (or more frequently if appropriate). The teacher rates (1 to 4) each student on multiple criteria divided into two categories—Skills and Performance—on the Class Assessment Sheet. On the Skills criteria, the teacher selects only those relevant to the course, and grades each student (1 to 4) on each Skills criterion. The standards for each value on the 1-to-4 scale are pre-specified.

In the Performance category, the Class Assessment Sheet provides six blank spaces allowing teachers or departments to develop and use their own criteria and better tailor the Sheet to their subject-matter and course learning goals. Teachers/departments are to devise their own 1-to-4 standards for these criteria. A student's ratings on these criteria are to be averaged to produce a summative rating on a criterion called "composite." Two other criteria provided in the Performance category are "perseverance" and "enterprise." In the example shown, the teacher uses knowledge, reasoning, presentation, imagination, and critical awareness as the criteria for the Performance category.

Pupil Profile Cards. Attached to the Class Assessment Sheet are detachable carbon copies—one card for each student, called Pupil Profile Cards (Figure 7.7b). Each Pupil Profile Card contains all the Skills and Performance criteria from the Class Assessment Sheet. Each student's Profile Card reproduces his or her (1-to-4) ratings and has a space for individual comments from the teacher. While the Class Assessment Sheet is a record for the teacher of the achievement of a class, the Pupil Profile cards, grading each student for each class, accumulate to create a comprehensive and individualized record of achievement.

School Leaving Report. Each student's record of achievement is summarized on a four-page School Leaving Report (one sheet folded to create four pages). The cover page provides biographical information. Page two, SKILLS, reproduces the eight individual criteria of the Skills category used on the Class Assessment Sheet. A summative rating over all courses is given for each of the criteria, along with a description of the 1-to-4 ratings standards). Page three, SUBJECT/ACTIVITY ASSESSMENT, gives detailed course information and reproduces the "composite" rating and the ratings on the "perseverance" and "enterprise" criteria included in the Performance category of the Class Assessment Sheet. The back page provides space for recognition of individual achievements and comments on other personal strengths. It is the responsibility of some adult(s) who know(s) the student well (homeroom teacher, guidance counselor) to develop the leaving report from the information contained in the student's Profile.

These three parts of the pupil profile system can contribute to several assessment goals. Teachers keep the Class Assessment Sheet as a record of achievement for their classes. The individual Pupil Profile Cards create a

FIGURE 7.7a

Class Assessment Sheet

CLASS ASSESSMENT SHEET		O. Quinn 3L	T. Johnson 3L	F. Fielding 3L	S. Retish 3L	F. Shack 3L	H. Hollis 3L	D. Kennedy 3L	B. McGregor 3L	R. Jones 3L	L. Frews 3L	M. Jackson 3L	F. Shaw 3L	S. Smith 3L	D. Gordon 3L	D. Brown 3L	P. Anderson 3L
SKILLS	Listening	2	3	2	4	2	1	3	3	2	2	4	2	3	1	3	3
	Speaking	2	4	2	3	3	2	3	2	2	2	4	2	1	3	3	1
	Reading	1	2	2	3	2	2	2	2	3	2	3	2	3	2	3	4
	Writing	2	3	1	4	3	1	3	2	4	2	4	2	4	3	4	4
	Visual understanding & expression	4	3	1	3	4	3	2			1	3	3	3		2	3
	Use of Number																
	Physical Coordination																
	Manual Dexterity				4		2	1				4			3		
PERFORM	Knowledge	1	4	3	4	3	1	4	2	3	4	3	3	4	1	3	4
	Reasoning	2	3	2	3	2	1	3	1	1	2	2	3	3	2	4	4
	Presentation	3	3	1	5	4	2	1	1	4	1	2	2	3	4	2	3
	Imagination	2	4	1	1	3	2	2	1	1	3	4	2	1	3	3	3
	Critical Awareness	2	3	2	2	4	1	3	2	1	2	4	2	2	2	4	4
	Composite Grades	2	3	2	3	3	1	4	1	2	1	4	2	3	2	3	4
PE	Perseverance	1	3	2	4	4	1	2	2	4	4	1	3	4	1	3	3
	Enterprise	3	4	1	1	3	1	2	2	1	3	2	2	4	3	3	2
	Subject/Activity	Hist.	Hist.	Hist.	Hist.	Hist.	Hist.	Hist.	Hist.	Hist.	Hist.	Hist.	Hist.	Hist.	Hist.	Hist.	Hist.
	Teacher	McG	McG	McG	McG	McG	McG	McG	McG	McG	McG	McG	McG	McG	McG	McG	McG
	Date	3/89	3/89	3/89	3/89	3/89	3/89	3/89	3/89	3/89	3/89	3/89	3/89	3/89	3/89	3/89	3/89

FIGURE 7.7b

Pupil Profile Cards

PUPIL PROFILE		Q. Quarry
Comments:		
Class Section		3 L
S K I L L S	Listening	2
	Speaking	2
	Reading	1
	Writing	2
	Visual understanding & expression	4
	Use of Number	
	Physical Coordination	
	Manual Dexterity	
P E R F O R M A N C E	Knowledge	1
	Reasoning	2
	Presentation	3
	Imagination	2
	Critical Awareness	2
	Composite Grades	2
	Perseverance	1
	Enterprise	3
Subject/Activity		Hist.
Teacher		Mcb.
Date		3/89

PUPIL PROFILE		T. Johnson
Comments:		
Class Section		3 L
S K I L L S	Listening	3
	Speaking	4
	Reading	2
	Writing	3
	Visual understanding & expression	3
	Use of Number	
	Physical Coordination	
	Manual Dexterity	
P E R F O R M A N C E	Knowledge	4
	Reasoning	3
	Presentation	3
	Imagination	4
	Critical Awareness	3
	Composite Grades	3
	Perseverance	3
	Enterprise	4
Subject/Activity		Hist.
Teacher		Mcb.
Date		5/89

detailed individualized longitudinal record of pupil achievement and progress. These cards can be used for conventional grading purposes as well as for diagnostic and guidance purposes. The School Leaving Report provides an informative summary of the pupil's high school achievement. Relatively detailed information that is both comparative and idiosyncratic is provided on course background, skills, achievements, and character.

FIGURE 7.8

School Leaving Report

SKILLS	
LISTENING	**SPEAKING**
Acts independently and intelligently on complex verbal instructions ☐	Can debate a point of view ☐
Can interpret and act on most complex instructions ☒	Can make a clear and accurate oral report ☐
Can interpret and act on straightforward instructions ☐	Can describe events orally ☐
Can carry out simple instructions with supervision ☐	Can communicate adequately at conversation level ☒
READING	**WRITING**
Understands all appropriate written material ☐	Can argue a point of view in writing ☐
Understands the content and implications of most writing if simply expressed ☒	Can write a clear and accurate report ☐
Understands uncomplicated ideas expressed in simple language ☐	Can write a simple account or letter ☒
Can read most everyday information such as notices or simple instructions ☐	Can write simple messages and instructions ☐
VISUAL UNDERSTANDING AND EXPRESSION	**USE OF NUMBER**
Can communicate complex visual concepts readily and appropriately ☐	Quick and accurate in complicated or unfamiliar calculations ☐
Can give a clear explanation by sketches and diagrams ☐	Can do familiar or straightforward calculations, more slowly if complex ☒
Can interpret a variety of visual displays such as graphs or train timetables ☒	Can handle routine calculations with practice ☐
Can interpret single visual displays such as roadsigns or outline maps ☐	Can do simple whole number calculations such as giving change ☐
PHYSICAL COORDINATION	**MANUAL DEXTERITY**
A natural flair for complex tasks ☐	Has fine control of complex tools and equipment ☐
Mastery of a wide variety of movements ☐	Satisfactory use of most tools and equipment ☒
Can perform satisfactorily most everyday movements ☒	Can achieve simple tasks such as wiring a plug ☐
Can perform single physical skills such as lifting or climbing ☐	Can use simple tools, instruments and machines such as a screwdriver or typewriter ☐

continued

The major advantage of portfolios and profiles is their recognition of multiple indicators of individual achievement. To be sure, they involve keeping more complex and comprehensive records than grades and test scores. There is also some risk that well-intentioned efforts to develop multiple indicators will lead to a proliferation of arbitrary and unnecessary criteria for achievement. If we are interested in more comprehensive indicators of student achievement, however, portfolios and profiles offer promising opportunities.

FIGURE 7.8

Continued

SUBJECT/ACTIVITY ASSESSMENT					
Curriculum Area	Subjects Studied (includes final year level where relevant)	Years of Study	Achievement	Enterprise (includes flair, creativity)	Perseverance (includes reliability, carefulness)
Aesthetic Subjects	Drawing	1-4	2	2	1
	Music	1-4	2	3	3
Business Studies					
Community/ Leisure Activities	Social Education	1-4	3	2	3
Crafts	Pottery	3-4	2	1	3
English	English	1-4	2	1	3
Mathematics	Arithmetic	1-4	1	1	2
Other Languages	German	2-4	2	2	3
Outdoor Studies	Outdoor Pursuits	3-4	2	2	3
Physical Education	General	1-4	3	1	3
Science	Biology	3-4	1	2	2
Social Subjects	History	1-4	2	1	3

SUMMARY

What kind of information might be gathered about the individual student to convey both to the student and to others a valid indication of the student's mastery of authentic academic challenges? The diverse approaches described in this chapter fall into three main categories, and each can make an important contribution to a school's assessment program.

Testing discrete competencies informs students about how well they meet specific standards for the performance of important skills in language use, problem-solving, and mastery of subject-based facts and concepts. It is crucial in testing discrete competencies to develop tasks that meet criteria of authenticity, but that also elicit performances that can be reliably measured with numerical rating systems.

The main strength of the exhibition is the opportunity it affords to demonstrate knowledge and skill in ways that are meaningful and interesting to others. Such demonstrations reveal authentic academic achievement, not only because they have public value beyond testing, but because they allow students to integrate knowledge in unique and useful ways. Exhibitions are perhaps the most authentic form of academic assessment, but at the same time the most challenging to assess.

Finally, portfolios and profiles present ways to summarize the variety of students' accomplishments comprehensively and parsimoniously, thus giving both students and the public a more complete record of students' achievement. These approaches are particularly useful for systematic assessment of academic growth and for summarizing competence and accomplishments for external audiences.

This chapter has documented a variety of authentic alternatives to standardized multiple choice testing. Wider use of these approaches could yield important benefits: teachers liberated from the strictures of atomistic objectives and minimum skills imposed by standardized multiple choice questions; students engaged in more meaningful and useful academic pursuits; and the public presented with clearer and more understandable measures of educational outcomes. Will there be wider use of these more authentic assessment alternatives?

Much depends upon whether decision-makers are persuaded by the message of this book and the arguments of testing reformers nationwide, such as those of "Coalition calls for Genuine Accountability" (1989–90) and The National Commission on Testing and Public Policy (1990). A critical mass of parents, teachers, and principals must come to believe that standardized tests are inadequate and that all new forms of assessment must be developed. Much work remains, both in designing alternatives and in illuminating their value for decision-makers and the public at large.

8

Toward the Development of a New Science of Educational Testing and Assessment

Harold Berlak

Introduction: Educational Tests as Scientific Instruments

Standardized and/or criterion-referenced tests are used by administrators, school governing bodies, lawmakers, courts, colleges, and professional schools for making comparative judgments about students, educational programs, and the quality of school programs, schools, and school districts. The credibility of these tests depends upon the claim that they are *scientific instruments*. The question I address here is whether this claim is tenable. I begin with a brief sketch of the origins of testing as a positive science, and then examine the basis of this claim.

The idea that educational testing could become a science was born in the United States prior to World War I, a time in history when the nineteenth-century social and economic order was in upheaval. The rapid industrialization following the Civil War created an unprecedented demand for labor, which was supplied by the immigration of almost forty million people from Europe and Asia in the last quarter of the nineteenth and the early years of the twentieth centuries. The newcomers, mostly poor and illiterate, looked different, practiced strange customs, spoke unfamiliar languages, and within a few years they had literally transformed the face of American society and culture. These changes were certainly not always welcomed; they bred xenophobia, hostility, widespread social unrest, political dissent, and on occasion violence. (Handlin, 1951; Zinn, 1980). Modern behavioral psychology and its subfield, mental measurement, gained a foothold in American universities after the turn of the century, in part because the leaders in these new emerging

fields argued quite openly that modern behavioral science could help manage
social unrest.

Mass testing as we know it today first appeared in the form of the
"Army Alpha," a test developed and administered to two million conscripts
during World War I at the urging of Robert Yerkes, then president of the
American Psychological Association, and chairman of the Committee on the
Inheritance of Mental Traits of the Eugenics Research Association. This test
was an adaptation of the Stanford-Binet, the nation's first IQ test, produced
by Lewis Terman, who drew upon the earlier work of the Frenchman Alfred
Binet. The Alpha was created by a committee composed of Yerkes, Terman,
and Henry Goddard, all of who were prime movers of the American eugenics
movement and leading advocates for developing mental measurements which
could be used to identify and classify mental incompetents and defectives.
Mental tests, they argued, were a scientific means of identifying and controlling social deviants (read: troublemakers and nonconformists).

The argument made to the War Department by Yerkes and his colleagues at the time was that results from the Alpha test would provide the
military with the scientific basis for routing draftees into the jobs that best
suited their abilities. But the war ended before the tests were used in this way.
After the war, however, Yerkes and his colleagues, with government encouragement and substantial foundation support, analyzed the data from a sample
of 125,000 draftees and published the results in several volumes. These and
other analyses were later introduced in testimony to a Congressional committee by Yerkes, Goddard, and Terman and used as the scientific basis for the
quotas and restrictions set in the National Origins Act of 1924, which heavily
favored northern European "Nordics" over southern and eastern Europeans
and barred all Japanese, Chinese and other Asians. During the 1920s Yerkes,
who was a professor at Princeton, and Terman, who was at Stanford, became
central figures in legitimating mental measurement, or psychometrics, as a
distinct area of academic specialization within the discipline of psychology
and in the newly founded schools of education.[1]

The leaders of this emerging field of psychometrics were associated
with the so-called "positivist" tradition of scientific psychology which by the
early 1930s was becoming dominant in many university departments of psychology and schools of education. Countless books and articles have been
written with complex arguments and counterarguments about the meaning
and viability of positivism as a philosphical position and as a general stance
toward social and behavioral research in psychology and education (Beyer,
1988; Fay, 1975). What is relevant to this discussion is the image of science
shared by the early leaders of the field of mental measurement that remains
fundamental to positive psychology, and is reflected in the everyday language
of contemporary psychometrics. Simply stated, it is a conception of psychol-

ogy and of the social sciences as "hard," precise sciences much like physics or chemistry. This image of mental measurement as a natural science is implicit in the technology of all forms of psychometrically-based educational tests. From this perspective, the psychological and social sciences, if they are to be genuinely scientific, must emulate the epistemology and methodologies used in the sciences. This is seen as necessary because, it is assumed, only by using the methods of the natural sciences is it possible to obtain truly objective and precise accounts about human characteristics, actions, and institutions. Older, prescientific approaches to the study of human behavior and institutions were considered inferior and unscientific, not only because they were imprecise, but also because they intermingled observed facts with values and subjective predispositions.

The field of mental measurement, borrowing metaphors from the natural sciences, conceived of their newly invented tests as "instruments" or things—tangible objects like thermometers, seismographs, or meter sticks. As "instruments" they stand outside history, apart from the flux of ordinary everyday events, and thereby are able to yield precise, quantifiable readings of human characteristics.

How can we determine whether a particular test, conceived as an instrument, is scientific, that is, capable of being used for measurements that provide information undistorted by the preconceptions, values, and interests of the observer? The answer is well known to anyone with an elementary knowledge of educational and psychological measurement. An instrument, to be scientific, must be shown to possess *reliability* and *validity*. It is important to note here that, as a consequence of conceiving of tests as objects, validity and reliability become qualities or attributes *of the instruments* themselves. The instrument's readings (i.e., test scores) are considered objective, that is, true measures free from subjective distortions of the observer only if the instrument is constructed, and the interpretations made from its readings conform to established *technical* standards for reliability and validity. Who is in the best position to establish these technical standards? The community of scientists, psychologists, and educational measurement specialists, of course, who are the experts in the theory and practice of test-making and interpretation.

According to the accepted technical standards, establishing reliability is reasonably clear-cut and straightforward. Using the thermometer analogy, reliability is established if the instrument can be shown to give nearly identical temperature readings, plus or minus a small and predictable margin of error, when used repeatedly under the same conditions. Obtaining objective observations and making scientific interpretations from these observations would not be possible if the instrument's readings were erratic. Similarly, an educational or psychological test is considered reliable only if it can be shown that a test (or essentially similar test) when administered to the same or similarly constituted sample of subjects yields nearly identical results. There are a variety of generally accepted techniques for establishing a test's reliability, but virtually no disagreements over the meaning of the concept of reliability itself, or that establishing test reliability is primarily a technical matter.

Not so for test validity. Controversies and confusions over the meaning of test validity and how it can be established are almost as old as the testing movement itself and the controversies extend to the present. The manual of *Standards for Educational and Psychological Tests* (American Psychological Association, 1963) prepared by a joint committee of the American Psychological Association, American Educational Research Association and the National Council for Measurement in Education, first published in 1963, and updated periodically, distinguishes three types of test validity: *content, criterion,* and *construct.*

According to these standards, *content* validity requires establishing that the material and tasks required in the array of test items—the set of skills and/or body of knowledge—are a representative sample of the universe of skills or knowledge in a particular domain or discipline. A test in American history, for example, must be shown to include an array of items that represents the field of American history. Whether the test items are an adequate sample of the content and skills in a given domain is established, in practice, by a panel of experts selected by the test-makers. A case for *criterion-related* validity requires demonstrating high statistical correlations between the scores obtained by using the test under development and one or more other tests considered criterial for the first test. In practice, criterion validity entails obtaining a set of statistical correlations between two or more tests. And what constitutes a credible criterion for determining validity in the end also rests on judgments made by testing experts.

If the distinctions among types of validities seem fuzzy, it is because, as Messick (1989), a well-known testing expert points out, the effort to distinguish them dissolves under close scrutiny; content and criterion-related evidence in the final analysis, are merely aspects of the case made for construct validity.

How is *construct* validity established? As I indicated in Chapter 1 establishing construct validity requires getting things straight among (1) the world of human events and experience, (2) the construct label, and (3) the test. This requires that a case for construct validity be woven from inferences based on empirical (that is, quantitative) evidence, philosophical and logical analysis of the construct, and an examination of the uses made of the test in the real world. As Messick (1989) and other testing specialists have come to acknowledge, value judgments and subjective choices are unavoidable in making a case for a test's construct validity. But as Cherryholmes (1989) argues, it is not only that subjective judgments are involved, it is also that constructs themselves are *products* of power and their use is an *exercise* of power. As my exposition in a subsequent section shows, not only are there are a multiplicity of contradictory positions with respect to all educational terms and schooling practices which are rooted in culture, gender, social class, ethnicity, and race, but the power that each position has in shaping everyday discourse and schooling practices differs enormously. Since neutrality is an impossibility, perspectives will invariably be reflected in assessment procedures which affirm the values and interests of the more powerful and influential individuals and groups while denying or ignoring the positions and perspectives of the least powerful and influential. Unless one believes it is the right of some in society to exercise dominion over others, there are no grounds for turning over to testing experts, indeed to any experts, decisions about which positions and values should be affirmed and which ignored in the assessment process.

Clearly, the validity of educational tests is not and cannot be regarded as a technical question to be left to testing specialists. If the meaning of educational constructs is not a matter that can be solved at the level of technical verification then the entire concept of "construct validity" itself as it is currently used in the field of mental measurement deconstructs or dissolves because it is self contradictory. It promises what it cannot possibly deliver: scientific measurement unsullied by subjective judgments, and power.

The promise of the psychometric paradigm is that tests as "instruments" can somehow transcend or stand outside of history and of everyday social practice. However, power invariably shapes of meaning and use of constructs, as Cleo Cherryholmes argues:

> Power refers to asymmetries by which some people are indulged and rewarded and others are deprived and penalized. Effects of power produce subjectivities, constructs, discourses, and practices. . . . [The] effects of power produce speech about construct validity as well as its silences. . . . Constructs, measurements, discourses and practices are objects of history. From this perspective construct validity is situated in a power-knowledge nexus over which the speakers have limited control. (pp. 115–116)

The promise of creating educational tests that are analogous to instruments used in the natural sciences, whose validity can be based on expertise, rationality, and authoritative knowledge uncorrupted by the passions and power of everyday existence, cannot be sustained. The view of tests as scientific instruments and more than a half century of futile debate among academics over the meaning of test validity have served only to obscure the fundamental differences in society over the purposes of schooling and to mask the control that testing experts, test producers, and upper-level administrators and governments exert over the schooling process through the use of testing.

Reconceptualizing Educational Assessment
and Testing as a Form of Practice

I begin with the proposition that tests are not objects, instruments that exist outside of history, independent of the schooling process. Rather, assessments are a form of schooling practice and a form of discourse about schooling practices. Tests and other forms of assessment are forms of schooling practice in the same sense that a school's curriculum, a teacher's pedagogy, or a school's or school district's policies and procedures with respect to student discipline, grading, or staff development are forms of schooling practice. Particular forms of tests and assessments represent particular forms of discourse, that is, they produce particular ways of talking and communicating with others about the schooling and educational process. The use of standardized tests, for example, leads to talking about academic achievement in terms of numerical scores, norms, and percentiles. Though it may appear to be a truism to say that assessments should be regarded as a particular form of practice and discourse, the implications of this view for the development of a science of assessment are not so immediately apparent.

What this reformulation of assessment and testing as an aspect of schooling practice and discourse does is to radically transform the problem of establishing credible indicators of educational achievement and performance. From this perspective, validity as technical concept is superfluous. The usefulness and credibility of any particular educational assessment procedure cannot be resolved with reference to a set of technical criteria established by experts in the science of testing; rather, making assessment policy, devising assessment procedures (including tests), and rendering judgments about the adequacy of any given assessment procedure are, in principle, no different than making policy, devising ways of carrying out these policies, and making judgments about their adequacy in all other areas of schooling practice. I should point out that abandoning validity as a technical concept does not automatically mean abandoning all standardized and conventional criterion-referenced tests. It does mean, however, that standardized and criterion-referenced tests may no longer be privileged as "scientific;" their usefulness and credibility are to be judged alongside any other form of assessment practice.

To assert that tests are a form of practice and discourse, of course, still leaves us with the nagging question of how judgments shall be made about the design, usefulness and credibility of any particular set of assessment practices. There are at least two needs a system of assessment must satisfy: First, it must serve as dependable national *educational currency* for individuals, that is to say, provide teachers, college admission officers, prospective em ployers, etc., as well parents and students with a record which accurately de picts a person's strengths, what he or she knows and can do best. This infor mation is necessary for institutions to make fair and reasonable decisions about who is most likely to profit from a particular educational program, and in order for educators within these institutions to know the needs and interests of students so that they may be better served. Dependable information about their strengths is also needed by students themselves so that they are able to make informed personal decisions, and have in their possession a publicly ac cepted record of their own educational accomplishments. Second, an assess ment system must also provide dependable information to public decision making bodies at all levels about the quality of programs, individual classrooms, schools, and other organizational entities so that these may be improved and/or so that unrecognized educational problems and community needs may be identified and addressed. I will address the question of how to devise an assessment system which serves these two purposes and which takes contradictions in values and differences in power as the norm. First, however, I will discuss several of the basic conflicts in our society over the purposes and practices of schooling.

The Purposes and Practices of Schooling

Schooling, or more specifically the *institutionalized process* of compul sory elementary and secondary schooling, is a complex set of functions or ganized and conducted by school professionals. It is often taken for granted that the sole and unique aim of schools and school systems is to educate. But the schools' job is at the same time both narrower than education (families and many other institutions educate) and much broader (schools do things other than educate). In addition to educating students, schools perform two other functions: they distribute social status and educational and job oppor tunities by their control of diplomas or credentials; and they provide care for children and adolescents during daytime hours. The former is what is some times called the school's *selection* function, the latter its *care-giving* function. Historical forces and contemporary circumstances have shaped and co-joined these three functions, education, selection, and care–giving, within schooling institutions.

Care-Giving. Schools act *in loco parentis,* that is to say that by law and tra dition schools have a mandate to care for and supervise children and adoles cents. Care of children in schools is necessitated by the realities of life in this society, and will remain as a necessary function unless other means are invented to fulfill the schools' caregiving role (Freedman, 1985).

The issue is not whether, but how schools will fulfill the care-giving role. Stated differently, the question is how should schools "parent". In our society, there are contradictory images of parenting rooted in history, culture, tradition, and social practice. One I call *traditional* the other *nurturant*. These perspectives represent contradictory positions on the nature of "childhood"; the proper authority relationship between child and adult; what children should learn at school; and how children think and learn. Not only do cultural, ethnic, and racial groups differ on these matters, but there are differences in perspectives within groups. Further, many of the contradictions in basic values and beliefs with respect to childhood are internalized *within* individuals. Though often deeply submerged in our subconscious, these differences and contradictions are manifested in our basic attitudes and opinions about the purposes and practices of schooling, which purposes and practices should take precedence, and on what basis and how should schools', teachers', and students' performance be assessed.

From the *traditional* perspective proper parenting of children is paternalistic and hierarchical. I use these two words here descriptively and not pejoratively. Because children are viewed as unformed adults, they must be civilized and moulded to the requirements of the adult world—as adults perceive and conceive of that world. From this viewpoint, children have few if any rights other than those granted by parents or the institutions acting on their behalf. This viewpoint is represented in the writings of the Reverend John Brown, who was often cited in early nineteenth century England as the defender of mass schooling: " 'Tis necessary, therefore, in order to form a good citizen to impress the infant with early habits: even to shackle the mind (if you so please to speak) with salutary prejudices, such as may create conformity of thought and action with the established principles on which his native society is built".[2]

From the *nurturant* perspective, children are seen not as unformed or deficient adults, but as qualitatively different. Childhood is viewed as a unique period of growth during a person's lifetime, wherein the adult caregiver is expected to exercise control in a way that stimulates the growth and development of each child to his or her fullest capacities. The metaphor for the caregiver's (teacher or parent) role is the gardener who has responsibility for cultivating the soil, maintaining optimum environmental conditions for full and healthy growth. Learning and development from this perspective requires a stimulating environment and guidance from knowledgeable and caring adults. The emotional climate of the schooling environment and a concern for the emotional well-being or "affective" aspects of learning are seen as inseparable from the cognitive or academic. There is also a strong strand within the nurturant view of human growth and development as social, that is as requiring a supportive environment wherein rights of children and adults are respected.

If the traditional view is associated with paternalism, the nurturant view is often associated with mothering. Mothering here does not refer to the gender of the care-giver (though historically mothering has been and remains largely the responsibility of women), but to care-giving and supervision characterized by love, patience, understanding, and empathy.

Selection. All societies have some mechanism for sorting persons into occupational roles. Sorting is never benign, because in modern society a person's place in the social order not only indicates status, but real and potential economic and political power. Because modern industrial societies rely heavily on scientific knowledge and technical proficiency, selection must to some significant degree be based on what individuals know and can do, not on whom they know—that is, on individual merit rather than on inherited or ascribed privilege. There is no claim here that technological societies are meritocracies, only that there are social and economic pressures for filling jobs outside the home based on competence. For this to occur, some flexibility in the social structure or "mobility" is essential. Sociologists speak of "ascribed" or "sponsored" mobility versus "contest" mobility. The former refers to position gained through tradition, connections, or family wealth, the latter through competition—fairly run.

Schools in the age of high technology increasingly take on the function of making a match between persons and positions through control of credentials, degrees and diplomas. Whether schools have ever made much of a difference in terms of social mobility is in dispute (Jencks 1979; Bowles and Gintis, 1976), but there is wide consensus that schools should aspire to sort and route based on merit—that is, on demonstrable individual achievements and competences. Individuals and cultural groups within a society, however, differ sharply among and within themselves over the way schools should sort and select.

One view is that schools should provide *equality of opportunity,* that is, offer every student, regardless of ethnic origin, religion, race, gender, or station in life of parents, equal access to courses and programs. Another view is that a guaranteed place at the starting gate is not sufficient for a fairly-run race for entire categories of people (women, African-, and Native Americans, Latinos, and other ethnic and religious minorities) who have been handicapped by years of discrimination and oppression. From this point of view a fair contest requires "positive discrimination" (Halsey, 1972) or "affirmative action.'' Still others hold that equality of opportunity, even with affirmative action, is insufficient in a society with enormous discrepancies in political and economic power between social classes, genders, white and nonwhite; and that schools in a democracy have an obligation to pursue policies aimed at achieving equality of outcomes or results—meaning a proportionately equal share of high status degrees and credentials which provide access to political power and wealth.[3]

Education. Education is a process which occurs in and outside of schools whereby some individuals pass on to others something presumed to be of worth or value. That ''something'' may be a body of knowledge, way of looking, thinking, interpreting, or doing things. The operative phrase here is ''of worth or value.'' Because all education cultivates attitudes, selects some bodies of knowledge and skills and ignores others, it transmits values.

Emile Durkeim, generally regarded as the first sociologist of education suggests that historically Western society has embraced contrasting conceptions of education and of the primary educational functions of schools—one I call *education-as-cultural-heritage,* the other the *education-as-use* perspective. Durkheim (1977 p. 96), quoting Erasmus, the sixteenth century Dutch theologian and humanist, associates the cultural heritage view with the process of refining the mind: ''The only way to succeed in ridding the human intellect of its courseness, to polish and refine it, was to introduce it to and make it intimate with an elegant and refined civilization so that it might become imbued with its spirit.'' This refinement requires that individuals ''are intimate with'' the highest accomplishments of culture.

The primary educational goal of schooling from the education–as–use perspective is to connect learning and life. To quote once again from Durkheim (1977 p. 97): ''[From this perspective] . . . the supreme need is survival, and what is needed in order to survive is not the art of subtle speech, it is the art of sound thinking, so that one knows how to act.'' A more recent statement of this view by Sir Toby Weaver (1986) former Deputy Secretary of the Department of Education and Science in Britain is as follows:

> [T]he definitive characteristic of *homo sapiens* [is the] capacity to form purposes, weigh alternative courses of action, to reach wise decisions and to act on them. In this process thought and reflection is to be regarded not as an end in itself, but as an inseparable component of rational action. Action indeed has been defined—to distinguish it from physical event or organic behavior—as human activity guided by knowledge. (p.54)

Quoting Whitehead, he goes on to say education is ''the art of the utilization of knowledge. . . . Pedants sneer at education which is useful. But if education is not useful what is it?'' From this point of view education is not mastering the great ideas, thoughts and refined intellectual traditions, but developing the person's capacity for bringing knowledge from any source to bear on the practical problems of life.

While some within the cultural heritage tradition may speak of knowledge for its own sake, most would likely argue that mastery of cultural heritage is the most useful form of education, indeed far more useful than an education which focuses specifically on contemporary problems or developing practical vocational skills. What distinguishes the knowledge-as-use from the cultural heritage view is the criterion for what knowledge is of most worth. From the former perspective, it is whether knowledge helps individuals to deal with the practical decisions and problems of daily living. For the latter it is whether the corpus of knowledge qualifies as a legitimate piece of the heritage.

The cultural heritage perspective is by no means a unitary point of view. For R. S. Peters, (1966) a contemporary English philosopher, the cultural heritage is composed of the "public traditions enshrined in public languages which it took our remote ancestors centuries to develop." For Peters and also for Allan Bloom (1987), author of the widely circulated *The Closing of the American Mind*, the final arbiters of what belongs in the corpus are university academics who are keepers of these traditions. Others, Robert Hutchins (1943) and Mortimer Adler (1982), for example, object to the narrowness and specialism within the university disciplines, and conceive of the heritage in terms of masterpieces of literature, philosophical, and scientific texts which represent the highest achievements of western civilization. Still others— E. D. Hirsch (1987) is the most recent example—attempt to develop taxonomies, or lists of concepts, generalizations, events, ideas and cultural myths that presumably constitute the essentials of the cultural heritage. Finally, there is a body of opinion that holds that the cultural heritage as represented by all the foregoing is narrowly Eurocentric and male-oriented. From this, a multicultural position, no one tradition has a superior claim than another, and there are a multiplicity of cultures and traditions with equally compelling arguments for inclusion in the schools' curriculum (Green, 1988; McCarthy & Apple, 1988; Sleeter & Grant, 1988; Ogbu, 1988).

Significant differences exist among those who profess a knowledge-as-use position. Perhaps the most commonly expressed view is that whatever else schools do, their primary obligation is to give students the knowledge and skills they need to compete in the job market. The position of *A Nation at Risk* (National Commission on Excellence in Education, 1983) the report of the Carnegie Forum on Education and the Economy (1986) *A Nation Prepared*, and most other highly visible reports is that the United States has lost the ability to compete in the high-tech age of tomorrow, and that the future economic well-being and growth of the nation depends on schools providing students with the job skills needed for the new global economy.[4]

Where those who defend this premise differ is on how narrowly or broadly to construe the skills and knowledge needed. Some see knowledge as job- or occupation-specific; others argue for a much broader conception of job related competencies:

> The uncertainty about the future requirements of work suggest that the best preparation should be general rather than job specific education and training. Jobs as we know them today may be radically different in the future. All workers will probably change jobs with continued or increased frequency. [Thus,] the best preparation for a changing work world is one that stresses flexibility and adaptability. Students will need to learn specific job skills not once, but many times throughout their work lives. This learning will take place at work, at home or in schools, and will require communication, comprehension and analytic skills. These skills will enable today's students to learn new specific job skills, and more importantly, to shape as well as adapt to a changing work environment. (Levin and Rumberger, 1985, p.1)

There are also others in this society who hold that educating for paid employment, even broadly conceived, is far too limited a conception of the school's proper educational responsibilities. Though they may accept the proposition that preparation for work is a valid educational purpose of schools, they would add that preparation for the future must include educating for democratic citizenship.[5] To be prepared, a citizen must possess knowledge and a range of competencies which enable them to be critical and responsible participants in the political life of their communities and the nation. Others, particularly some feminists, have made a compelling case that this position perpetuates the invisibility of women. Dichotomizing the political and personal, in effect, emphasizes as most useful the knowledge and skills in those areas which have been and remain bastions of male privilege (government, law, business). They would likely argue for the need to develop in students knowledge and skills that are instrumental to building caring communities, recognizing and mediating differences. (de Laurentis, 1986; Ellsworth, 1989; Martin & Mohanty, 1988; Weiller, 1988)

The foregoing is only a partial representation of the controversies and contradictions in contemporary America over the purposes and practices of schooling. I have not, for example, represented the positions of those who regard the non-instrumental, spiritual, or religious dimensions of human experience as vital to the school's educational functions (Oliver, 1989; Purpel,

1989), nor have I fully represented the child-centered traditions which hold that schooling above all else should stimulate and nurture persons' interests, regardless of whether these interests are to connected to an accepted intellectual tradition or have any foreseeable practical use. And last but not least, the foregoing analysis deals only in a limited way with multicultural questions, the positions and concerns of women, and of African-, Native, Asian-, and Latino- Americans, both male and female, whose voices have been silenced or largely ignored in all areas of social policy, including schooling.

The Structure and Process of a Contextual Assessment Paradigm

I begin with the claim that fundamental contradictions and differences over what are the legitimate or rightful purposes of schooling outlined above are inevitable. They are manifest (1) in the discourse of educational professionals, public officials, and ordinary citizens about the nature of schooling, what's wrong and right with schools, and what can and should be done to improve individual schools and the entire system of elementary and secondary education; (2) in schooling practices, which include the ways schools are structured and governed, all everyday social relationships, schooling routines with respect to curriculum, pedagogy, organization of space and time, student discipline, and all testing and assessment procedures. Discourses about policies and practices shape or produce practices; practices shape or produce other practices and discourses about practices. For example, public discussion about the weaknesses of the American economy and the schools' failure to educate a technically competent workforce produced more standardized testing, and discourse about standardized testing produced more time devoted in classrooms to workbooks and time spent on practicing for tests, as well as talk among teachers, school board members and in the mass media about the improvement or lack of improvement of schools based on rising and falling test scores. Such discourse produced other practices—such as programs for the gifted and talk about "excellence", "the culturally deprived" or "at-risk" students—which in turn produced other practices, and discourses, and on and on. My use of the word "produce" does not imply that there is a one to one or determinate relationship between discourses and practices, or between one form of practice and another. The foregoing illustration which implies linear causality (X causes $a, b, c,$ which in turn causes Y, causing $d, e, f,$ etc.) is a vast oversimplification. There are simultaneously ocurring matrices of mutually influencing practices and discourses in response to particular interventions, including some which may be completely unexpected and/or directly contrary or oppositional to those intended by the individual or body initiating the intervention. For example, increases in standardized testing not only produced the discourses and practices suggested above, but also several

forms of covert resistance to testing, such as cheating by teachers and principals, student absenteeism, formations of new coalitions among parents,
teachers groups, and children's advocates opposed to increased centralized
decision-making, spurring more talk about and efforts to develop alternative
forms of testing and assessment.

While the relationships and interconnections among practices, between
discourses and practices, and among discourses are problematical and uncer-
tain, some discourses and practices are clearly more authoritative or privileged than others, that is, far more likely to produce discourses and practices
which regulate and authorize some forms of social relationships and structures
while suppressing others. Assessment practices and discourses are uniquely
privileged because the results of assessments are singled out by the public,
policy-makers, and by educational administrators to serve as criteria for making judgments about the successes and failures of other schooling practices,
that is, for making policy determinations about whether or not given schools,
school districts, or particular programs are effective, whether teachers are
competent, or students are being properly educated. And among all assessment procedures, standardized and criterion-referenced tests are particularly
privileged, that is, they serve as the single most powerful regulators of schooling practice, shaping the language used in public discussions about schooling,
the criteria for judging the competence of students, and the range of possibilities considered for reforming the schools.

Why do standardized and criterion-referenced tests enjoy such a highly
privileged status? Since the turn of the century in North America, psycho-
metricians have laid claim to providing the most, if not the only, *scientifically*
valid means of measuring academic achievement. A major reason why these
tests are privileged is because the discourse surrounding their use is itself
nested in the discourses which have been dominant in Western philosophy and
political practice since the Enlightenment,—the discourses of rationality, instrumental and critical reasoning. These dominant discourses marry social,
political, and economic progress to science. Indeed, science and social
progress are seen as inseparable.

I do not fault standardized and criterion-referenced tests because they
regulate and control educational practices and discourses; all forms of educational assessment regulate and control educational practice. Indeed shaping
practice is what assessment is all about. My point here is that the psychometric paradigm embodies a particular regime of scientific truth. This regime
produces assessment discourses and practices which control schooling practices and stuctures in directions driven by the assumptions accepted as truths
within this regime. These assumptions, outlined and examined in Chapter 1,
are:

1. There are or can be universally accepted meanings of educational constructs, or where conflicts and contradictions exist, these may be transformed into technical problems which may be settled by experts.
2. Tests constructed according to established technical requirements are morally neutral scientific instruments which stand outside of history and culture.
3. Human cognition and affect may be separated at least for the purposes of measurement.
4. Schools and educational systems can and should be managed and controlled from the center, the center here referring to the central office of a local school district, a district-wide governing board, state educational bureaucracy, a national governmental or non-governmental testing agency, an accrediting body, or some combination of the foregoing.

If these assumptions of the psychometric paradigm are questioned or abandoned, then on what grounds would it be possible to devise a usable and credible system of assessment given the deeply held and often contradictory positions on schooling purposes an practices? If there are no technical solutions to disagreements over values, no ultimate authority scientific, or otherwise, no universally accepted moral code to appeal to in order to settle contending positions, then the solution that remains in a culturally diverse democratic society is *political.* Put more precisely, the only way to deal with fundamental differences where there are conflicting interests and positions, and where there is a need for a common solutions to mutually acknowledged problems, is to develop political structures and processes for mediating differences which do not privilege the perspectives and interests of those whose policies and perspectives predominate within government the major universitites, the high-prestige foundations, and public policy think-tanks.

I will not attempt to make a detailed set of recommendations for a national system of schooling assessment, a task far beyond the capacity of any individual, and one which requires a significant investment of resources and a comprehensive examination of a wide range of legal, economic, political, cultural, and strategic questions. However, I will outline a possible set of structures, and discuss a number of the problems related to establishing processes and procedures. My purpose is to demonstrate that though the issues related to structure and process are extraordinarily complex, practical solutions are possible, if the political will exists to address the task.

Four general propositions have guided my effort to address the issues related to structure and process:

1. Differences and contradictions in positions, and conflicts in interests over the purposes and practices of schooling among individuals and groups are normal in a multicultural, polylingual society.
2. All assessment procedures, including tests, are privileged forms of schooling practice; they are not and cannot be morally neutral scientific instruments.
3. There are wide discrepancies in power among individuals and groups, and because coercive power is capable of being exercised by the more powerful groups, assessment structures and processes should deliberately diffuse and decenter power in order to limit centralized, coercive control.
4. Assessment systems should provide for both *horizontal* and *vertical* accountability.

By horizontal accountability, I mean control exercised at the local school-community level by professional peers who work in a given school and by citizens who reside within the areas the school serves. By vertical control, I refer to control exercised at the district, state, or national levels by individuals or bodies who have been granted the legal authority to exercise control.

Bodies exercising vertical and horizontal control will have different and sometimes conflicting preoccupations and interests requiring different sorts of information. Thus, there will need to be some form of checks and balances within the system of assessment.

Structures

There are at least three distinguishable classes of tasks which must be performed if a system of assessment is to serve its purposes.[6]

Creating Systems and Procedures for Recording Information about Students' Talents and Achievements. The two fundamental problems or sets of issues related to this task are: (1) how to define the categories or areas of educational achievements and talents, and (2) what procedures should be used for collecting and summarizing information.

Teachers, principals, and counsellors at the school level would have the primary (but not the sole) responsibility for defining areas and domains of achievement, and for developing assessment systems and procedures. A student's record of achievement would likely include testimonials from persons who have first-hand knowledge of his or her accomplishments, portfolios of a student's writings, artistic productions, examples of practical work, summaries of performance on tasks specifically designed as assessment tasks, which could include oral and written examination results. Assessment policies and procedures have a direct bearing on, indeed are impossible to separate from, other educational decisions made by teachers and principals at the school level. Though primary responsibility should rest with professionals at the school level, their powers are limited by the curriculum and assessment guidelines established by governing bodies, and district- and national-level accrediting agencies. School-level decisions with regard to assessment, as with school practices in all other areas, must respect the constitutional and other rights of students and parents.

Validating Students' Records. Each school would have a school-level validating board. The validation function, in effect, is oversight of an individual school's educational programs. A validating board at each school site would have the continuing responsibility for reviewing the quality of all school programs and activities indicated on students' records. The board would also have the associated responsibility of periodically forwarding recommendations about needed changes in curriculum, pedagogy and assessment procedures to the school staff, and the district-level accrediting body. The school-level validating board would be elected, or appointed by an elected school-level body. In England each school has a lay board of governors which carries statutory responsibility for overseeing a schools' programs. In the United States elected school-level governing bodies are rare, and where they do exist are a recent phenomenon whose powers and functions are often ill-defined. The validation function could be undertaken by an extant body, or by a newly created entity. Each board would be composed of lay members, parents and citizens from the local community; it could also include teachers, principals and student members. I cannot here resolve the complex issues about how such boards may be legally established and their members selected. However, the principle that should govern the creation of such boards is that validating responsibility should rest with a body composed of persons with divergent economic and cultural histories, reflecting the racial, ethnic, social class, occupational, and gender composition of the school-community.

Accrediting Students' Records. The accreditation process is intended to provide assurance to the public that the individual records of students' achievement are reliable and credible. Reliable in this context means that the records themselves are accurate and conscientiously kept; and credible in this context means that the claims records make are true, that is to say, if the record indicates a student writes well, that he or she, in fact, does write well. The accrediting process would be undertaken at two levels; the school district and national. A school district under authority granted by the state would establish one or more district-level accrediting boards depending on the size of the districts. The boards would be composed of lay and professional members who represent a cross-section of the communities the district serves.

The district-level accrediting boards' basic responsibility would be to accredit each student's record every three years or so. This board would systematically review all (or perhaps a carefully selected sample of) student records. They would accomplish this task by examining the specific procedures used by the school for developing, collecting and summarizing individual students' records, and the quality of the work included and summarized with each record. If, for example, the summary record indicated a student exhibited superior competence in writing narrative prose, this claim would be checked by reading students' compositions included in their portfolios. On the basis of these reviews of records, the district-level accrediting board would put their stamp of approval on (or accredit) each student's record. On the basis of an examination of student records from a given school, the district-level accrediting board would make recommendations to district-level administrators, the elected district-wide school board, and to the school-level validating board with respect to needed changes in record-keeping and assessment procedures, curriculum offerings, and/or staffing.

Individual students would not be penalized if their records had been inappropriately evaluated by the school-level validating board, rather, the process would be aimed at identifying the sources of the problem and finding systemic solutions. Let us say that a district-level board found the general quality of writing of ninth graders in a given school was below par, and that the evidence suggested that the source of the problem was weaknesses in the writing curriculum. The school-level validating board might respond by agreeing with the finding about the quality of writing, but indicating that their investigation suggested that the deficiencies were due to excessively heavy teaching loads which left writing teachers very little time to provide feedback to students. Assuming a conscientious effort to address the problem by all parties, this process while it would certainly not solve all problems, would have the the effect of clarifying the sources of the problems, and initiating a process at the school and district levels that could lead to practical efforts to improve educational standards.

The primary purpose of national accreditation is to establish a national currency of records. National accreditation boards' responsibility would differ from district-level boards' in that national boards would not accredit individual students' records. Rather their job would be to accredit the district-level accrediting boards. This would be accomplished by reviewing at set intervals selected samples of student records from a given district-level accrediting board, and conducting periodic site visits in order to review the work and operating procedures of each district-level accrediting board. Based on these reviews, a national board would make recommendations to state and local educational officials for correcting deficiencies, and for developing new programs for serving neglected or changing national, regional or local needs.

They might suggest to state officials, for example, that if the quality of writing is to improve markedly, there must be reductions in size of writing classes accompanied by inservice programs programs for writing teachers. Or they may suggest that district resources while only marginally adequate, are inappropriately allocated within the district. It also would be the national board's responsibility to devise, revise, and publish accreditation standards for district-level boards and to withhold accreditation if necessary.

To avoid concentrations of coercive power by national accrediting boards, there would be created perhaps a dozen or more national boards, each independent of the other and free of government control. Also, consideration could be given to creating some boards which specialize in particular types of educational programs (in the performing arts, for example). The structure and functions of each national accrediting board would resemble in some ways the independent regional agencies that currently accredit secondary schools, colleges, and universities in the United States, except that the focus of activities of the former would be solely on assessment, and each school district would be free to choose one from among the several accrediting agencies serving a particular region. Districts would contract with a national board of their choice for a specified period, perhaps five to seven years. An additional safeguard to minimize the possibility of undue influence by particularly influential constituencies, or by powerful interest groups would be for local school districts to receive direct state funding based on average daily attendance to pay for services provided by the national accrediting boards. In this way the national boards would not be beholden to state departments of education or foundations. A code of ethics and set of ground rules for districts concluding contracts with national boards could also be established by individual states, or perhaps by the Education Commission of the States.

Processes

There is a long history of democratic forms being subverted by privileged elites. Democratic structures with specified roles and duties of group members alone will not suffice to assure that the concerns and interests of all are seriously addressed.[7] Careful attention must be given to developing procedures which increase the chances that differences in perspectives and conflicts in interests among individuals and groups are heard and addressed, and to insuring that validation and accreditation guidelines are being conscientiously followed. I will briefly discuss several issues and concerns that will need to be addressed.

I will assume that each validation and accreditation body assents to the principle of equal regard for the positions and interests of each member and the constituencies whom they represent. However, as I have already noted, there will persist wide differences in power and status among group members rooted in history, culture, educational background, wealth, race, gender, and occupation. In addition, there are strong cultural and political supports in the United States for defining unpopular positions as extremist, dangerous, irrational, or un-American. Consequently, some positions are far more likely than others to be heard, and taken into account, and some voices are far more likely than others to be marginalized or silenced. If validating and accrediting bodies are to avoid recapitulating the power relations in the community and in the society as a whole, there must be an open acknowledgement that there are differences both in status and power among constituencies and within the group. Even if acknowledged in advance, discrepancies in power (which are often hidden or denied) will surface in unexpected ways during day-to-day operations. Each body, then, must not merely proclaim tolerance for difference, but self-consciously develop procedures which treat differences of oppositional and marginalized groups as positive contributions to the group's efforts to find practical solutions (Hartsock, 1987).

Many groups after a period of time often develop an unspoken consensus to avoid controversy in order to reach closure on specific tasks or issues. The unspoken suppression and silencing of differences, and a facade of unity is often strengthened by the group members' shared interest in defending the group from outside criticism and by a tendency of those within the group to view those not party to the group's deliberations as outsiders, naive or ill-informed about the complexities of the issues. All these pressures toward homogenization, both internal and external to the group, suggest that the integrity of an assessment system which assumes plurality of positions and sees differences as an assets will require a continuously and rigorously monitored set of proactive and retroactive practices.

Among the proactive measures which might be taken to insure decentralization of coercive power is requiring that validation and accreditation boards actively involve less powerful, oppositional groups in the formulation and implementation of assessment criteria, policies and procedures. For example, at regular intervals boards might be obliged to ask such groups for detailed criticisms and proposals for alternative approaches, and to respond publicly to these criticisms and their proposed alternatives. In addition, boards might be required to request that oppositional groups select persons from within and outside the communities the boards serve who are experienced in areas of achievement being assessed or in methods of assessment. Local writers, auto mechanics, musicians, accountants, social workers, community activists or business executives, for example could be asked to review records of achievement, assessment procedures, and evaluate educational programs relevant to their area of knowledge and experience. Such experts could include academics and technical specialists in educational testing.

Retroactive measures might include creating an office of "ombudsman" to hear complaints, and/or establishing an appeals procedure which allows individuals, schools, or local educational authorities to bring their objections and grievances to an independent, standing or *ad hoc* body.

Finally, I bring the readers' attention to what is probably the single most troublesome and difficult procedural question: the uses and limits of rational discussion and debate in resolving differences and contradiction. A number of recent writers have pointed out that the modern age of science and technology initiated by the Enlightenment rests upon an assumption that rationality will enable homo sapiens to control the physical, biological, and social worlds. Rousseau, Bentham, Adam Smith, Thomas Jefferson, Marx, Weber, Durkheim, and Dewey for all their differences elevated reason to a universal. It is true that the force of the best argument—rational, dispassionate testing of empirical claims and logical examination of contending arguments— may clarify positions, and locate common ground for action, thereby resolving conflicts in human interests and values. But science and reason have also served as ideological weapons of the powerful and the privileged to silence and suppress the perspectives of women and minorities, and to rationalize oppression. Questions about the possibilities and limits of reason cannot be resolved here and will doubtless continue to preoccupy philosophers and social critics for many years to come. As a practical matter, many individuals and cultural groups will not accept as self-evident the primacy of reason, particularly when fundamental interests are at stake. What this suggests is that in the end persuasion, rational analysis, and logical argumentation within accreditation and validation bodies will not, cannot, dissolve all differences, and individuals and groups will continue to have conflicting interests and hold contradictory values. The challenge facing the body, then, is how to mediate differences, to search for common ground *within these differences,* even when oppositional perspectives could be silenced by a strong majority.[8]

The foregoing discussion of structures and processes should not be construed as a comprehensive solution to the educational assessment problem. Educational assessment is enormously complex, politically and conceptually, and the practical question of what the contextual paradigm would look like in practice cannot be easily answered. The most common response even from those who are highly critical of current assessment practices and existing test is, "What will replace them?" It is quite understandable why we look for new instruments to replace the old. Most of us socialized in the empirical social sciences find it next to impossible to free ourselves of the conception of assessment as dependent on the use of "instruments." It is difficult to conceive of assessment as a political practice, as an ongoing process of identifying

common interests and negotiating differences. We easily fall back into the
mindset that the answer to flawed tests are new or alternative forms of testing
which will correct the flaws.

Also seriously flawed is the view that in order to redesign the system of
testing and assessment, we must first define and establish criteria for ''authentic achievement,'' and on the basis of these criteria construct more authentic forms of testing (Newmann, Chapter 4). This solution sidesteps the
validity problem, but replaces it with the issues of what is the ''true'' meaning
of authentic achievement, and who has the right to decide what is and what is
not authentic achievement. Stated differently, this view cannot avoid the value
questions of what schools are for, and what knowledge and ways of thinking
are of most worth. Unless imposed, there is no way to achieve universal
agreement on the ''authenticity'' question. The position I take here, is that if
assessment structures and processes are developed so that power is decentered
(that is, shared by the local-school community, school districts, the state, and
bodies which represent the national interests) there can develop in each
school-community a working consensus on the purposes of schooling and the
knowledge questions which will serve the collective national interest, and at
the same time acknowledges and validates the of diversity in cultures within
and among school-communities, and differences in philosophical outlook,
and interests.

I anticipate many objections to the position on assessment and testing I
take here and I will briefly address two of them. The first objection is that the
sort of solution I am suggesting will further politicize the schools, leaving
them vulnerable to interference from powerful interest groups. An answer to
this charge is implied by my earlier discussion of the construct validity question. Current forms of testing already give administrative bodies, testing experts, and testing agencies an inordinate amount of political power, power that
permeates the entire system, but is masked by the claim that current forms of
standardized and criterion-referenced tests are scientific instruments. A second and far more difficult question is, whether those groups which are already
very powerful, well-organized and well funded, will not somehow find ways
of controlling whatever bodies or structures and procedures are devised. This
is a serious problem which requires a much lengthier response than is possible
here. There is no easy answer to this criticism. It is the same problem that
threatens all democratic institutions, all efforts to create institutions which
acknowledge the legitmacy of unpopular positions and attempt to protect the
interests of the least powerful and most oppressed social groups. A partial response to this objection is that the current system of assessment leaves the
schools no less at risk and far more open to the undue influence of dominant
groups since much of this influence is indirect and hidden. One, and perhaps
the only, protection against undue political influence over the schooling pro-

cess is a system of assessment that explicitly acknowledges the problem of differential and coercive power and attempts to decenter power by deliberately creating multiple centers of power for controlling the assessment process at several points throughout the system, each with procedural safeguards for teachers, students, and for those individuals and groups whose positions and interests are most likely to be suppressed or ignored.

Prospects for Change and Some Conclusions

The psychometric assessment paradigm is embedded not only in the way we have come to think about education and schooling, but is interwoven in the structures and everyday practices of all educational institutions. The power of the psychometric paradigm to control practice and dominate discourse about schooling and the possibilities for change does not rest in its superior logic and scientific standing, but in the political and economic influence of the many institutions and public and private agencies—national, state and local—who publish, administer, or whose everyday activities depend upon the continued use of standardized and criterion-referenced tests. The livelihood and professional status of many thousands of people who work in these institutions at all levels would be seriously threatened if there were to be a basic reorientation in the practice of educational assessment and testing. Also, there are court decisions, legislation, and administrative practices at the national, state, and school district levels, many instituted with the good intentions of serving the interests or safeguarding the rights of particular populations of students—the handicapped, poor, various minorities, women—which mandate or assume the need for continued use of psychometrically-based testing. For many—citizens, students, and educational professionals—schools without the anchor of standardized and criterion-referenced tests are simply unimaginable.

It is wishful thinking to expect that the psychometric paradigm, as a result of the impersonal march of history toward enlightenment, will quietly fade away. Changes only look inevitable peering backwards. Institutions and social practices change as a consequence of real people taking real risks often in the face of uncertainty and massive resistance. This book, indeed no book or treatise, will revolutionize the field of educational assessment. What this book may do for those who believe that structural changes in schools are essential is convince them that basic changes in schooling practices and significant improvement in the quality of schools will become widespread and take root only if they are accompanied by basic changes in the assessment paradigm, and that the many difficult conceptual, technical, and organizational problems of abandoning the psychometric paradigm and the transition to a nationwide system of contextual assessment can be solved if our national, state, and local political leaders are ready to devote sufficient energy and resources to the task.

For this to occur there must be concerted action on the political front, major investments in research and development, and last, but by no means least, a new and compelling vision of democratic schooling.

Political Action. Political action is required to challenge the deeply entrenched interests in maintaining current forms of assessment. Such action is highly unlikely unless many disparate groups—educational professionals, teachers, principals, and ordinary citizens across racial, gender, ethnic, and social class lines—can come together to bring political pressure to bear at the national, state, and local community levels for changes in laws and regulations which encourage rather than obstruct efforts to institute major changes in testing and assessment procedures. The prospect of a single-issue coalition developing around reforming testing and assessment is problematical. Such a movement most likely would need to be linked to a broader democratic movement to change not only schools, but also other political economic and social institutions.

Investment in Research and Development. All paradigms include what Kuhn has called "puzzle solutions," ways of conducting investigations, handling data, and solving specific methodological problems. Several chapters have suggested specific models, approaches, and procedures for gathering, summarizing, and interpreting information about educational programs, the performance of schools, students, teachers and other educational professionals. I also have argued in this chapter that an assessment system must also include *organizational* "puzzle solutions," that is, structures, roles and processes for solving problems and dealing with conflicting interests and positions. While the puzzle solutions, methodological and structural, discussed in this volume appear promising, they still must be regarded only as modest beginnings.

It is not difficult to understand why, historically, changes in paradigms and development of new puzzle solutions generally do not arise from those in the existing community of experts who are entangled in the boundaries of the received traditions of their fields. The record of the established testing organizations such as Educational Testing Service and other major test publishers over the years is not encouraging; they generally have ignored criticism and resisted change while absorbing the largest share of private and public research and development funds. The efforts of these major testing agencies and publishers to develop alternative forms of assessment have been minimal, confined at best to adapting the familiar psychometric technology for use on desktop computers. Indeed, however, well-intentioned, the creators and purveyors of tests and most educational testing specialists within independent agencies, universities, or school districts have very little to gain and a great deal to lose from a decentered system of educational assessment. School districts, state departments of education, foundations and the federal government must be willing to make major long term investments in necessary research and development to address the problems only touched upon in this book. If there are to be significant moves toward the development of a new science of educational testing and assessment along the lines suggested here, funding agencies, foundations, states, and school districts must have the political will to bypass established research a development agencies and testing experts many of whom have a material interest in maintaining the use of current test technologies.

A Vision of Democratic Schools. Finally, the need to reform testing clearly cannot be separated from the need to reform the nation's schools. Reforms at best will remain marginal, confined to a scattering of districts and demonstration projects, unless coalitions of men and women, teachers, educators, parents, and ordinary citizens are able to join together to envision new possibilities—schools where all children, male and female, of all races, cultures, ethnic groups, and social classes can realize their aspirations and talents and experience the joy and power of learning.

If as a society we are committed to diversity and democratic decision-making, then it is clearly inconsistent with this commitment for national, state, or local educational authorities, elected officials, or experts to assess schooling and educational performance using the psychometric paradigm which rests upon the assumption that there is or can can be a unitary view of schooling and education. Given the fundamental differences and multiplicity of perspectives, there clearly is not now, nor is there ever likely to be a national, state, or even district-wide consensus on, or single vision of schooling purposes and policies.

Schooling has a direct and indirect impact on all of us—our material interests and our social and cultural values. It follows that decisions about *all* school practices, including assessment practices, should be arrived at with the participation and consent of those who must live with the consequences of these decisions. Since they are closest to, and bear the everyday moral responsibility for the growth and development of children, the local school-community (teachers, principals, counselors, parents, and other members of the immediate community the school serves) must have a substantial voice. However, in a democracy, school-level professionals and the local community the school serves must share the responsibility for deciding upon the school's purposes and how a school shall fulfill those purposes.

While a system of assessment which is responsive to community interests and values is vital, if professionals and citizens are to know whether and how well these purposes are being fulfilled, each school community cannot completely go its own way. There are legitimate district-wide, state-wide, region-wide and nation-wide interests in what purposes individual schools pursue and how they pursue them. The needs, priorities, and standards of performance seen from the vantage point of an entire district, state, region, and the nation as a whole will undoubtedly differ from, and in some instances be in conflict with, those of the local school-community. Local, state and national government officials, who are elected to represent the collective interests of the people, have a right and responsibility to participate in shaping the schools' purposes, priorities, and standards. If all interests and concerns— national, state, regional and local—are to be addressed, the assessment system, must provide structures and procedures whereby differences in positions and interests are dealt with fairly and openly. Devising such structures and procedures is, of course, a very difficult and politically complex process. But as several writers in this volume attempt to show, the conceptual and technical problems are not insurmountable. Finally, it should be noted that the role of testing and assessment specialists is not eliminated in a system of contextual assessment, but it is substantially different. The job of assessment experts would *not* be to make value judgments for the community, as is often the case now; rather it would be to help unmask and clarify hidden assumptions and to use their specialized knowledge and training to devise and refine assessment procedures and techniques which facilitate democratic decision-making.

Notes and References

Chapter 1

Notes

1. *New York Times* on February 17, 1990, citing 1986–87 U.S. Department of Education statistics reported that almost 30% of American youth do not complete High School. This figure obscures the wide range of graduation rates which vary by region, state, social class, and race. Minnesota's rate is reported at 90.6%, while in the poor urban and rural areas, rates dip below the 50% mark. These statistics do not include those who complete high school requirements as adults, nor those who complete the GED, the national high school equivalency examination.

2. See, for example, Alan Graubard's (1972) analysis of the nations schooling problems describing the problems and issues facing schools in the fifties, sixties, and early seventies. With minor changes, it could have been written today.

3. See, for example, Henry M. Levin (1985), an occasional paper published by the Institute for Research on Educational Finance and Governance at Stanford University. This Institute, now defunct, produced a series of reports by Henry Levin, Russell W. Rumberger and others which challenged the assumptions of *A Nation at Risk* and the Carnegie report, *A Nation Prepared*. Two reports which received limited national notice were: *Choosing Equality: The Case for Democratic Schooling*, (New World Foundation, 1985); and *Equity and Excellence: Toward an Agenda for School Reform*, (The Public Education Information Network, 1985).

4. See "Looking Backward at Educational Reform", Education Week (1989).

5. Efforts to develop practical alternatives have accelerated in the last several years, and a great deal of attention has been given to the development of so-called performance-based tests. A survey of efforts to develop alternatives across the United States and several other English-speaking nations was undertaken by the National Center on Effective Secondary Schools at the University of Wisconsin, and selected examples of these alternatives are included in Chapter 7.

6. This is an overly simplified picture. As Raven (1989) points out, the distributions produced by standardized tests rarely, if ever, are normally distributed.

7. This discussion draws from Cherryholmes (1989).

References

Apple, M. (1986). *Teachers and texts: a political economy of class and gender relations in Education*, New York: Routledge and Kegan Paul.

Bloom, B. (1956) *Taxonomy of educational objectives*, David McKay.

Carnegie Forum on Education and the Economy (1986), *A Nation prepared*. New York: The Carnegie Foundation.

Cherryholmes, C. (1989) *Power and criticisms; poststructural investigations in education*. New York: Teachers College Press.

Cronbach, L. J. (1987) Construct validity after thirty years. In Linn (ed.) *Intelligence: measurement theory and public policy*, Urbana: University of Illinois Press.

Education Week (1989) "Looking backward at educational reform", November 1, p. 27.

Foucault, M. (1979) *Discipline and punish: the birth of the prison*. New York: Vantage Books.

Graubard, A. (1972). *Free the children: radical reform and the free shcool movement*. New York: Vintage Books.

Kuhn, T. S. (1970). *The structure of scientific revolutions*. Enlarged edition. Chicago: University of Chicago Press.

Levin, H. M. (1985) *State planning for higher education and jobs in an age of high technology*, Palo Alto: Institute for Research on Educational Finance and Governance, Stanford University.

Medina, N. & Neil, D.M. (1989) *Fallout from the testing explosion: how 100 million standardized exams undermine equity and excellence in America's public schools*. Cambridge MA: The National Center for Fair and Open Testing.

Messick, S. (1989) Meaning and values in test validation: the science and ethics of assessment, *Educational Researcher;* March, 1989.

National Center on Effective Secondary Schools (1988) *Beyond standardized tests: Assessing authentic achievements in the secondary school*. Published in collaboration with the National Association of Secondary School Principals. Reston, VA.

National Commission on Testing and Public Policy (1990) *From gatekeeper to gateway: transforming testing in America*. Chestnut Hill, MA.

New World Foundation (1985) *Choosing equality: the case for democratic schooling,;* and *Equity and Excellence;*, New York: New World Foundation.

Public Education Information Network (1985) *Toward an agenda for school reform*, St. Louis: Public Education Information Network.

Raven, J. (1989) Questionable assumptions in test construction. *Bulletin of the International Test Commission*, 28 & 29. (combined issue).

Sarason, S. (1989). *The predictable failure of educational reform*. San Francisco: Jossey-Bass.

Chapter 2

Notes

1. Described in *A Nation at Risk* (National Commission on Excellence in Education 1983), or *Educating Americans for the 21st Century* (National Science Board Commission on Precollege Education in Mathematics, Science, and Technology 1983).

2. *The Agenda for Action* (National Council of Teachers of Mathematics 1980), *New Goals for Mathematical Sciences Education* (Conference Board of the Mathematical Sciences 1983) and *School Mathematics: Options for the 1990s* (Romberg 1984).

References

Anick, C. M., T. P. Carpenter, and C. Smith (1981). "Minorities and Mathematics: Results from the National Assessment of Educational Progress." *Mathematics Teacher, 74,* 560–66.

Bloom, B. S. (Ed.). (1956). *Taxonomy of Educational Objectives: The Classification of Educational Goals. Handbook 1: Cognitive domain.* New York: Longman, Green, and Company.

Bobbitt, F. (1924). *How to Make a Curriculum.* Boston: Houghton Mifflin.

Chang, L. and E. J. Ruzicka. (1985). *Second International Mathematics Study (United States Technical Report I, Item Level Achievement Data, Eighth and Twelfth Grades.* Champaign, IL: Stipes Publishing Company.

Collis, K. F. (1987). "Levels of Reasoning and Assessment of Mathematical Performance." In T. A. Romberg and D. M. Stewart (Eds.), *The Monitoring of School Mathematics: Background Papers.* Madison, WI: Wisconsin Center for Education Research.

Collis, K. F., T. A. Romberg, & M. E. Jurdak, (1986). "A Technique for Assessing Mathematical Problem-Solving Ability." *Journal for Research in Mathematics Education, 17*(3), 206–21.

Conference Board of the Mathematical Sciences (1983). *New Goals for Mathematical Sciences Education.* Report of a conference sponsored by the Conference Board of the Mathematical Sciences, Airlie House, Warrenton, VA, November 13–15, 1983. Washington, DC: Author.

Freudenthal, H. (1983). "Major Problems of Mathematics Education." In M. Zweng, T. Green, H. Pollak, and M. Suydam (Eds.), *Proceedings of the Fourth International Congress on Mathematical Education* (pp. 1–7). Boston: Birkhauser.

Glaser, R. (1984). "Education and Thinking: The Role of Knowledge." *American Psychologist, 39*(2), 93–104.

Gorth, W. P., P. E. Schriber, and R. P. O'Reilly (1974). *Comprehensive Achievement Monitoring: A Criterion-Referenced Evaluation System*. New York: Educational Technology Publishers.

Kirsch, I. S. and A. Jungeblut (1986). *Literacy: Profiles of America's Young Adults* (Report No. 16–PL–02). Princeton, NJ: Educational Testing Service, National Assessment of Educational Progress.

Lesh, R. (1985). "Conceptual Analyses of Mathematical Ideas and Problem-Solving Processes." In L. Streefland (Ed.), *Proceedings of the Ninth International Congress for the Psychology of Mathematics Education. Volume 2: Plenary Addresses and Invited Papers*. Noordwijkerhout, The Netherlands (pp. 73–97).

Lipson, J. I., E. Koburt, and B. Thomas (1967). *Individually Prescribed Instruction (IPI) Mathematics*. Pittsburgh: Learning Research and Development Center.

Maurer, S. B. (1985). The Algorithmic Way of Life is Best. *The College Mathematics Journal, 16,* 2–5.

McLean, L. D. (1982). *Report of the 1981 Field Trials in English and Mathematics: Intermediate division*. Toronto: The Minister of Education.

National Coalition of Advocates for Students (1985). *Barriers to Excellence: Our Children at Risk*. Washington, DC: Author.

National Commission on Excellence in Education (1983). *A Nation at Risk: The Imperative for Educational Reform*. Washington, DC: U.S. Government Printing Office.

National Council of Teachers of Mathematics (1980). *An Agenda for Action: Recommendations for School Mathematics of the 1980s*. Reston, VA: Author.

National Science Board Commission on Precollege Education in Mathematics, Science, and Technology (1983). *Educating Americans for the 21st Century: A Plan of Action for Improving the Mathematics, Science, and Technology Education for all American Elementary and Secondary Students so that their Achievement is the Best in the World by 1995*. Washington, DC: National Science Foundation.

National Science Foundation (1982). *Science Indicators, 1982*. Washington, DC: U.S. Government Printing Office.

Pollak, H. (1987). Notes from a talk given at the MSEB Frameworks Conference, Minneapolis, May.

Pressley, M. (1986). "The Relevance of the Good Strategy User Model to the Teaching of Mathematics." *Educational Psychologist, 21*(1&2), 139–61.

Ralston, A. (1986). "Discrete Mathematics: The New Mathematics of Science." *American Scientist, 74,* 611–18.

Resnick, L. B. (1987). *Education and Learning to Think.* Washington, DC: National Research Council.

Resnick, D. P., and L. B. Resnick (1977). "The Nature of Literacy: An Historical Exploration." *Harvard Educational Review, 47,* 370–85.

Rice, J. M. (1913). *Scientific Management in Education.* New York: Hinds, Noble, and Eldredge.

Roberts, F. S. (1984). "The Introductory Mathematics Curriculum: Misleading, Outdated, and Unfair." *The College Mathematics Journal, 15,* 383–85.

Romberg, T. A. (1976). *Individually Guided Mathematics.* Reading MA: Addison-Wesley.

Romberg, T. A. (1983). "A Common Curriculum for Mathematics." In G. D. Fenstermacher and J. J. Goodlad (Eds.), *Individual Differences and the Common Curriculum.* Chicago: The University of Chicago Press.

Romberg, T. A. (1984). *School Mathematics: Options for the 1990s* (Chairman's report of a conference). Washington, DC: U.S. Government Printing Office.

Romberg, T. A. (1988) "Curricular Interfaces in School Mathematics: The 'Ideal' with the 'Real.' " In J. Pegg (Ed.), *Mathematical Interfaces: The Proceedings of the 12th Biennial Conference of the Australian Association of Mathematics Teachers* (pp. 22–37). Newcastle, New South Wales: Australian Association of Mathematics Teachers.

Romberg, T. A., and T. P. Carpenter (1986). "Research on Teaching and Learning Mathematics: Two Disciplines of Scientific Inquiry." In M. C. Wittrock (Ed.), *Handbook of Research on Teaching: A project of the American Educational Research Association* (3rd Edition), (pp. 850–73). New York: Macmillan.

Romberg, T. A., J. G. Harvey, J. M. Moser, and M. E. Montgomery (1974, 1975, 1976). *Developing Mathematical Processes.* Chicago: Rand McNally.

Schoenfeld, A. H., and D. J. Herrmann (1982). "Problem Perception and Knowledge Structure in Expert and Novice Mathematicl Problem Solvers." *Journal of Experimental Psychology: Learning, Memory, and Cognition, 8,* 484–94.

Shane, H. I., and M. B. Tabler (1981). *Educating for a New Millennium: Views of 132 International Scholars.* Bloomington, IN: Phi Delta Kappa Educational Foundation.

Steen, L. A. (1986). "Living with a New Mathematical Species." In A. G. Howson and J. P. Kahane (Eds.), *The Influence of Computers and Informatics on Mathematics and Its Teaching* (pp. 52–60). Cambridge: Cambridge University Press.

Swan, M. (1987). *The Language of Functions and Graphs.* Nottingham: Shell Centre for Mathematical Education.

Tyler, R. W. (1931). "A Generalized Technique for Constructing Achievement Tests." *Educational Research Bulletin, 8,* 199–208.

Venezky, R. L., C. F. Kaestle and A. M. Sum (1987). *The Subtle Danger: Reflections on the Literacy Abilities of America's Young Adults* (Report No. 16–CAEP–01). Princeton, NJ: Center for the Assessment of Educational Progress, Educational Testing Service.

Weinzweig, A. I., and J. W. Wilson (1977, January). *Second IEA Mathematics Study: Suggested Tables of Specifications for the IEA Mathematics Tests. Working Paper I.* Wellington, New Zealand: IEA International Mathematics Committee.

Welch, W. (1978). "Science Education in Urbanville: A Case Study." In R. Stake and J. Easley (Eds.), *Case Studies in Science Education.* Urbana, IL: University of Illinois Press.

Chapter 3

Notes

An earlier version of this paper was commissioned in August 1986 for the Study Group on the National Assessment of Educational Progress by the Scretary of the United States Department of Education, with substantial assistance from Mary Louise Gomez of the University of Wisconsin, Madison.

1. This problem has been most succinctly addressed by Oliver (1957).

2. Discourse analysts (e.g., Halliday and Hasan, 1976) often define discourse as any natural language occurrence or utterance in which a speaker/writer tries to communicate with a listener/reader. According to such a broad defintion, the number of words or other linguistic criteria are not significant (e.g., an EXIT sign or single-word answer to a question would count as discourse). But some authors (e.g., Stubbs 1983) focus on conversation and written text that extend beyond sentences. To emphasize the importance in social studies of student language that *elaborates* human experience, we have added to the definition the criterion that formal knowledge is integrated into the student's interpretation of social experience through several words and/or sentences.

3. See Newmann and Archbald (Chapter 4 in this volume) for a full discussion of the nature of authentic achievement.

4. Higher-order thinking has recently attracted increasing attention from psychologists, educational leaders, and policy-makers (Resnick 1987). It has been tied not only to citizenship, but also to economic productivity on the grounds that problem solving skills are increasingly needed by workers. Career changes demand new forms of adaptation and, as jobs become more complex, they challenge workers not merely to find answers to problems but also to identify the problems themselves and to create processes for developing solutions.

5. For example, see Chi et al. (1987), Gelman and Brown (1986), Resnick (1987), and Romberg and Zarinnia (1987).

6. This discussion of how to develop indicators of discourse assumes that a major feature of NAEP assessment can be retained; namely, that whether testing at the school, district, state, or national level, items will be distributed among samples of students such that no individual student will be asked to show compentence on all of the topics to be assessed. Indicators of the quality of discourse within a system can be constructed by different students addressing different topics.

7. Efforts to outline critical topics that could form the basis for discourse include National Council for the Social Studies (1979; 1984), Boyer (1983), College Entrance Examination Board (1983; 1986).

8. Alternative approaches to assessment in mathematics and science are suggested by Collis (1987), Murnane and Raizen (1988), Romberg and Zarinnia (1987).

9. Carlson (1986) estimated that only 8 percent of the 1981–82 NAEP objectives for social studies dealt with discourse, and his analysis of released items agrees with these points.

10. The following material on writing assessment was developed by Mary Louise Gomez.

11. Discussions of this issue from diverse perspectives include Apple (1979, 1986), Dickenson and Lee (1978), Erickson (1984).

12. Care must be taken, of course, to avoid unfair comparisons. For example, comparing discourse indicators of schools whose student bodies differ greatly in socioeconomic background will give misleading conclusions regarding school effectiveness.

References

Adler, M. J. (1982). *The Paideia Proposal: An Educational Manifesto*. New York: Macmillan.

Apple, M. W. (1979). *Ideology and Curriculum*. New York: Routledge and Kegan Paul.

Apple, M. W. (1986). *Teachers and Texts: A Political Economy of Class and Gender Relations in Education*. New York: Routledge and Kegan Paul.

Applebee, A. N. (1984). "Writing and Reasoning." *Review of Educational Research,* *54*(4), 577–96.

Applebee A. N., J. A. Langer, and I. V. S. Mullis (1986). *NAEP: Writing Trends across the Decade, 1974–84.* Washington, DC: National Assessment of Educational Progress.

Boyer, E. L. (1983). *High school: A Report on Secondary Education in America.* New York: Harper and Row.

Burstall, C. (1986). "Innovative Forms of Assessment: A United Kingdom Perspective." *Educational Measurement: Issues and Practice, 50*(1), 17–22.

Carlson, K. (1986). *The National Assessment of Educational Progress in Social Studies.* (Commissioned paper prepared for the Lamar Alexander-H. Thomas James Study Group Report). Washington, DC: National Academy of Education. (ERIC Document Reproduction Service No. ED 279 665)

Chi, M. T. H., M. Bassok, M. W. Lewis, P. Reimann, and R. Glaser (1987). *Self-Explanations: How Students Study and Use Examples in Learning to Solve Problems.* Pittsburgh: Learning Research and Development Center, University of Pittsburgh.

College Entrance Examination Board. (1983). *Academic Preparation for College: What Students Need to Know and Be Able to Do.* New York: Author.

College Entrance Examination Board. (1986). *Academic Preparation in Social Studies: Teaching for Transition from High School to College.* New York: Author.

Collis, K. T. (1987). "Levels of Reasoning and the Assessment of Mathematics Performance." In T. A. Romberg and D. M. Stewart (Eds.), *The Monitoring of School Mathematics: Background Papers. Vol 2: Implications from Psychology; Outcomes of Instruction* (Program Report 87–2, pp. 203–26). Madison, WI: Wisconsin Center for Education Research.

Conlan, G. (1986). " 'Objective' Measures of Writing Ability." In K. L. Greenberg, H. S. Wiener, and R. A. Donovan (Eds.), *Writing Assessment: Issues and Strategies* (pp. 109–25). New York: Longman.

Cooper, C. R. (1977). "Holistic Evaluation of Writing." In C. R. Cooper and L. Odell, *Evaluating Writing: Describing, Measuring, Judging* (pp. 3–32). Urbana, IL: National Council of Teachers of English.

Dickinson, A. K., and P. J. Lee (Eds.). (1978). *History Teaching and Historical Understanding.* London: Heinemann.

Erickson, F. (1984). "School Literacy, Reasoning, and Civility: An Anthropologist's Perspective." *Review of Educational Research, 54*(4), 325–46.

Fader, D. (1986). "Writing Samples and Virtues." In K. L. Greenberg, H. S. Wiener, and R. A. Donovan (Eds.), *Writing Assessment: Issues and Strategies* (pp. 79–92). New York: Longman.

Frederiksen, N. (1984). "The Real Test Bias: Influences of Testing on Teaching and Learning." *American Psychologist, 39*(3), 193–202.

Frederiksen, N. (1988). "Indicators of Learning in Science and Mathematics." In R. J. Murnane and S. A. Raizen (Eds.), *Improving Indicators of the Quality of Science and Mathematics Education in Grades K–12* (pp. 40–72). Committee on Indicators of Precollege Science and Mathematics Education, Commission on Behavioral and Social Sciences and Education, National Research Council. Washington, DC: National Academy Press.

Gelman, R., and A. L. Brown, (1986). "Changing Views of Cognitive Competence in the Young." In N. J. Smelser and D. R. Gerstein (Eds.), *Behavioral and Social Sciences: Fifty Years of Discovery: In Commemoration of the Fiftieth Anniversary of the "Ogburn Report," Recent Social Trends in the United States* (pp. 175–207). Washington, DC: National Academy Press.

Giroux, H. A., and P. McLaren (1986). "Teacher Education and the Politics of Engagement: The Case for Democratic Schooling." *Harvard Educational Review, 56*(3), 213–38.

Greenberg, K. L., H. S. Wiener and R. A. Donovan (Eds.). (1986). *Writing Assessment: Issues and Strategies.* New York: Longman.

Halliday, M. A. K., and R. Hasan (1976). *Cohesion in English.* London: Longman.

Hirsch, E. D. (1987). *Cultural Literacy: What Every American Needs to Know.* Boston: Houghton Mifflin.

Hunt, M. P., and L. Metcalf (1968). *Teaching High School Social Studies.* New York: Harper and Row.

Lazerson, M., J. D. McLaughlin, B. McPerhson, and S. K. Bailey (1985). *An Education of Value: The Purposes and Practices of Schools.* New York: Cambridge University Press.

McPeck, J. E. (1981). *Critical Thinking and Education.* Oxford: Martin Robertson.

Murnane, R. J., and S. A. Raizen (Eds.) (1988). *Improving Indicators of the Quality of Science and Mathematics Education in Grades K–12.* Washington, DC: National Academy Press.

Meyers, M. (1980). *Procedures for Writing Assessment and Holistic Scoring.* Champaign, IL: National Council of Teachers of English.

National Council for the Social Studies (1979). *Social Studies Curriculum Guidelines.* Washington, DC: Author.

National Council for the Social Studies Task Force on Scope and Sequence (1984). "In Search of a Scope and Sequence for Social Studies." *Social Education, 48* (4), 249–62.

Newmann, F. M. (1975). *Education for Citizen Action: Challenge for Secondary Curriculum*. Berkeley, CA: McCutchan.

Newmann, F. M. (1990). "Higher-order Thinking in Teaching Social Studies: A Rationale for the Assessment of Classroom Thoughtfulness." *Journal of Curriculum Studies, 22*(1), 41–56.

Nystrand, M. (1977). "Language as Discovery and Exploration: Heuristic and Explicative Uses of Language." In M. Nystrand (Ed.) *Language as a way of knowing* (pp. 95–104). Toronto: Ontario Institute for Studies in Education.

Nystrand, M. (1986). *The Structure of Written Communication: Studies in Reciprocity Between Writers and Readers.* New York: Academic Press.

Nystrand, M., and M. Wiederspiel (1977). "Case Study of a Personal Journal: Notes Toward an Epistemology of Writing." In M. Nystrand (Ed.), *Language as a way of knowing*, (pp. 105–12). Toronto: Ontario Institute for Studies in Education.

Oliver, D. W. (1957). "The Selection of Content in the Social Studies." *Harvard Educational Review, 27*(4), 271–300.

Oliver, D. W., and J. P. Shaver (1966). *Teaching Public Issues in the High School.* Logan: UT: Utah State University Press.

Resnick, L. B. (1987). *Education and Learning to Think*. Washington, DC: National Academy Press.

Romberg, T. A., and E. A. Zarinnia (1987). "Consequences of the New World View to Assessment of Students' Knowledge of Mathematics." In T. A. Romberg and D. M. Stewart (Eds.), *The Monitoring of School Mathematics: Background Papers. Vol. 2: Implications from Psychology; Outcomes of Instruction* (Program Report 87–2, pp. 203–26). Madison, WI: Wisconsin Center for Education Research.

Sizer, T. R. (1984). *Horace's Compromise: The Dilemma of the American High School.* Boston: Houghton Mifflin.

Stubbs, M. (1983). *Discourse Analysis: The Sociolinguistic Analysis of Natural Language*. Chicago: University of Chicago Press.

Tyler, R. W. (1983). "Testing Writing: Procedures Vary with Purposes." In R. W. Bailey and R. M. Fosheim (Eds.), *Literacy for life: The Demand for Reading and Writing* (pp. 197–206). New York: Modern Language Association.

White, E. M. (1986). "Pitfalls in the Testing of Writing." In K. L. Greenberg, H. S. Wiener, and R. A. Donovan (Eds.), *Writing Assessment: Issues and Strategies* (pp. 53–78). New York: Longman.

Chapter 4

Notes

1. This chapter is an expanded treatment of material that appeared in Archbald and Newmann (1988) and Newmann (1991).

2. Commitment to depth over coverage entails no retreat from liberal education into narrow forms of vocationalism, as some might suspect. The effort to concentrate on complex understanding welcomes study of a wide variety of disciplines and paths to knowledge. In reducing the emphasis on superficial exposure, it implies no necessary narrowing of the curriculum as a whole. For a more detailed discussion of depth in curriculum, see Newmann (1988).

3. This analysis is based in part on the work of Nystrand and Gamoran (1991).

4. Even criterion-referenced tests based initially on substantive performance standards may ultimately be converted to norm-referenced reporting schemes (e.g., where a particular success rate for a task or item is considered a satisfactory norm for a particular grade or group of students). The main point, however, is to make sure that the assessment provides useful information about substance and content of the performances, not simply about success rates.

References

Archbald, D. A., and F. M. Newmann (1988). *Assessing Authentic Academic Achievement in the Secondary School.* Reston, VA: National Association of Secondary School Principals.

Elmore, R. F. and Associates. (1990). *Restructuring Schools: The Next Generation of Educational Reform.* San Francisco: Jossey Bass.

Newmann, F. M. (1988). "Can Depth Replace Coverage in the High School Curriculum?" *Phi Delta Kappan, 69*(5), 345–48.

Newmann, F. M. (1991). "Linking Restructuring to Authentic Student Achievement." *Phi Delta Kappan, 72*(6), 458–463.

Nystrand, M., and A. Gamoran (1991). "Student Engagement: When Recitation Becomes Conversation." In H. Waxman & H. Walberg (Eds.), *Contemporary research on teaching.* Berkeley, CA: McCutcheon.

Resnick, L. B. (1987). "Learning in School and Out." *Educational Researcher, 16*(9), 13–20.

Wiggins, G. (1989). "A True Test: Toward More Authentic and Equitable Assessment." *Phi Delta Kappan, 70* (9), 703–13.

Wigginton, E. (1985). *Sometimes a Shining Moment: The Foxfire Experience.* Garden
City, NY: Anchor Press/Doubleday.

Chapter 5

Notes

1. The term *value* is not quite right because the behaviors in question often seem
to be rather compulsive. People engage in them "despite themselves." This is difficult
to reconcile with the term *valued activity,* which conjures up an image of a "freely
chosen" activity. Yet people do usually agree that these activities are important to
them, and it is in this sense that they can truly be said to value them. McClelland has
tried to avoid the difficulty by using the term *need.* Unfortunately, this has led him
to claim that his measures are not measures of values. This is not only untrue, as I
have shown in Raven (1988), it has also caused endless confusion and unnecessary
argument.

2. The conative components are those concerned with determination, persistence, and will. In the American literature other than that associated with McClelland,
these components have either been ignored or inappropriately subsumed under *affective.* Yet a person can very much enjoy doing something without being determined
to see it through—and he or she can hate doing something but still be determined
to do it.

3. This does not mean that it is not useful to think about behavior in terms of
these categories, only that, in practice, attempts to assess the components separately
are mistaken.

4. Greeno and his colleagues would add that the latter will only be developed in
particular circumstances. See Greeno (1989) and Brown and Collins and Duguid
(1989).

5. The diagram can also be used to illustrate the fact that other people's ratings
of observed behavior—the resultant—are even less valid indices of the ratee's competence than is the behavior itself, for what raters perceive depends on their own values
and priorities, what they take to be the demands of the task and situation, and their
subjective ability to manage the ratee—who has values, priorities, and talents which
may well differ from their own. Many teachers (and managers) lack confidence in their
own ability to manage independent, thoughtful, questioning students. This makes them
unwilling to create situations in which such qualities could be developed and displayed. And it has a marked effect on the interpretation they place on such behavior
when it occurs.

Having said that, it is important to note that it is only the (already "contaminated") "resultant" behavior, further contaminated by their own values and abilities,

which any observer can see with the unaided eye. The only way around this difficulty involves, on the one hand, getting inside the ratee's head and, on the other, making the values, priorities, assumptions, and competencies of the rater as explicit as possible.

6. McClelland, Atkinson, Clark, and Lowell (1958).

7. Raven, Molloy, and Corcoran (1972), Raven (1977a).

8. These components of competence are spelled out in more detail in Raven (1977b) and Raven (1984a).

9. It is not, in fact, difficult to reconcile some such model with the facts to which factor-analysts point as a justification for their model. They point out that most human traits are correlated with each other. They go on to argue that it is unnecessary to retain a large number of independent dimensions, or categories. However, many of the correlations are of the order of .2 and most are of the order of .3 to .5. Even the latter leave some 75 percent of the variance on one trait "unexplained" by the variance on the other. There is, therefore, a *good* chance that someone who is not good at one thing will be good at another. Even factor-analysts point out that this is because the second ability has probably caught the interests of the person concerned and, therefore, been practiced and developed. While the factor-analysts's model does, in fact, provide for such possibilities (by including provision for specific factors) these are generally neglected in practice. If we were forced to state our case in factor-analytic terms, we would therefore find ourselves arguing that the important things to record about an individual are his specifics, not his generalities.

10. See Greeno (1989) and Brown, Collins, and Duguid (1989).

11. In setting appropriate expectations it is also important to say that, precisely because there has been no continuity in funding or projects, there has been no continuity in staffing either. No sooner have those concerned been socialized into (earlier versions) of the way of thinking presented here than—complete with their hard-won insights and expertise—they have had to move on. In this context, the progress which has been made looks more significant.

12. This was a Levenstein-like program of adult education designed to "emphasize the unique and irreplaceable role of the mother in promoting the development of her children" (Raven 1980b; McCail 1981).

13. Raven, Johnstone, and Varley (1985).

14. Raven (1984a); Graham and Raven (1987).

15. Raven (1984a).

16. Raven (1980b).

17. Klemp, Munger, and Spencer (1977).

18. Smith and Kendall (1963); for a summary of the procedure as we have used, see Raven (1977a).

19. McClelland (1978); Spencer (1983).

20. Stansbury (1976, 1980).

21. Burgess and Adams (1986).

22. Fishbein (1967); Fishbein and Ajzen (1975). However, see also Vroom (1964), Porter and Lawler (1968), Feather (1982), and Mitchell (1982).

23. This is the explanation of the still widely encountered statement that "there is little relationship between attitudes and behavior." It is true that there is little relationship between behavior in a particular situation and scores on a single, factorially pure attitude or personality scale. But there is a very close relationship between behavior and "attitudes" (or behavior tendencies) indexed by identifying and summating the perceptions, beliefs, and feelings which come into play in the particular situation using the techniques under discussion here.

24. This evidence is reviewed in Raven and Dolphin (1978b).

25. Raven (1977a); Walberg and Haertel (1980); Walberg (1979, 1984, 1985); Howard (1982a, b, c).

26. Additional, convincing, evidence of the validity of value-expectancy methodology, applied and interpreted more narrowly, will be found in Feather (1982) and Messick (1989). It is, perhaps, useful to mention that, although the evidence of validity cited here has not been expressed in the form of correlation coefficients, it provides exactly the information which those coefficients seek to provide, namely, evidence that scores based on verbal behavior relate to other aspects of behavior and vary with experimental manipulation.

27. The scheme is fully described in McCail (1981) and the evaluation in Raven (1980b). For earlier applications of the partially-developed model see Raven, Molloy, and Corcoran (1972).

28. Raven and Varley (1984).

29. I am talking here at a fairly gross level. Teachers varied a great deal from one to another in their educational objectives. In relation to this variation between teachers, the slippage between one teacher's objectives and what he or she did looks less stark than it does when researchers focus on such things as the discrepancy between teachers' reporting that they have conducted an "open-ended" discussion lesson, and external observers' ratings of the "openness" of that discussion. What was striking in our study was how few teachers thought it was important to have open-ended discussions. Those teachers who thought it was important to do so got with it, albeit imperfectly. Not surprisingly, the rest conducted no such discussions.

30. Raven (1982a, 1984a).

31. Graham and Raven (1987).

32. Additional, convincing, evidence of the validity of value-expectancy methodology, applied and interpreted more narrowly, will be found in Feather (1982).

33. Peters (1987).

34. Flanagan (1958, 1976).

35. Goodlad (1983).

36. Educational Testing Service (1985); see also Eyde (1987).

37. Joint Committee (1981).

38. Travers (1973); Wittrock (1986).

39. American Educational Research Association (1982).

40. Husen and Postlethwaite (1985).

41. McClelland (1961).

42. Roberts (1968); Oeser and Emery (1958).

43. Kanter (1985).

44. Lerner (1987).

45. I have discussed these issues at some length in Raven (1975, 1981, 1984c&e, 1985, 1989a, 1990).

46. Winter, McClelland, and Stewart (1981).

47. Schon (1987).

48. Cf. Schon (1987); Klemp, Munger, and Spencer (1977); Winter, McClelland, and Stewart (1981); Hope (1985); Raven (1984c&d); Raven, Johnstone, and Varley (1985).

49. Cf. De Bono (1980); Emery et al. (1974); Kanter (1985); Morgan (1986); Toffler (1981); Raven (1981, 1982b, 1983b, 1984a&c, 1986b&c, 1987a, 1988, 1989).

50. Morton-Williams et al. (1968).

51. Fortunately, both summary articles and books are already available (Raven, 1977a&b, 1984a,b,&f, 1985, 1986a, 1987b).

52. E.g., Goodlad (1983); Carnegie Report.

53. Dore (1976).

References

American Educational Research Association (1982). *Encyclopedia of Educational Research* (5th ed.). New York: AERA.

Boyer, E. L. (1983) *High School: A Report on Secondary Education in America.* The Carnegie Foundation for the Advancement of Teaching. New York: Harper and Row.

Brown, J. S., A. Collins and P. Duguid (1989). "Situated Cognition and the Culture of Learning." *Educational Researcher, Jan-Feb.*, 32–42.

Burgess, T., and E. Adams (1986). *Records of Achievement at 16.* Windsor NFER-Nelson.

The Carnegie Report: see Boyer (1983); Perrone (1985).

De Bono, E. (1980). *Future Positive.* Middlesex, England: Pelican.

Dore, R. (1976). *The Diploma Disease.* London: Allen and Unwin.

Emery, F. et al. (1974). *Futures We're In.* Centre for Continuing Education, Australian National University.

Educational Testing Service (1985). *The Redesign of Testing for the 21st Century.* Princeton: NJ, ETS.

Eyde, L. E. (Ed.) (1987). "Computerised Psychological Testing." Special issues: *Applied Psychology, 36,* nos. 3 and 4.

Feather, N. T. (1982). "Human Values and the Prediction of Action: An Expectance-Valence Analysis." In N. T. Feather (Ed.), *Expectations and Actions: Expectancy-Value Models in Psychology.* Hillside, NJ: Erlbaum.

Fishbein, M. (Ed.) (1967). *Readings in Attitude Theory and Measurement.* New York: Wiley.

Fishbein, M., and I. Ajzen (1975). *Belief, Attitude, Intention and Behavior.* Reading, MA: Addison Wesley.

Flanagan, J. C. (1958). *Personal and Social Performance Record: Teachers Guide and Materials.* Palo Alto, CA: American Institute for Research.

Flanagan, J. C. (1976). *Implications for Improving Education from a Study of the Lives of 1000 30-Year Olds.* Palo Alto, CA: American Institute for Research.

Goodlad, J. (1983). *A Place Called School.* New York: McGraw-Hill.

Graham, M. A., and J. Raven (1987). *International Shifts in the Workplace—Are We Becoming an "Old West" in the Next Century?* Provo, UT: Brigham Young University Department of Organisational Behavior.

Greeno, J. G. (1989). "A Perspective on Thinking." *American Psychologist, 44,* 134–41.

Hope, K. (1985). *As Others See Us: Schooling and Social Mobility in Scotland and the United States.* New York: Cambridge University Press.

Howard, E. (1982a). Involving Students in School Climate Improvement. *New Designs for Youth Development*. Tucson, AZ: Associations for Youth Development, Inc.

Howard, E. (1982b). *Successful Practices for Making the Curriculum More Flexible*. Denver: Colorado Department of Education.

Howard, E. (1982c). *Instrument to Assess the Educational Quality of Your School*. Denver: Colorado Department of Education.

Husen, T., and N. Postlethwaite (Eds.) (1985). *International Encyclopedia of Education*. London: Pergamon.

Johnson, R. Conference paper, c. 1986.

Joint Committee on Standards for Educational Evaluation (1981). *Standards for Evaluations of Educational Programs, Projects and Materials*. New York: McGraw-Hill.

Kanter, R. M. (1985). *The Change Masters: Corporate Entrepreneurs at Work*. Hemel Hempstead, UK: Unwin.

Klemp, G. O., M. T. Munger, and L. M. Spencer (1977). *An Analysis of Leadership and Management Competencies of Commissioned and Non-Commissioned Naval Officers in the Pacific and Atlantic Fleets*. Boston: McBer.

Lerner, B. (1987). "A National Census of Educational Quality—What is Needed?" *NASSP Bulletin, March*, 42–60.

McCail, G. (1981). *Mother Start, An Account of an Educational Home Visiting Scheme for Pre-School Children*. Edinburgh: Scottish Council for Research in Education.

McClelland, D. C. (1961). *The Achieving Society*. New York: Van Nostrand.

McClelland, D. C. (1973). "Testing for Competence rather than for 'Intelligence'." *American Psychologist, 28*, 1–14.

McClelland, D. C. (1978). *Guide to Behavioral Event Interviewing*. Boston: McBer.

McClelland, D. C., J. W. Atkinson, R. A. Clark, and E. L. Lowell, (1958). "A Scoring Manual for the Achievement Motive; Heynes, R. W., Veroff, J., & Atkinson, J. W. "A Scoring Manual for the Affiliation Motive"; Veroff, J. "A Scoring Manual for the Power Motive." Respectively, chapters 12, 13, and 14 in J. W. Atkinson (Ed.), *Motives in Fantasy, Action and Society*. New York: Van Nostrand.

Messick, S. (1989). "Meaning and Values in Test Validation: The Science and Ethics of Assessment." *Educational Researcher, 18, No. 2*, 5–11.

Mitchell, T. R. (1982). "Expectancy-Value Models in Organisational Psychology" (pp. 293–312). In N. T. Feather (Ed.), *Expectations and Actions: Expectancy-Value Models in Psychology*. Hillside, NJ: Erlbaum.

Morgan, G. A. (1986). *Images of Organization.* Beverly Hills, CA: Sage.

Morton-Williams, R., S. Finch, C. Poll, J. Raven, and J. Ritchie (1968). *Young School Leavers.* London: HMSO.

Oeser, O. A., and F. E. Emery (1958). *Information, Decision and Action.* Melbourne: University of Melbourne Press.

Perrone, V. (1985). *Portraits of High Schools.* New York: Carnegie Foundation for the Advancement of Teaching.

Peters, R. (1987). *Practical Intelligence.* New York: Harper and Row.

Porter, L. W., and E. E. Lawler (1968). *Managerial Attitudes and Performance.* Homewood, IL: The Dorsey Press.

Raven, J. (1975). "Social Research in Modern Society; I: The Role of Social Research; II: The Institutional Structures and Management Styles Required to Execute Policy-Relevant Social Research." *Administration, 23,* 225–45 and 247–68.

Raven, J. (1977a). *Education, Values and Society: The Objectives of Education and the Nature and Development of Competence.* Oxford: Oxford Psychologists Press.

Raven J. (1977b). "On the Components of Competence and their Development in Education." *Teachers' College Record, 78,* 457–75.

Raven, J. (1980a). "The Most Important Problem in Education is to Come to Terms with Values." *Oxford Review of Education, 7,* 253–72.

Raven, J. (1980b). *Parents, Teachers and Children.* Edinburgh: The Scottish Council for Research in Education.

Raven, J. (1981). Social Research and Development in the Doldrums. *New Universities Quarterly, 36,* 72–86.

Raven J. (1982a). *The Edinburgh Questionnaires: A Cluster of Questionnaires for use in Organisational Development and in Staff Guidance, Placement and Development.* Oxford: Oxford Psychologists Press.

Raven, J. (1982b). "Public Policy in a Changed Society." *Higher Education Review, 14,* 80–89.

Raven, J. (1983a). "The Relationship Between Educational Institutions and Society with Particular Reference to the Role of Assessment." *International Review of Applied Psychology, 42,* 249–74.

Raven, J. (1983b). "Towards New Concepts and Institutions in Modern Society." *Universities Quarterly, 37,* 100–18.

Raven, J. (1984a). *Competence in Modern Society: Its Identificaton, Development and Release.* Oxford: Oxford Psychologists Press; distributed in North America by the Ontario Institute for Studies in Education, Toronto.

Raven, J. (1984b). "Quality of Life, the Development of Competence, and Higher Education." *Higher Education, 13,* 393–404.

Raven, J. (1984c). "The Role of the Psychologist in Formulating, Administering and Evaluating Policies Associated with Economic and Social Development in Western Society." *Journal of Economic Psychology, 5,* 1–16.

Raven, J. (1984d). "Some Barriers to Educational Innovation from Outside the School System." *Teachers College Record, 85,* 431–43.

Raven, J. (1984e). "Some Limitations of the Standards." *Evaluation and Program Planning, 7,* 363–70.

Raven, J. (1984f). "What is Language Teaching?" *New Horizons, 25,* 82–90. Also published in *Teaching English, 18, No. 1,* 23–27.

Raven, J. (1985). "The Institutional Framework Required for, and Process of, Educational Evaluation: Some Lessons from Three Case Studies." In B. Searle (Ed.), *Evaluation in World Bank Education Projects: Lessons from Three Case Studies.* Washington, DC: The World Bank, Education and Training Department. Report EDT5 141–170.

Raven, J. (1986a). "Fostering Competence." In T. Burgess (Ed.), *Education for Capability.* London: NFER-Nelson.

Raven, J. (1980b). "A Nation Really at Risk: A Review of Goodlad's 'A Place Called School'." *Higher Education Review, 18,* 65–79.

Raven, J. (1986c). "Review Article: The Future of Work." *Journal of Occupational Psychology, 84,* 343–48.

Raven J. (1987a). "Choice in a Modern Economy: New Concepts of Democracy and Bureaucracy." In S. Maital (Ed.), *Applied Behavioural Economics.* Brighton, England: Wheatsheaf.

Raven, J. (1987b). "The Crisis in Education." *The New Era, 68,* 38–44.

Raven, J. (1988). "Toward Measures of High-Level Competencies: A Re-examination of McClelland's Distinction Between Needs and Values." *Human Relations, 41,* 281–94.

Raven, J. (1989a). "Democracy, Bureaucracy and the Psychologist." *The Psychologist, Vol. 2, No. 11,* November, 458–66.

Raven, J. (1989b). "Equity in Diversity: The problems Posed by Values—and Their Resolution." In F. Macleod (Ed.), *Families and Schools: Issues in Accountability and Parent Power* (pp. 59–101). Brighton, England: Falmer.

Raven, J. (1989c). "Parents, Education and Schooling." In C. Desforges (Ed.), *British Journal of Educational Psychology, Monograph Series No. 4, Special Issue on Early Childhood Education,* 47–67.

Raven, J. (1990). "The Barriers to Achieving the Wider Goals of General Education." *The British Educational Research Journal, 16,* 273–96.

Raven, J., & T. Dolphin, (1978a). *The Consequences of Behaving: The Ability of Irish Organisations to Tap Know-How, Initiative, Leadership and Goodwill.* Edinburgh: The Competency Motivation Project.

Raven, J., & T. Dolphin, (1978b). *Toward Value-Expectancy Measures of Human Resources.* Edinburgh: The Competency Motivation Project.

Raven, J., J. Johnstone, and T. Varley. (1985). *Opening the Primary Classroom.* Edinburgh: The Scottish Council for Research in Education.

Raven, J., E. Molloy and R. Corcoran (1972). "Toward a Questionnaire Measure of Achievement Motivation." *Human Relations, 25,* 469–92.

Raven, J., and T. Varley (1984). "Some Classrooms and their Effects: A Study of the Feasibility of Measuring Some of the Broader Outcomes of Education." *Collected Original Resources in Education, 8, No. 1,* F4–G6.

Roberts, E. B. (1968). "A Basic Study of Innovators: How to Keep and Capitalize on their Talents." *Research Management, XI,* 249–66.

Schon, D. (1987). *Educating the Reflective Practitioner.* San Francisco: Josey-Bass.

Smith, P. C., and L. M. Kendall (1963). "Retranslation of Expectations." *Journal of Applied Psychology, 41,* 149–55.

Spencer, L. M. (1983). *Soft Skill Competencies.* Edinburgh: The Scottish Council for Research in Education.

Stansbury, D. (1976). *Record of Personal Experience, Qualities and Qualifications* (plus tutor's handbook). South Brent, UK: RPE Publications.

Stansbury, D. (1980). "The Record of Personal Experience." In T. Burgess and E. Adams, *Outcomes of Education.* Basingstoke, UK: Macmillan Education.

Taylor, C. W. (1976). *All our Children are Educationally Deprived.* Salt Lake City: University of Utah Press.

Taylor, C. W. (1985). "Cultivating Multiple Creative Talents in Students." *Journal for the Educationally Gifted, Vol. VIII, No. 3,* 187–98.

Toffler, A. (1981). *The Third Wave.* New York: Bantam.

Travers, R. M. W. (Ed.) (1973). *Second Handbook of Research on Teaching.* Chicago: Rand McNally.

Vroom, V. H. (1964). *Work and Motivation.* New York: John Wiley.

Walberg, H. J. (Ed.). (1979). *Educational Environments and their Effects.* Berkeley, CA: McCutchan.

Walberg, H. J. (1984). "Improving the Productivity of America's Schools." *Educational Leadership, 41, No. 8,* 19–30.

Walberg, H. J. (1985). "Classroom Psychological Environment." In T. Husen and N. Postlethwaite, *International Encyclopaedia of Education.* London: Pergamon.

Walberg, H. J., and D. Haertel (1980). "Validity and Use of Educational Environmental Assessments." *Studies in Educational Evaluation, 6,* 225–38.

Winter, D. G., D. C. McClelland, and A. J. Stewart (1981). *A New Case for the Liberal Arts.* San Francisco: Jossey-Bass.

Wittrock, M. C. (Ed.) (1986). *Handbook of Research on Teaching: Third Edition.* New York: AERA.

Chapter 6

References

Adams, E. & T. Burgess (1989). *Teachers' Own Records.* Windsor, England: NFER-Nelson.

Burgess, T. & E. Adams (1985). *Records of Achievement at 16.* Windsor, England: NFER-Nelson.

Task Group on Assessment and Testing (1987). *National Curriculum: A Report.* London Department of Education and Science and the Welsh Office.

The Newsom Report (1963). *Half our Future.* A report of the Central Advisory Council for Education, London, HM Stationery Office.

The Beloe Report (1960). *Secondary School Examinations other than the General Certificate of Education.* A report by a Committee of the Secondary School Examinations Council, Ministry of Education, London, HM Stationery Office.

Records of Achievement National Steering Committee (1989). Report: *Records of Achievement.* London, Department of Education and Science and the Welsh Office.

The Secretaries of State for Education and Science and for Wales (1984). *Records of Achievement, A Statement of policy.* London, Department of Education and Science and the Welsh Office.

Burgess, T. (1986). "Performance appraisal the DIY way", in London *Times Educational Supplement,* May 2, 1986.

Rogers, C. R. (1951). *Client-Centered Therapy.* Cambridge Mass, Houghton-Mifflin Company.

Dewey, J. (1900). *The School and Society.* Chicago, University of Chicago Press.

Chapter 7

Notes

1. This chapter is an updated version of similar material in Archbald and New-mann (1988). The examples were selected through a search of the literature, an announcement in the NASSP *Newsleader,* (October, 1986), and solicitation of suggestions from authorities in numerous research centers and professional organizations.

2. According to research on the method, the inter-rater reliability of holistic grading is high, in the .7 to .9 range (Hogan and Mishler 1981). The extent to which inter-rater scores match depends on the level of training of the raters, the clarity of guidelines, and the range in scores used in judging. Generally, fewer than 10 percent of papers need to be reread; 5 percent or less is considered desirable. For discussions of specific programs and issues in the assessment of writing, see Greenberg, Wiener, and Donovan (1986) and articles in the Spring 1984 issue of *Educational Measurement: Issues and Practice.*

3. For further discussion see Greenberg, Wiener, and Donovan (1986).

4. For more information about the APU and a complete description of the assessment tasks described in "The Assessment of Speech," see Gorman, White, and Brooks (1982), Gorman (1986), and Maclure and Hargreaves (1986).

5. Adapted from a task developed by Great Britain's Assessment of Performance Unit.

6. For a summary of some of this research, see Hirsch (1987).

7. For more information on student competency testing see (Klein 1983–84).

8. See Gibbons (1976, 1984). The latter reference is accompanied by seven other articles describing the development of Walkabout or "challenging education" in schools since 1974.

9. The following draws from the 1984 student handbook, *Walden III's Rite of Passage Experience* by Tom Feeney, a teacher at the school.

10. For more on portfolios, see Committee for the Assessment of Experiential Learning (1975) and Forrest (1975).

11. See PROPEL (1987).

12. We are grateful to W. Ross Brewer of the Vermont Department of Education; Drew Gitomer of Educational Testing Service, Princeton, New Jersey; and Tom

Kosmala of the Pittsburgh Public Schools for their helpful contributions to this section on portfolios.

13. The examples are drawn from Burgess and Adams (1980).

References

Adler, M. (1982). *The Paideia Proposal: An Educational Manifesto.* New York: MacMillan.

Archbald, D., and F. M. Newmann (1988). *Beyond Standardized Tests: Assessing Authentic Academic Achievement in the Secondary School.* Reston, VA: National Association of Secondary School Principals.

Boyer, E. L. (1983). *High School: A Report on Secondary Education in America.* New York: Harper and Row.

Burgess, T., and E. Adams, (1980). *Outcomes of Education.* London: Macmillan.

Committee for the Assessment of Experiential Learning. (1975). *A Guide for Assessing Prior Experience Through Portfolios* (Working Paper No. 6). Princeton, NJ: Educational Testing Service.

Coalition for Genuine Accountability. (1989–90, Winter). *Fair Test Examiner, 4*(1), 1, 6–7.

Forrest, A. (1975). *A Student Handbook on Preparing A Portfolio for the Assessment of Prior Experiential Learning.* (CAEL Working Paper No. 7.) Princeton, NJ: Educational Testing Service.

Gibbons, M. (1974). "Walkabout: Searching for the Right Passage from Childhood and School." *Phi Delta Kappan, 55,*(9), 596–602.

Gibbons, M. (1976). *The New Secondary Education: A Phi Delta Kappa Task Force Report.* Bloomington, IN: Phi Delta Kappa.

Gibbons, M. (1984). "Walkabout Ten Years Later: Searching for a Renewed Vision of Education." *Phi Delta Kappan, 65,*(9), 591–600.

Gorman, T. (1986). *The Framework for the Assessment of Language.* Windsor, England: NFER-Nelson.

Gorman, T., J. White, and G. Brooks (1982). *Language Performance in Schools.* Report on the 1982 secondary survey from the Language Monitoring Team at the National Foundation for Educational Research in England and Wales to the Department of Education and Science, the Welsh Office and the Department of Education for Northern Ireland.

Greenberg, K. L., H. S. Wiener, and R. A. Donovan (Eds.) (1986). *Writing Assessment: Issues and Strategies.* White Plains, NY: Longman.

Hirsh, E. D. (1987). *Cultural Literacy: What Every American Needs to Know.* Boston: Houghton Mifflin.

Hogan, T. P., and C. Mishler (1981). *Relationship Among Measures of Writing Skill.* Green Bay, WI: University of Wisconsin-Green Bay.

Klein, K. (Ed.) (1983–84). *Phi Delta Kappa Hot Topics Series: Student Competency Testing.* Bloomington, IN: Phi Delta Kappa, Center on Evaluation, Development and Research.

Loacker, G., L. Cromwell, J. Fey, and D. Rutherford (1984). *Analysis and Communication at Alverno: An Approach to Critical Thinking.* Milwaukee: Alverno College.

Maclure, M., and M. Hargreaves (1986). *Speaking and Listening: Assessment at Age 11.* Windsor, England: NFER-Nelson.

National Assessment of Educational Progress. (1987). *Learning By Doing: A Manual for Teaching and Assessing Higher-Order Thinking in Science and Mathematics.* The NAEP study was supported by the National Science Foundation through a grant to the Center for Statistics, Office for Educational Research and Improvement, U.S. Department of Education.

National Commission on Testing and Public Policy. (1990). *From Gatekeeper to Gateway: Transforming Testing in America.* Chestnut Hill, MA: Author.

PROPEL (1987). The Arts PROPEL Project, Harvard Project Zero. Cambridge, MA: The Harvard Graduate School of Education.

Sizer, T. S. (1984). *Horace's Compromise: The Dilemma of the American High School.* Boston: Houghton Mifflin.

Valencia, S. W., and P. D. Pearson (1988). "Principles for Classroom Comprehension Assessment." *RASE, 9*(1), 26–35.

Chapter 8

Notes

1. Sources for this analysis include Gould (1981); Kamin (1974); Karier (1975); White (1977). For a comprehensive review of the concept of intelligence and an exposition of a theory of "multiple intelligences" which challenges the unidimensional view of intelligence and human development which is assumed in the Stanford-Binet and all tests which rely on the psychometric paradigm, see Gardner (1983). Gardner's critique of the single factor paradigm of intelligence is parallel to the critique of the view of educational achievement as a unitary construct offered in this chapter and in Chapters 1 and 5.

2. Quoted by Johnson (1976). His (incomplete) reference is to John Brown, *Sermons on Various Subjects,* London, 1764, p. 8.

3. For examinations of the equality issues, see Oakes (1985) and Karabel and Halsey (1977).

4. For a discussion of these questions see Aronowitz and Giroux (1985).

5. For a liberal view of citizenship education see Engle and Ochoa (1988). For a more radical conception see Giroux (1988).

6. The discussion of structure is freely adapted from Adams and Burgess (Chapter 6). For a detailed account of their proposals see Adams and Burgess (1985).

7. The discussion of process draws from three general sources; writings in the tradition of critical research particularly Berlak and Berlak (1981); Fay (1987); Smyth (1989); Gitlin and Smyth (1989); Blackmore (1988). The second source are the writings of Michael Foucault (1972; 1979). The final source are several postmodernist writers in the feminist tradition, particularly Hartsock (1987), Nicholson (1990), and Young (1990).

8. Several writers exploring the theoretical and practical questions related to a "politics of difference" have suggested strategies for making it more likely that silent voices are heard. See Berlak (1991) and Young (1990); nevertheless, a great deal of theoretical and practical work remains.

References

Adams, E, and Burgess, T. (1985). *Records of achievement at 16.* Windsor, UK; NFER-Nelson.

Adler, M. (1982) *The padeia proposal.* New York: Macmillan.

American Psychological Association (1963). Published in association with the American Educational Research Association and the National Council for Measurement in Education. *Standards for educational and psychological tests.* Washington, DC.

Apple, M. (1986). *Teachers and texts: a political economy of class and gender relations in education.* New York: Routledge and Kegan Paul. New York: 1986.

Aronowitz, S. and Giroux, H. (1985). *Education under siege; the conservative, liberal, and radical debate over schooling.* So. Hadley, MA: Bergin and Garvey.

Berlak, A. and Berlak, H. (1981). *Dilemmas of schooling.* London and New York: Methuen.

Berlak, A. (1991). An exploration of anti-racist teaching in a college classroom. A paper delivered at the annual meeting of the American Educational Research Association, Chicago April 1991.

Beyer, L. E. (1988). *Knowing and acting: inquiry ideology and educational studies.* London, New York and Philadelphia: Falmer Press.

Blackmore, J. (1988). *Assessment and accountability.* Geelong, Victoria: Deakin University Press.

Bloom, A. (1987). *The closing of the American mind.* New York: Simon and Shuster.

Bloom, B. (1956). *Taxonomy of educational objectives.* David McKay, 1956.

Bowles, S. and Gintis, H. (1976). *Schooling in capitalist America.* New York: Basic Books.

Burgess, T. ed. (1986). *Education for capability.* Windsor, UK: NFER-Nelson.

Carnegie Forum on Education and the Economy (1986). *A Nation prepared.* New York: The Carnegie Foundation.

Carnoy, M. and Levin, H. (1985). *Schooling and work in the democratic state.* Palo Alto: Stanford University Press.

Cherryholmes, C. (1989). *Power and criticisms; poststructural investigations in education.* New York: Teachers College Press.

Cronbach, L. J. & Meehl P. E. (1955). Construct validity in psychological tests. *Psychol. Bull.* 281–302.

Cronbach, L. J. (1987). Construct validity after thirty years. In Linn (ed.) *Intelligence: measurement theory and public policy.* Urbana: University of Illinois Press.

de Laurentis, T. (ed). (1986). *Feminist studies/critical studies.* Bloomington: Indiana University Press.

Durkeim, E. (1977). On education and society. In Karabel & Halsey, (eds). *Power and ideology in education.* New York: Oxford University Press, pp. 92–105.

Ellsworth, E. (1989). Why doesn't this feel empowering? working through the repressive myths of critical pedagogy. *Harvard Educational Review, 59* 297–324.

Engle, S. & Ochoa, A. (1988). *Education for democratic citizenship.* New York: Teachers College Press.

Fay, B. (1987). How people change themselves: the relationship between critical theory and its audience. In Ball, T. (ed.). *Political theory and praxis: new perspectives.* Minneapolis: University of Minnesota.

Fay, B. (1975). *Social theory and political practice.* London: Allen & Unwin.

Foucault, M. (1972). *The history of sexuality; an introduction.* New York:

Foucault, M. (1979). *Discipline and punish: the birth of the prison.* New York: Vantage Books.

Freedman, S. (1985). Master teacher/merit pay—weeding out women from women's 'true' profession. *Radical Teacher, 25.*

Gardner, H. (1983). *Frames of mind.* New York: Basic Books.

Giroux, H. (1988). *Schooling and the struggle for public life.* Minneapolis: University of Minnesota Press.

Gitlin, A. (1990). Educative research, voice, and school change. *Harvard Educational Review, 60,* 443–466.

Gitlin, A. D. & Smyth, J. (1989). *Teacher evaluation: educative alternatives.* London, New York and Philadelphia: Falmer Press.

Gould, S. J. (1981). *The mismeasure of man.* New York: Norton.

Greene, M. (1988). *The dialectic of freedom.* New York and London: Teachers College Press.

Halsey, A. H. (1972). *Educational priority, vol 1, problems and policies,* London: Department of Education and Science and Social Science Research Council, HMSO.

Handlin, O. (1951). *The uprooted.* New York: Grosset & Dunlap.

Hartsock, N. (1987). Rethinking modernity: minority vs majority theories, *Cultural Critique,* Fall.

Hirsch, E. D. (1987). *Cultural literacy: what every American needs to know.* Boston: Houghton Mifflin.

Hutchins, R. (1943). *Education for freedom.* Baton Rouge: Louisiana State University Press.

Jencks, C. et al (1979). *Inequalty: a reassessment of family and schooling in America.* New York: Basic Books.

Johnson, R. (1976). Notes on the schooling of the English working class. In Dale, R, Esland, G. and MacDonald, M. *Schooling and capitalism; a sociological reader.* London and Henley: Routledge & Kegan Paul in association with Open University Press.

Kamin, L. (1974). *The science and politics, of I.Q.* New York: John Wiley.

Karabel, J. and Halsey, A. H. (eds.) (1977). *Power and ideology in education.* New York: Oxford University Press.

Karier, C. J. (1975). *The shaping of the American educational state.* New York: Free Press.

Kirp, D. L. (1982). *Just schools.* Berkeley and London: University of Calfornia Press.

Levin, H. and Rumberger, R. W. (1985). Education for the high tech future. *Policy Perspectives*, Institute for Research on Educational Finance and Governance, Stanford University. Summer.

Lubeck, S. (1988). Nested contexts. In Weiss, L. (ed.) *Class, race, & gender in American education.* Albany: State University of New York Press.

Martin, B. and Mohanty, C. T. (1986). Feminist politics: what's home got to do with it? In de Laurentis, T. ed. *Feminist studies/critical studies.* Bloomington: Indiana University Press.

McCarthy, C. & Apple, M. W. (1988). Race, class, and gender in American educational research: toward a nonsynchronous parallelist position. In Weiss, L. (ed). *Class, race, & gender in American education.* Albany: State University of New York Press.

Messick, S. (1989). Meaning and values in test validation: the science and ethics of assessment. *Educational Researcher*, March, 1989.

Mishler, E. G. (1990). Validation in inquiry-guided research. *Harvard Educational Review, 60,* 415–442.

National Commission on Excellence in Education (1983). *A Nation at risk: the imperative for educational reform.* Washington DC: Government Printing Office, 1983. Stock #065-000-00177-2.

National Commission on Testing and Public Policy (1990). *From gatekeeper to gateway: transforming testing in America.* Chestnut Hill, MA.

Nicholson, L. J. (ed). (1990). *Feminism and postmodernism.* New York and London: Routledge.

Oakes, J. (1985). *Keeping track; how schools structure inequality,* New Haven and London: Yale University Press.

Ogbu, J. U. (1988). Class stratification, racial stratification, and schooling. In Weiss, L. (ed.) *Class, race, & gender in American education.* Albany: State University of New York Press.

Oliver, D. W. (1989). *Education, modernity and fractured meaning.* Albany: State University of New York Press.

Peters, R. S. (1966). *Ethics and education.* London: George Allen & Unwin, London, 1966.

Purpel, D. (1989). *The moral and spiritual crisis in education: a curriculum for justice and compassion in education.* So. Hadley MA: Bergin and Garvey.

Raven, J. (1989). Questionable assumptions in test construction. *Bulletin of the International Test Commission,* 28 & 29. (combined issue).

Raven, J. (1986). Fostering competence. In Burgess, T. (ed.) *Education for capability.*
London: NFER-Nelson.

Sleeter, C. E. & Grant, C. (1988). A rationale for integrating race, gender, and class.
In Weiss, L. (ed.) *Class, race, & gender in American education.* Albany: State
University of New York Press.

Smyth, J (1989). A pedagogical and educative view of leadership. In Smyth, J (ed.)
Critical perspectives on educational leadership, Deakin Studies in Education: 3.
London, New York and Philadelphia: Falmer Press.

Weaver, T. (1986). Education for what? In Tyrrell Burgess, (ed.) *Education for capability.* Windsor: NFER-Nelson, 1986, pp. 52–59.

Weiler, K. (1988). *Women teaching for change; gender class & power.* So Hadley MA:
Bergin and Garvey.

White, S. (1977). Social implications of IQ. In Houts, P. (ed.) *The myth of measurability.* New York: Hart Publishing Co.

Young, I. M. (1990). The ideal community and the politics of difference. In Nicholson, L. J. (ed.). *Feminism and postmodernism.* New York and London:
Routledge.

Zinn, H. (1980). *People's history of the United States.* New York: Harper.